Learning through
  community : exploring
    c2008.

Learning through Community

Exploring Participatory Practices

Kathryn Church • Nina Bascia • Eric Shragge

Editors

Learning through Community

Exploring Participatory Practices

 Springer

Kathryn Church
Ryerson University
Toronto, ON
Canada

Nina Bascia
OISE/UToronto
Toronto, ON
Canada

Eric Shragge
Concordia University
Montreal, QC
Canada

ISBN 978-1-4020-6653-5   e-ISBN 978-1-4020-6654-2

Library of Congress Control Number: 2007939170

Printed on acid-free paper.

9 8 7 6 5 4 3 2 1

springer.com

Preface

The Turbulence of Learning to Publish

> As researchers, we learned about working together and collaborating across multiple dimensions of space, time and our own identities. ... We learned and we are still learning. We are learning as we write and revise this book. We learn as we begin to see this book through the eyes of others who have not lived through the process of discovery with us in the field. ... We learn as we go "back to work," ... to try to figure out how our learnings can make a difference. (Jackson, 2004, p. 289)

It took 10 years to create this book. Of course, none of us intended to take so long. Like a lot of things that appear to be individual pathology, our tardiness was socially produced. The first defining relation was the collegial way in which Nina Bascia, Eric Shragge and I selected contributors for this volume. As co-editors, we sought contributions from academics who had produced case studies for the Toronto-based research network called NALL: *Network for New Approaches to Lifelong Learning*.[1] However, we selected from what we knew to be the periphery of that network rather than from what we referred to as "NALL Central." Many of us were studying the lives and learning of people considered to be marginal to society or becoming increasingly marginalized within more mainstream locations. Some of us collaborated for several years to foster an understanding of other themes that our studies held in common. While our collectivity might not "make sense" in the canon of work and learning, we wanted a book that would juxtapose these particular studies: for the affiliations that underpin them as well as the "off-centre" quality of their knowledge.

The second defining relation was the major constriction of academic publishing that occurred in Canada during the late 1990s, and our frustrated enmeshment in that shrinkage. We secured our first book contract in 2002, when the case study results were as fresh as new-mown grass. The manuscript was then titled *Making Sense of Turbulent Times: Informal Learning*. However, before our signatures were even dry, the publisher informed us that work could not actually proceed without external funding. This meant applying for assistance to a Canadian programme intended to support scholarly publication. We negotiated with that programme for 3 years. We believed that we were moving forward right up to the moment that we were rejected: an "insufficient contribution to the discipline," said the letter. In that moment, our contract also evaporated.

Inherent in all of this was our sweaty, gerbil-like cycling within the peer-review process. To be brief, between 2003 and 2007, this manuscript was assessed by four sets of reviewers. ("Greetings to all," I wrote repeatedly to the book's contributors, "This is, wryly, my annual update on our manuscript.") Reviewer comments were generally positive: "timely and significant" said our peers, "a welcome relief," and "genuinely enlightening." However, some reviewers claimed that the notion of "informal learning," supposedly our common thread, was "not clarified in a consistent manner across the cases." They proposed that the manuscript needed a concluding chapter to "tie it all together." The work was, it appeared, difficult to characterize and to position. Eventually, a new criticism emerged: that the references were somewhat old and the individual authors "should be given the opportunity to revise their chapters to include recent literature."[2] We viewed this criticism as "iatrogenic:" makeable only because of the review process itself.

Rather than arguing the point, let us simply agree that this book does not unify or synthesize. However, this "failure" is not simply a matter of sloppy intellectual work. Again, the roots are relational. When NALL assembled for the first time in 1997, "informal learning" was already in place as a key term of the approved funding proposal. Through the network's circulation of core papers, members received it as the organizing concept for our work. But we did not necessarily "buy" it, at least, not without critique. In fact, any conceptual "wanderings" evidenced by contributors to this volume can best be understood as resistance. They demonstrate our willingness to take "informal learning" seriously as a category, or, more to the point, to take learning as categorical at all. Thus, in the chapters that follow, while we write about "informal learning" as if it was a fact, we search repeatedly for some means to acknowledge the definitional blurring and fluidity that we find in our own data. Our struggles with this situation and their relevance to research on learning are well articulated in the editors' introductory chapter.

The contributors to this volume were, then, highly tolerant of different ways in which the notion of "informal learning" could be taken up and explored – and the range of theoretical orientations and lived experience that could be brought to bear on the case studies. Such multiplicity diffused rather than concentrating the definition of the term. As co-editors, we took that occurrence seriously. It was connected to our own discovery that a loose coalition of thinkers/actors worked better within the research network than a unified or synthesized group. The reviewers' desire for a concluding chapter seemed always in aid of a "total cohesion" that our contributors did not seek and were not organized to produce. We were and remain a "ragtag" group whose research efforts were sufficiently diverse, across disciplines and sectors, that a singular conclusion is not possible. What we have done instead is generate a profusion of new questions, and openings into unexplored field sites.

Our story took a final turn in 2002. That year marked the emergence of a second Toronto-based research network, titled *The Changing Nature of Work and Lifelong Learning (WALL)*.[3] Organized much more tightly than its predecessor – 12 case studies instead of 46 – it renewed the resources for us to probe the dilemmas of learning we had encountered in our original fieldwork. The new network had a strong international advisory committee, including Stephen Billett from Griffith University in Brisbane, Australia. Stephen shared our concerns with the division of learning into categories. "Informal learning" was a prime example, but he was also critical of the increasing association of "lifelong learning" with "a rather one-dimensional view of securing economic goals for individuals and the enterprises that employ them" (personal correspondence, 2004). In Stephen, we found an ally who recognized the strength of our contribution to more mainstream debates over learning and development, but who expressed that contribution in terms quite different from those to which we were originally bound.

So it is – after 10 years, two publishers, four peer-reviews, two research networks and one substantive reorganization – that we offer you this slim, stubborn volume re-titled *Learning through Community: Exploring Participatory Practices*. The new title reflects the editors' passage from "informal learning" where we began our engagement to, as Stephen says, "a conception of learning premised on (people's) participation in communities." To recognize this shift, we present the book in two parts. Part I, titled "Out of Bounds," comprises two chapters. The first articulates the turbulent learning that we did as academics orchestrating cross-project research collaboration. The second is a further introduction to the book that was written by Stephen Billett at our invitation. His task was to attempt "a conceptual reconciliation" that profiles "the ways that informal learning is a contested concept across all chapters in this volume." Part II, titled "From the Margins," presents eight Canadian case studies that profile the research conducted by our contributors within NALL from 1997 to 2002. Thus, we preserve the integrity of their original work while situating it more fully within the debates that shape the present moment.

Kathryn Church

Endnotes

[1] Funding for the Network for New Approaches to Lifelong Learning came from the Social Sciences and Humanities Research Council of Canada (SSHRC#818-96-1033). Results of all these studies are reported in a series of working papers available on the NALL web site at *www.nall.ca* or its "sister" web site *www.wall.ca*.

[2] The editors wish to acknowledge the generous support of the Faculty of Community Services at Ryerson University in Toronto for a publication support grant (2006) that enabled us to hire a research assistant to update the citations in this manuscript.

[3] Manuscript revision was supported by WALL. It was funded by the Social Sciences and Humanities Research Council (SSHRC) from 2002 through 2006 as a Collaborative Research Initiative on the New Economy (Project No. 512-2002-1011). This network is composed of a large national survey and 12 case study projects. For further information see the network web site at *www.wallnetwork.ca*.

Reference

Jackson, N., 2004, Appendix: notes on ethnography as research method, in M.E. Belifiore, T.A. Defoe, S. Folinsbee, J. Hunter, and N.S. Jackson (Eds.), *Reading Work: Literacies in the New Workplace*, Lawrence Erlbaum Associates, Mahwah, NJ/London.

Acknowledgements

We acknowledge the Social Sciences and Humanities Research Council of Canada for its support of the OISE/University of Toronto-based networks called NALL and WALL: New Approaches to Lifelong Learning, and The Changing Nature of Work and Lifelong Learning. We owe a debt of gratitude to David W. Livingstone, director of both networks for his commitment to debate; to Reuben Roth, NALL's Senior Research Officer, for his skillful constancy in all things; and to Jill Given-King for crucial but sometimes hidden labour in terms of administrative assistance and upgrading of references. We are grateful as well to the Faculty of Community Services at Ryerson University, and specifically to Jiji Voronka, Research Assistant, who laboured so diligently over the formatting of our text. We wish to acknowledge all our colleagues in NALL. With special affection and solidarity, we thank the feisty misfits of Group Five, in particular, the contributors of this volume. We appreciate the high quality of the chapters submitted to us, and the opportunity to work with the authors who were responsive, constructive and patient. In profiling their work, we simultaneously acknowledge the diverse communities – some struggling against great odds in these turbulent times – that are the source of their data and inspiration. Finally, we acknowledge the pleasure of working with each other. Putting this volume together was a social process, one that enabled us to learn and savour each other's intellectual and political contributions.

Contents

Contributors

Editors

Kathryn Church is Associate Professor in the School of Disability Studies at Ryerson University in Toronto, Canada. She teaches courses in community organizing and research methods and directs the School's affiliated research programme through the Ryerson-RBC Institute for Disability Studies Research and Education. She is the author of *Forbidden Narratives: Critical Autobiography as Social Science* (1995).

Nina Bascia is Professor and Chair of the Department of Theory and Policy Studies at OISE, University of Toronto. She has been researching and working with teacher unions in Canada and the United States since 1987. She is the author of *Unions in Teachers' Professional Lives* (1994) and co-editor of *The Sharp Edge of Educational Change: Teaching, Leading and the Realities of Reform* (2000).

Eric Shragge is Director of the Graduate Diploma in Community Economic Development in the School of Community and Public Affairs, Concordia University, Montreal, Canada. His books include *Activism and Social Change: Lessons for Community and Local Organizing* (2003). He is active in community organizations such as the Immigrant Workers' Centre.

Contributors

Stephen Billett has worked as a vocational educator, educational administrator, teacher educator, professional development practitioner and policy developer within the Australian vocational education system, and more recently as a teacher and researcher at Griffith University. His research interests include the social and cultural contributions to vocational knowledge and its learning by individuals. Learning in and through working life has been the focus of his research work, particularly how vocational practice can be developed in workplace settings. In addition, he has a broad interest in policy and practice within adult and vocational education. He has published in *Culture and Psychology, Learning and Instruction* and *Mind, Culture and Activity, Studies in Continuing Education*, as well as sole-authored books such as *Learning through Work: Strategies for Effective Practice* (2001) and *Work, Change and Workers* (2006). He is currently on the editorial boards of five refereed journals, including the *American Education Research Journal*. He is also the Founding Editor and Editor-in-Chief of *Vocations and Learning*, a journal of professional and vocational education which will commence publication in 2008, by Springer.

Kari Dehli is Associate Professor and Associate Chair in the Department of Sociology and Equity Studies in Education at OISE, University of Toronto, where she teaches and supervises students in the graduate programme. Her research interests and publications include education policy and governance, feminist cultural studies and media education. She is co-editor of *Discipline, Moral Regulation and Schooling: A Social History* (1997) and is currently working on a co-edited book on *The Uses of Foucault in Education Research*.

Karen Edge is Lecturer in Education Leadership and Management at the London Centre for Leadership in Learning, Institute of Education, University of London. She is also an educational consultant and has recently completed her Ph.D. in knowledge management and educational reform. Her research and publications focus on policy implementation, knowledge management, organizational learning, school improvement and reform. She is co-author of *Educational Accountability: State of the Art* (1999).

Jean-Marc Fontan has a Ph.D. in sociology from the University of Montreal, Canada. He is a professor-researcher at the Department of Sociology at the University of Quebec in Montreal (UQAM). He works mainly on social economy, local development and community economic development. In 1994, he co-published an important book on local development in Quebec. He is co-director with Nancy Neamtan of the Community–university research alliance on social economy (ARUC-ES) and member of the Centre de recherche sur les innovations socials (CRISES).

Stephen Friedman is an Organizational Development and Human Resource Consultant and a Ph.D. candidate in Applied Psychology at the University of Toronto. He specializes in teaching business people about various aspects of interpersonal communication and their applications at work. Stephen's research has focused on making the most of cross-functional work teams through the enhancement of interpersonal communications. Stephen is also a part-time faculty at the Schulich School of Business at York University where he teaches Organizational Behaviour and Human Resource Management, coordinates the MBA orientation programme and teaches MBA students about teamwork. He operates a private consulting, coaching and learning practice, and is an associate with several consulting EAP and training centres in Toronto.

Doreen Fumia is Assistant Professor in the Department of Sociology at Ryerson University. Consistent with years of trying to theorize community activism as well as activate theory in community activism, she is interested in the relationship between and amongst the production of knowledge, moral regulation, citizenship and identity formation. Her doctoral work examined a local site of writing equity policy in public education where Muslims and Lesbians and Gays competed for, and staked claims to, legitimized identities within Canadian national identities. Building on this work, she is currently looking at the current gentrification projects in Cabbagetown, Toronto, and the surrounding areas. By focusing on the interlock of race and sexuality, she continues to participate in local community struggles that she theorizes as broader claims to national identity and citizenship.

Edward T. Jackson is Associate Dean in Research and Graduate Affairs at the Faculty of Public Affairs at Carleton University in Ottawa, Canada. He is a founder of the pan-Canadian Community Economic Development Technical Assistance Program and a board member of the National Social Economy Research Hub supported by SSHRC, and has served as Lansdowne Visiting Scholar in community–university partnerships at the University of Victoria. He has published extensively in the areas of community economic development, participatory research and evaluation, and civil-society financing.

Marilyn Laiken is a professor at the Department of Adult Education and Counseling Psychology at OISE, University of Toronto, and Director of the OISE, University of Toronto Certificate Program in Adult Training and Development. Marilyn combines an interest in adult education and organizational change through research, teaching and field development in such areas as organizational learning and change, system redesign, work team development, participative leadership and experiential, transformative adult education. She speaks internationally and has published widely in all of these areas, and her book, entitled *The Anatomy of High Performing Teams: A Leader's Handbook* (1998), focuses on work team facilitation concepts and skills. She has been honoured with the prestigious Ontario Confederation of University Faculty Association (OCUFA) award for Excellence in Teaching, and the Canadian Society for Training and Development President's Award for her contributions to the field of Adult Education.

Susan McDonald is a lawyer with a doctorate in Adult Education from OISE, University of Toronto. She is currently a Senior Research Analyst with the Department of Justice, Canada. Her areas of interest include adult learning, immigration, violence against women, public legal education and poverty law.

Diane Meaghan is a professor in the Liberal Studies Division at Seneca College and a community activist in the areas dealing with women, anti-racism and class issues. Her research interests include the restructuring of post-secondary education, international sex trade and equity. She is the author of over 70 journal publications and texts predominantly dealing with education and feminism.

Shahrzad Mojab is Associate Professor in the Department of Adult Education and Counselling Psychology at OISE, University of Toronto, and the Director of Women and Gender Studies Institute at the University of Toronto. Her areas of research and teaching are minority women's access to education; critical and feminist pedagogy; women, state, globalization and citizenship; and women, war, violence and learning. She is the editor of *Women of a Non-state Nation: The Kurds* (2001); with Himani Bannerji and Judy Whitehead co-editor *Of Property and Propriety: The Role of Gender and Class in Imperialism and Nationalism* (2001) and with Nahla Abdo co-editor *Violence in the Name of Honour: Theoretical and Political Challenges* (2004). She is currently conducting SSHRC-funded research on war, diaspora and learning; women political prisoners in the Middle East; and war and transnational women's organizations.

John P. Myers is Assistant Professor in the Department of Instruction and Learning at the University of Pittsburg, USA. He completed his Ph.D. in 2005 at OISE, University of Toronto in the Curriculum, Teaching and Learning Department, with a specialization in Comparative, International, and Development Education. His research interests include cross-cultural perspectives on citizenship education, globalization and curriculum, and teacher education reform in developing nations.

Roxana Ng has been working with immigrant women in Canada since the mid-1970s, and has published extensively on immigrant women, community–state relations, and gender, race and class. Her major publications include *The Politics of Community Services* (2nd edition, 1996) and *Anti-Racism, Feminism and Critical Approaches to Education* (1995). Her current research concerns the experiences of immigrant garment workers in Toronto. She is a professor in the Adult Education and Community Development Program at OISE, University of Toronto.

Daniel Schugurensky is Director of the Collaborative Master's Program in Community Development at the University of Toronto, and Associate Professor at the Department of Adult Education and Counseling Psychology at OISE, University of Toronto. Among his teaching and research interests are the connections between informal citizenship learning and participatory democracy practices.

Mary Stratton is the Research Director for the Canadian Forum on Civil Justice, based in Edmonton, Alberta. Since 2001, she has been coordinating the *Civil Justice System and the Public*, an innovative national collaborative research project available at *www.cfcj-fcjc.org*. Previously, she was a researcher for *Women and Community Economic Development: Changing Knowledge, Changing Practice*, a project conducted by what is now the Centre for Community Innovation at Carleton University. Mary has been actively involved in community development, action research, education and organizational change for over 15 years. She has a Ph.D. in sociology from Carleton University and an interdisciplinary M.A. in Child and Human Development from Laurentian University.

Karima West is a doctoral candidate at the Centre for Applied Cognitive Science, Department of Human Development and Applied Psychology, OISE, University of Toronto. Currently based in Montreal, she is a freelance research consultant and analyst, specializing in qualitative research in education, psychology and sociology fields. Recent projects include evaluation of new technology approaches in medical student education and impact assessment of community development programmes in Europe and South America. Her thesis examines the creative process in knowledge building in the industry.

Part I
Out of Bounds: Situating Ourselves

Chapter 1
The Turbulence of Academic Collaboration

Kathryn Church, Nina Bascia, and Eric Shragge

Introduction

This book is a collection of Canadian case studies about informal learning – what it looks like and how it happens in a range of different social, political and organizational settings. In this declaration there is already a question: "What is informal learning?" For the purpose of beginning a discussion, let us say that informal learning is any learning process that occurs outside of the context of school programmes or continuing education courses. This basic notion was the starting point for each of the contributors to this volume. Each researcher then studied how different groups lived the experience of this learning during a time of turbulent social and economic change.

In the chapters that follow, we articulate our discoveries, beginning with groups that are highly marginalized in Canadian society and moving through to groups that are less (or differently) so. This collection's major contributions to understanding informal learning are:

- Its sensitivity to the rapidly changing socio-economic context
- Its focus on *collective* learning
- Its consistent probing for the possibilities of learning that arises from oppositional action – including our own as researchers

In emphasizing these themes, we demonstrate the ways in which informal learning is contested terrain, its definitional boundaries fluid and blurred. The cases in this book describe how what is learned and how it is learned often challenges conventional understandings about the distinctions between formal learning, non-formal learning and informal learning. Informal learning is both voluntary and involuntary, sometimes simultaneously. It blurs the boundaries between intellectual, technical, social, political and emotional forms of knowledge. It is embedded in the processes of daily life as a means for coping, survival and change. The chapters in this book demonstrate the ways that individuals and groups learn when their life circumstances demand it, and in ways that reflect those circumstances.

This book is noteworthy for its unusual hybridization of concepts, made necessary by the interdisciplinary nature of our contributors and the conceptual tradi-

K. Church et al. (eds.), *Learning through Community: Exploring Participatory Practices.*

tions surrounding the groups and situations that are the subjects of their research. The collective framework includes critical theory and conscientization theory; transformative learning theory; critical materialism; theory of communicative action; contemporary Marxist feminist standpoint theory; self-directed learning theory; neo-Vygotskian activity theory; situated learning theory; social learning theory; cultural capital theory; social structuration theory and postmodern standpoint theory. Working across this intricate backdrop promises to inform not just informal learning theory, but also the literature on the groups and phenomena that are the focus of the case studies.

Although the trend is not easy to trace, Canadians are spending more and more time on informal learning. Writing in 2005, Livingstone notes the methodological problems that haunt empirical studies of informal learning, specifically the conflation of what he refers to as informal education and self-directed learning. He goes on to summarize known study results beginning with Tough's case studies in the 1970s. They pegged the average number of hours that respondents devoted to informal learning at around 10 hours per week. Critical of flaws in survey research done abroad in the 1990s, Livingstone is more satisfied with Canadian surveys from the mid-1990s to the current moment. A countrywide survey conducted in 1998 assessed the participation of the adult population in four aspects of informal learning: employment related, community volunteer work related, housework related and general interest related. A key finding was that, in the previous year, Canadian adults devoted an average of 15 hours per week to informal learning activities (Livingstone, 1999). This is a significant amount of time, and significantly greater than the 4 hours per week they reported spending on organized courses.

Summarizing his reading of survey research in this area, Livingstone uses the metaphor of an iceberg to argue that:

> Clearly, the overwhelming majority of Canadian adults are now spending a substantial amount of time regularly in these pursuits and are able to recognize this intentional informal learning as a significant aspect of their daily lives ... virtually all empirical studies to date that have estimated the extent of adults's intentional informal learning have confirmed that it is a very extensive activity. (2005:9)

A major implication is that, while informal learning as a term may not be widely familiar, the activity itself deserves considerably more attention (Harrison, 2003).

In putting this book together, part of our motivation has been to profile informal learning and the debates that surround it, particularly within the field of adult education. But we also want to suggest what might be learned if the boundaries between adult education and other fields were to be transgressed. Thus, while it uses "informal learning" as an organizing concept, this volume makes important contributions to the fields of community development, occupational sociology, organizational learning and socialization, professional learning and development, and citizenship education, among others. Our intent is to speak to – to "talk back" to – some of the conventions that have been established in these domains as well.

How This Book Came to Be

This book was developed under the auspices of a research initiative known as the Network for New Approaches to Lifelong Learning (NALL). Active from 1997 to 2001, NALL was comprised of almost seventy academic researchers and their community partners across the country.[1] Its central purpose was to document the processes and contents of informal learning in Canada and to explore ways of facilitating better linkages between informal learning and organized (formal and non-formal) education programmes. Members advanced this objective through the research and programme development activities of 46 projects structured by 6 working groups. One group undertook a national survey of informal learning practices; other groups studied Prior Learning Assessment and Recognition (PLAR), informal learning cultures, learning and work transitions, and computer-based informal learning.[2]

NALL members whose research did not fit in these categories were clustered together under the title "Informal Learning in Different Workplaces," also known as "Group Five." Unlike other groups within the Network, we had no single task and no single focus. Instead, the group was an "umbrella" for 15–20 projects, each with separate goals and resources. Our stated purpose was to investigate and compare approaches to informal learning in corporate, cooperative, union, school and community settings, and to map relations with formal/non-formal education activities. Because of the differences between these sites, collaborating across them turned out to be quite a challenge.

Initially, we were disgruntled. We speculated that we had been hastily thrust together – ragtag bits that did not fit into the more focused, higher profile NALL groups. We felt alienated from each other and from the larger Network. Pressed to function as a unit, we were awkward, uncomfortable and edgy. We spent our early meetings just trying to figure out who was there – invariably a different combination of people – and listening to each other describe the projects that brought us to the table. We struggled with obvious questions: Why are we a group? What do we have in common with each other? How could our work together advance our primary project? And, underlying these questions, who has the time and energy on top of everything else that they are doing to make this group work? It took several years of meetings for us to become conversant across our diverse range of topics and fields and for common thematic concerns to surface.[3]

The three of us – co-editors of this collection – entered NALL as researchers and participated in the Network at a number of levels. Our most significant learning occurred when we decided to band together to organize and animate Group Five. Nina Bascia's recollection of her entry point describes a shift that all of us felt as we took up this work:

> I was somewhat impatient with much of the discussion at the early NALL conferences but, well-socialized academic that I am, I knew that this impatience would serve as a constructive foil for my own writing and, further, I was willing to endure some of it in exchange for

my bit of research funding. Later, when we decided to see what we could do to bring the group together, I became more engaged, curious to see how the dynamic interaction between ideas and power positions might play out.

As members, we perceived early on that Group Five could constitute a vital alternative space within the Network, one that would be more collaborative and reflective than other projects or networks we had experienced. We began tentatively, without really knowing how to proceed or what we might accomplish. We learned the work that was necessary and how to do it as we went along. Our process is documented through 4 years of email correspondence – roughly 65 pages all told. Those missives became the chewy "crumbs" that we followed to pull together this opening chapter. In these pages, we not only identify the major understandings about informal learning that emerged from the Group Five sites, we also situate them within our own lived experience of informal learning.

Group Five itself is a useful case for understanding how informal learning occurs in the context of an academic research network, and by extension, the Canadian research establishment. Working at various locations in relation to these structures, members came to better understand the ways in which peripheral spaces (such as the one Group Five occupied in relation to NALL) are not only possible but also necessary. Thus, as we introduce this volume and the work of its contributors, we also bring forward some of the informal learning necessary to produce it. One of our major contributions to the field of informal learning is what we learned about doing research and analysis together.

Conceptual Antecedents and Trajectories

In their summary monograph, British theorists Percy et al. (1994) identify 1961 as the date marking the emergence of self-directed learning – a concept roughly equivalent to informal learning. Since then, there has been at least one major shift in how the concept is understood: from a sociological paradigm based on structural functionalism (1950s–1960s) to a model of social action (1970s–1980s). "The latter emphasized the role of adult education to empower people. [It] has opened up the 'space' for individuals to evaluate critically all aspects of their lives" (1994:10). Percy et al. locate this definitional shift in relation to the social and economic demands of a post-industrial society. "Accounts such as these," they argue, "have stressed the need for individuals consistently to acquire new skills and knowledge as previous skills and knowledge become redundant" (1994:10).

Watching (perhaps enviously) from across "the pond," Percy and colleagues note an outpouring of North American research, theory and discussion on self-directed, informal and/or independent learning by adults: whole books written just to index previous research and major literature reviews often "hedged around with definitional confusions and fraught with methodological uncertainties and frustrations" (1994:6).[4] Their review of definitions of self-directed learning reveals an enormous range of concepts and terms indicating to them that it is not a single phenomenon. "Clearly there is a range of foci and they cannot necessarily be tied down within a single definition or set of criteria" (1994:7). The frustration of finding so many terms in use is that "All of them seek to transfer conceptual material appropriate to the formal system of education – a socially and historically constructed professional artefact – to the heterogeneity of frontier-less adult learning in the community" (1994:7).

In seeking to clean up the debate somewhat, the Percy team cites a threefold adult learning typology initially advanced by Coombs et al. (1973), and strongly reinforced through NALL three decades later. The first site is formal schooling defined as "an age-graded, hierarchically organized, formally constituted system that requires compulsory attendance until at least mid-adolescence and provides the major credentialing programmes to certify our knowledge competencies" from early childhood into the adult years (Livingstone, 1999:50). The second site is non-formal learning, a term referencing all other organized educational activities including further courses, training programmes, and workshops. The third site is informal learning, defined as:

> Any activity involving the pursuit of understanding, knowledge or skill that occurs outside the curricula of institutions providing educational programs, courses or workshops. Informal learning may occur in any context outside institutional curricula. The basic terms of informal learning (e.g. objectives, content, means and processes of acquisition, duration, evaluation of outcomes, applications) are determined by the individuals and groups that choose to engage in it. Informal learning is undertaken on our own; either individually or collectively, without either externally imposed criteria or the presence of an institutionally-authorized instructor. (Livingstone, 1999:51)

Livingstone has since shifted so that his current schema includes formal education, non-formal education or further education, informal education or informal training, and self-directed or collective informal learning (2005). This is a useful refinement but it continues to be a formulation more amenable to survey research than to case studies in the interpretive paradigm.

Initially, those of us who constituted Group Five tried to fit our work into the tri-partite formal/non-formal/informal learning categories. But it was not always easy to feel a resonance with what we were observing in our various sites. In these contexts, where persistent inequality and magnified turbulence converge, what fosters learning, what is learned and how it is learned often challenges conventional understandings about the distinctions between formal learning, non-formal learning and informal learning (Longworth, 2003; Tusting, 2003).

These challenges are not simply intellectual; they pass into and trouble the lives and responses of researchers who are engaged with particular sites. Kathryn Church's experience is a good case in point:

> For the first half of NALL's life, I was documenting what low income and psychiatric survivor communities in Toronto were learning through community economic development. I spent my days with people who live on the fringes. I came to know them as colleagues, board members and employees of economic enterprises. In the process, I absorbed a lot of difficult personal stories and lived through some highly intractable organizational dilemmas. I didn't realize how raw that had made me until I found myself causing a small scene at a NALL event in Ottawa. "What is going on here?!" I blurted

into the middle of what felt like an interminable debate on the proper dividing line between formal, non-formal and informal learning. My anger was a response to what I perceived as the privilege of abstract discussion in the face of daily tragedies that I was exposed to down on Queen Street.

Sharing a similar kind of turbulence, members of Group Five plotted ways to unsettle the conceptual framework advanced by NALL's primary organizers. "Where does formal learning end and informal learning begin?" we asked. "Are the boundaries fixed? Should they be? Must we be able to fix the meaning of informal learning?" Interestingly enough, this dissent was also our first point of coalescence, our first sense of working collectively (against). We remember jesting that, "If you want to create a group under difficult circumstances, the thing you need is a common enemy." For us, at least initially, NALL Central (as we came to call it) was that useful "enemy."

In a recent, first stage report, Colley et al. (2004), analysed a major "literature trawl" on informal learning with the following key results:

- While the terms formal, non-formal and informal are used to distinguish some types of learning from others, they are, in fact, "contradictory and contested across the literature as a whole."
- There is "no clear difference between informal and non-formal learning"; the terms are practically interchangeable.
- It is "more sensible to see attributes of informality and formality as present in all learning situations."
- All forms of learning have the potential to be either emancipatory or oppressive depending on the wider contexts in which learning takes place (2004:3).

These results mirror Group Five's discoveries. As researchers, we searched repeatedly for some conceptual means to acknowledge definitional blurring and fluidity. Kari Dehli and Doreen Fumia's work is a good example. It analyses localized practices and relations of informal learning that are embedded in elementary school teachers' work. For these researchers, informal learning is both voluntary and involuntary. Their study suggests that it is difficult to maintain boundaries between formal and informal, voluntary and involuntary learning. It suggests that boundaries between formal and informal learning "are vague and permeable and in some ways imposed by researchers on participants' activities" (Church, 2000:29). With coming changes in regulation and certification of teachers' competence, the boundaries between formal and informal learning are likely to become even more contentious.

Similarly, Group Five members' work blurs the boundaries between emotional, social, political, intellectual and technical forms of knowledge. For example, Mary Stratton and Edward Jackson explore the ways that front line workers doing community economic development (CED) gained the information they needed to work with women participants. In CED initiatives, the practitioner's craft confounds the usual ways in which governments and educational systems recognize knowledge. Also relevant is Diane Meaghan's chapter on sex trade workers' learning and teaching of safer sex practices, and Nina Bascia's chapter on how the Alberta Teacher's Association "maintains an even keel." As Meaghan's prostitutes and

Bascia's teachers discovered, carrying out daily work independently, interacting with others of the same occupational group, and successfully negotiating legislative systems and the popular press are mutually reinforcing rather than disconnected realms of knowledge.

Within NALL, Group Five struggled to position itself in relation to three other conceptual debates: over the legitimacy of incidental learning; over the question of experience; and, over learning as liberation versus learning as regulation.

Incidental Learning

In his summary of the literature on informal learning, Livingstone begins with Knowles' concept of andragogy (e.g. Knowles, 1975), the inspiration for the Ontario-based research that Tough carried out through the late 1960s and the 1970s. Tough noted that adults were learning independently of educational institutions and professional educators (Percy et al., 1994). He argued that they were "planning programs of learning, using learning resources, and learning intentionally and rationally" (Percy et al., 1994:12). Over a couple of decades, Tough's work gave particular emphasis to deliberate, intentional efforts to learn. As a result, argues Livingstone, there are now a large number of case studies and several North American surveys that constitute a body of work on informal learning. His own survey research is built directly on the prior research of Tough and Penland (e.g. Tough 1968, 1971; Penland, 1979).

According to some, Tough's strong influence led to 30 years of American research "characterised by methodological hegemony and by a rationalistic, time-segmented, project-based and quantitatively defined series of related concepts such as 'learning projects' and 'learning episodes'" (Percy et al., 1994:36–37). Other critiques of Tough's studies honed in on his use of leading questions and preference for individually conducted learning among members of dominant social groups (Livingstone, 1999). Tough suggested that people in lower socio-economic groups did less self-directed learning. However, participants in Leean and Sisco's (1981) study of "under-educated" adults in Vermont "commented on how much more they had learned outside the school system. They enjoyed working at their own pace without anyone judging their learning ability. The value of common sense thinking and rational problem solving was expressed by both women and men" (1981:28).

Tough's contention that adult self-directed learning is deliberate and linear was called into question by Spear and Mocker's (1982, 1984) research, which found that pre-planning occurs with a small minority of learners and then only vaguely. Discovering that planning did not always rest with the individual, they turned their attention to the environments in which the learning took place. This line of enquiry led to the concept of the "organizing circumstance" as the directing force for learning: "circumstances created by one episode are used as a stepping stone to the next step of the process" (Percy et al., 1994:30). Perhaps the biggest challenge to Tough's work came from researchers who took seriously the "dormant, unintentional, incidental self-directed learning (that) fell outside (his) frame of reference" (1994:17). Early examples include Peterson (1979), Melville (1987) and Berger (1990). The relationship between incidental (ad hoc, spontaneous) and planned (deliberate, intentional) learning remains a key dimension of current studies on informal learning (Livingstone, 1999).

Watkins and Marsick (1992) attempted to resolve the deliberate versus incidental debate by distinguishing between informal and incidental learning. "Informal learning can be planned or unplanned," they maintain, "but it usually involves some degree of conscious awareness that learning is taking place. Incidental learning is largely unintentional; it is unexamined and embedded in people's closely held belief systems" (1992:16). For these theorists, informal learning includes self-directed learning, networking, coaching, mentoring and trial and error learning. Incidental learning refers to, for example, learning from mistakes or covert experiments such as trying out a new boss. Both informal and incidental learning tend to occur in non-routine situations.

After weighing all the evidence, Percy et al. suggest using the term informal learning to refer to "learning which takes place outside formal education institutions. However, it can also include learning in voluntary organizations and, as a subset, incidental learning" (1994:16). They are attracted to the post-Tough work from the 1980s and beyond because it broadens the scope of research to include women, ethnic minorities, and people with limited formal education. A particular controversy remains whether learning must be chosen. "One of us has tried to argue elsewhere," they confess, "that learning among adults in voluntary organizations can empirically be shown to be an extension of, to be continuous with, doing. There is no moment of deciding what or how or from what or from whom to learn. There is an intentional and progressive pursuit of an activity that we – the observers – may argue cannot proceed without learning. But it may not be labelled by the doer" (1994:37). And so the arguments continue.

The Question of Experience

John Garrick suggests that the best way to deal with the definitional confusion over informal learning is to locate it within what he sees as the broader category of experiential learning. He draws his support from Andresen et al. (1995) who argue that "experiential learning is of particular interest to adult educators because it encompasses formal learning, informal learning, non-formal education, lifelong learning, incidental learning and workplace learning" (Garrick, 1996:26). He then provides a major criticism of experiential learning.

Garrick questions the assumption that people actively give personal meaning to their reality. He takes a post-modernist position that subjects are meaning-takers rather than meaning-givers. In arguing this point, he links himself with contemporary radical thinkers who draw on Foucault's "counter-history of ideas" and particularly his early concern for the ways in which "external authorities shaped the structures of the mind" – and by extension, of meaning (1996:31). Garrick thus questions the degree to which people are intentional learners – a point that also goes to the matter of human agency. He references Foucault as refuting the idea of individual agency in favour of giving primacy "to 'historical situatedness' and 'disciplinary processes' (power/knowledge formations)" (1996:31; Foucault, 1980).

Garrick's position seriously challenges "the foundations of conventional adult education theory based on personal empowerment and autonomy" (Garrick, 1996:31). Like other postmodernists, he asserts that human intentions are distorted and compromised by "certain dynamics of asymmetrical power (which are) inherent to institutional and informal patterns of life" (1996:41). Some of the limits have to do with the way that language in use "colours and shapes our ways of living and being in the world" (1996:41). As a result, Garrick perceives the need to separate emancipatory intent from emancipatory outcomes. There is no guarantee that one produces the other. More to the point, "What tends to be unaddressed in the discourse of experiential learning is the ethical question about whether emancipatory intent and so-called 'liberating' reform processes do not merely lead to other forms of control" (1996:32).

If Group Five has postmodernist tendencies, they appear in our common attentiveness to discursive practices: words and meanings embedded in words that reflect shifts in understanding that signify learning. Most of the chapters explicitly treat language as the medium by which knowledge is negotiated and transformed – not only in helping the individuals make sense of their own experiences but also in transforming knowledge at a social level. Many researchers attempted participatory or interactive strategies, returning to their interviewees to ask them to reflect on the researchers' understanding, resulting in further learning on both sides. (See in particular Chapter 3 by Mojab and McDonald, Chapter 7 by Stratton and Jackson and Chapters 1 and 6 by Church et al.) In many cases, the authors capture the broader discursive contexts – both historical and contemporary – in which their subjects lived and worked. Dehli and Fumia present instances of government rhetoric about teachers; Bascia provides a history of the teachers' association and of teachers' organizations more generally; and Meaghan situates her case study in a broader history of social policy concerning sex work.

Liberation or Regulation?

In the Tough tradition, Livingstone argues for "explicit informal learning" that can be consciously identified as significant by the learner and retrospectively recognized both in the form of knowledge and the process of acquisition. His preference is for discrete rather than diffuse learning experiences. The conceptual exercise is to distinguish informal learning from socialization or tacit informal learning. With the latter "learning and acting constitute a seamless web in which it is impossible to distinguish informal learning in any discrete way" (Livingstone, 1999:51). Against the grain of this view, members of Group Five returned repeatedly to Polanyi's (1967) notion of "tacit" knowledge/s, namely, learning that is embedded in the processes of daily life as a means for coping, survival and change. It is not surprising, as we said in our opening remarks, that the chapters in this book demonstrate the ways that individuals and groups learn when their life circumstances demand it, and in ways that reflect those circumstances. Ranging from formal work settings to attempts to engage successfully in legal, political and social activities, the situations covered shape the kinds of learning that were taken up by our studies' participants.

In these situations, and taking up some of Garrick's concerns, the distinction between liberation and regulation is not always perfectly clear. Contradictions and tensions are part of the cognitive, emotional and political landscape in which learning occurs and action is taken. So, for example, Marilyn Laiken and her colleagues analyse several organizations in the public, private and not-for-profit sectors that provide contexts for individuals and teams to negotiate workplace change. Employees move from performing discrete tasks on an assembly line to managing their entire work process, but clearly many parameters of control remain in the hands of managers, owners and regulatory agencies. Similarly, Bascia's research investigates provincial unions as a vehicle that teachers can use to come into a broader understanding of the educational system, education policy and reform. The association she studied is able to introduce a counterdiscourse to that of the provincial government. But as the story captured by the chapter draws to a close, educational policy is still in the hands of government; political engagement does not lead to absolute victory as much as it relocates the arena of action from internal to public space.

Sometimes these kinds of ambiguities and contradictions manifest in terms of distinctions between entrepreneurial and policy activity. Speaking in relation to distinct fields of policy and research, the chapters in this book represent different positions in a debate about whether informal learning should serve the market or promote active engagement in social and political change. This question of purpose in many ways parallels the more common public debate that rages over the purposes of formal learning: should schools be training workers or citizens? Many chapters suggest that, at least in the current context, this is a somewhat false dichotomy: entrepreneurial engagement can be a kind of political action and vice versa. It is not absolutely clear whether those who control the substance and processes of learning also dictate the rules of the market and government or those who struggle to maintain some degree of autonomy in relation to those powerful forces.

The way this sorts out often depends on the structure and intention of the learners' organizational context. When organizations are balancing multiple pressures and agendas, as is often the case in our case studies, an oppositional perspective will often not be formally supported. Instead, it must be fostered in the gaps and holes between other more structurally valued and recognized activities. Church and her colleagues explore this point as they summarize fieldwork in three community/union organizations that work with people who are excluded from the labour market. Their study picks up on tensions between public policies that enable programme funding and organizational definitions of practice/s. The ability of these groups to resist becoming part of the regulatory apparatus of the state is linked to their visions, traditions and social/political power. The construction of citizenship in many cases is related to the degree of activity of the members in defending their organizations and constructing counterdefinitions of their personal situations and collective solutions to the problems that they face.

Positioning the Book

John Garrick (1996) identifies five prevailing philosophies in adult education: liberal, behaviourist, progressive, humanist and radical. They give rise to four core traditions: training and efficiency in learning; self-directed learning and the andragogy school; learner-centred education and the humanistic educations; and critical pedagogy and social action. Given this mix, there are "considerable theoretical as well as political differences and discontinuities" among people writing on the subject of informal learning. Garrick notes a fundamental distinction between those who privilege social/cultural context and those who privilege the individual. "Important differences exist between adult education as practiced within an individualistic discourse of personal empowerment, and a pedagogy of critical social theory" (1996:27). This book is clearly aligned with the latter.

Sensitivity to Socio-Economic Context

The chapters in this book reference, sometimes obliquely and sometimes as a major focus, a socio-economic context that is changing, possibly threatening, and most certainly challenging – physically, economically and/or politically. Involved in research during a time of significant social redefinition and reorganization, the authors and the subjects of these case studies often articulate an awareness of "globalization," "neo-liberal policies," and/or "social and economic turbulence." However you characterize it, this is the major force affecting our research participants: their personal and work lives, organizational boundaries, and whether what they know is defined as useful and legitimate.

Perhaps the strongest example of this is provided by Shahrzad Mojab and Susan McDonald as they investigate the lives of refugee women in two Toronto communities: the Latin Americans and the Kurds. The women who participated in this study have experienced war in their countries of origin and domestic violence in their present home lives. They face tremendous difficulties in their struggle to establish a political and legal footing in Canada. Equally dramatic in its own way is Dehli and Fumia's exploration of how public school teachers articulate their emerging senses of professional identity after a sudden, drastic change in educational policy direction. Laiken and her colleagues focus on how employees of several different kinds of organizations labour in redefined work environments to improve the quality of service and products in an increasingly competitive global marketplace.

And while all of the chapters focus on Canadian experiences, the sensibilities of the authors ensure that readers come to understand the conditions and responses as particular instances of events and actions that can and do occur in many parts of the world. Domestic violence, for example, is and has been a fact of life for women worldwide. The de-professionalization experienced recently by teachers in Ontario is similar to that encountered by educators across Canada, North America and many other countries.

While "globalization" is often understood as a recent phenomenon, day-to-day turbulence is not necessarily a new experience, particularly for individuals in subordinate positions. As Mojab and McDonald's chapter suggests and as Meaghan's chapter makes quite explicit, women often are in particular danger of violent assault from men. Like Laiken's rendering of employees who work in hierarchical organizations, Bascia, along with Dehli and Fumia, reveals how teachers' subordination in educational systems has endured over historical time. Stratton and Jackson's discussion of the discursive and knowledge "collisions" between academics and "front line" workers exemplifies enduring patterns between members of such groups. Perhaps the magnitude of such turbulence in the current era, and the discourse of globalization are useful in allowing greater access to understanding what subordinated groups have contended with, and what they have been able to achieve, however temporarily, over greater spans of time.

A Focus on Groups

The authors of this book address a weakness in the literature on informal learning by focusing on collectively conducted learning processes. In the cases we studied, relationships are integral to knowledge acquisition. People are thrown together (or deliberately choose to meet), groups form and learning results from the social interaction. Some of the studies profile groups on the social and economic margins of Canadian life. They investigate the experience of immigrant women, sex trade workers, senior citizens, social assistance recipients and psychiatric survivors. Contributing a rare "fringe" quality, these studies include locations, groups and organizational cultures that are typically left out of discussions about learning. Perhaps the most intriguing example is Meaghan's attempt to resituate sex workers as adult learners and the questions this raises about the possibility of developing a prostitute pedagogy concerning safer sex practices. Our intent in profiling groups such as this is to illuminate the social positions represented by the people who inhabit these spaces, and to articulate the challenges they represent to informal learning.

We juxtapose these studies with cases that, while also exploring new terrain, are less characterized by marginalized knowledge. They investigate informal learning practices that are typically hidden within, and unrecognized by, the formal practices of more mainstream organizations. These are environments that recognize and validate formal learning, the kind of knowledge that has academic currency, yet they are also sites where informal learning occurs by necessity and, sometimes, by design. Major examples focus on workplace learning in both private for-profit and public not-for-profit organizations and on the identity transformations of teachers in response to changing school curricula and the political strategies that they generate collectively through union activities. In the organizations that Laiken and her student team studied, employees' capacity to learn was shaped in significant part by that organizational context, and by the understandings (and ongoing learning) of others at multiple levels or locations: not only other workers, but also managers and executives (Boud and Middleton, 2003). We find sites such as these interesting in terms of the dynamic tensions of organizational learning; indeed, this concept is threaded through all of our chapters.

In bringing these studies into conversation with each other, our intent is to make visible the learning of people who are at the interface between formal organizations and social movements. Some have carved informal learning spaces out of environments that are typically perceived as conventional structures. Others have taken their learning directly out of struggle, without an organizational or institutional context. While these rough categories mark the scope of our endeavour, the boundaries between them are not fixed.

Nor are groups simple aggregates of individuals. Rather, individual learning is to some extent interdependent with group and societal learning. Individual learning is socially embedded, but social learning is also shaped by how individuals understand and articulate their realities. So, for example, in working across three employment-related community sites, the Church team's primary interest was not in job market preparation, but in the social processes that go on around that preparation and the impact they have on participants. The informal processes examined are not explicitly planned by the organizations. They emerge from the day-to-day interaction between participants and staff, and are shaped by the wider culture of the organization. These are discussed as informal "social learning" and are linked to such issues as personal and political identification, citizenship, participation and the building of networks of solidarity.

Probing for Oppositional Possibilities

All of the contributors to this volume have had to contend with the enduring nature of power relations. Most locate themselves on the political Left. We have made personal and professional commitments to work for social change. It follows that opposition is an important focus for us. Most of our projects probe the capacity for informal learning to contribute to resistance and/or opposition in response to government "reform" in various areas. "Where are the spaces of resistance?" we have wondered as we listened and watched. "How do participants work the cracks and holes between possibilities and limitations?"

Daniel Schugurensky and John Myers explicitly address the question of collective learning that involves political action. Their study explores Toronto's

Healthy City Project and its claim that a key to achieving healthy cities is the political skills of its citizens, in this case, its senior citizens. As a result of their deliberation process, the members of the Seniors Task Force pressed Toronto City Council to adopt all 55 recommendations from its final report in 1999. The creation of the Seniors' Assembly was particularly important and innovative. By sharp contrast, Mojab and McDonald's refugee women lacked this kind of context for learning and action. Instead, they were learning to trust others and to put in words the emotional challenges of their own experience in order to be able to organize and to navigate the systems of law and social services. For Mojab and McDonald, the most exciting part of the research was noting the growing interest and group formation among women. "The women involved ... are calling themselves 'The Right to Know' group, indicating a growing sense of collective purpose. Such purpose does not occur easily. ... Evidence of group cohesion was a turning point in the research experience" (Church, 2000:36).

While our primary interest was in what was happening in our research sites, we became increasingly attentive to our own oppositional activities as researchers attempting to implement studies within NALL. The Network's grant application structured Group Five's work. In that sense, some of the discussion in this opening chapter is characteristic of academic research more generally, with its tendencies towards scientific assumptions, formats and procedures. At the same time, our grant incorporated an expectation for diverse participation and representation from groups and interests outside of academia. In that historical moment, the proposal writers' belief in "partnerships" came together with the funding body's interest in fostering research that bridged different sectors of society. However, by incorporating partner organizations and their concerns, NALL's organizers introduced a tension that then worked its way through the Network. The network design set us up to struggle with the contradictions of collaboration – between researchers on individual projects, between projects clustered together in the same group, and with our community partners.[5]

As Group Five organizers, our informal learning experience thus was shaped by the dynamic interplay of opportunities and constraints within a large research network attempting to be credible on the national research scene as well as relevant to a range of community partners. To create collaborative learning under these conditions, we had to confront and find ways of working through at least some of the structural separations between the academics in our group and our various partners in community-based organizations. Like the refugee women of Mojab and MacDonald's study, we had to organize. We used three major strategies.

1. We escaped the university setting. The first independent meeting of Group Five took place in the offices of the 761 Community Development Corporation located on Queen Street West in Toronto. This was Kathryn Church's base of operation for the early part of Group Five's existence. We consciously used its vibrant, somewhat off-beat attractions to lure people into attendance:

   We have a good meeting space in an interesting part of the city, in an interesting site. 761 CDC is located in an old United Church that has been renovated and turned into a community

action center. On the main floor there is a consignment store called Prezents of Mind. It sells
arts and crafts made by people in long-term poverty from all over Ontario; many are psychiatric survivors. There is also a psychiatric survivor-run restaurant called The Raging Spoon,
and other smaller initiatives within the building. (Memo of Invitation)

Our decision to hold meetings outside the university environment was crucial. In
the sun-filled CDC boardroom, it was easier to feel like and become a group, to
think outside of institutional frames, and to have atypical conversations. Coffee
and snacks and a nice lunch were also important to the group-building process, to
socializing the knowledge that we were attempting to develop together.

2. We set limits on the impact of NALL Central on Group Five's work. Nina and
   Kathryn developed questions for the group's first independent meeting that were
   outside the Network's framework for informal learning, including the request that
   each person describe their own learning process. Things went as we hoped in the
   morning but in the afternoon Nina left to keep other commitments and NALL
   leader David Livingstone arrived to join the discussion. The dynamic of the group
   changed as members took the opportunity to ask him questions; we also deferred
   to his answers. After this experience, the three of us knew that if we were serious
   about generating broad participation, we had to convene the group by itself for
   most of the day and to make more strategic use of David's defining presence.

3. We took advantage of informal spaces. Most academics were too overwhelmed
   by other work demands to give the Group Five process much time. Thus, while
   full group meetings were important, most of the group's work was accomplished
   through informal discussion, by phone or email. Members met in two's and
   three's – a good example being the lunches that Nina and Kathryn shared in the
   winter of 1999. In these more casual spaces and lower profile moments, we
   debriefed the larger, more structured group meetings and evolved strategies for
   how to proceed. Important decisions about future steps were made in this way.

Ironically, these strategies not only helped Group Five become more cohesive,
they helped the Network as well. As Kari Dehli recalled:

The initial discussions with Group Five 'misfits' were very helpful and important because
they enabled us to question some of the key assumptions of the NALL process. Subsequent
discussions in meetings and email exchanges have continued these discussions and this
networking has been very useful. (Church, 2000:12)

We are reminded here of a point made by Sennett in his discussion of how
communities actually hold together:

In conflict, (people) have to work harder at communicating; as often happens in labour or
diplomatic negotiations, gradually, the ground rules of engagement bind the contending
parties together. … Differences of views often become sharper and more explicit even
though the parties may eventually come to agreement: the scene of conflict becomes a
community in the sense that people learn how to listen and respond to one another even as
they more keenly feel their differences (1998:143).

In pointing to the binding effects of verbal conflict, Sennett argues that there is no
community without the acknowledgement of difference.

David Livingstone responded to our agitation by encouraging Group Five to develop a proposal for group support. Heartened by this, the three of us followed up with a submission for funding that made our ragtag group of studies the only NALL group to secure resources specifically for its own coordinator. By capturing a funded space in the midst of the broader research network, Group Five moved into a new position, ultimately ensuring that the blurry boundaries of informal learning were taken up as the focus of the Network's final conference.

As a result of our oppositional organizing we became – unexpectedly – a "model" of group functioning for NALL Central. We discovered that while marginal to the Network, we were also necessary, and this gave us food for thought about our own projects. Of course, it is possible that we were simply co-opted, easily bought off with a fairly modest grant. While this may be true, the lesson we took away is that compromise and trade-offs are often part of political struggle. Indeed, our informal learning through NALL was frequently about political and social process.

Conclusion

The case studies that constitute this book are snapshots of learning, struggle and redirection. In developing them, we have come to some understanding of the liberatory potential for informal learning. We see it, as least partly, as a process through which people come to contest the challenging changes that are taking place in their lives. Finding ways to engage as citizens, to participate as workers in the organization of that work, to understand the broader parameters of the production process, to work the legal system, to control the quality and safety of sexual encounters, to seize the reins of public discourse – these are understandings that lead to greater determination.

However, while we are hopeful about the potential of informal learning for personal and social transformation, we are also clear that this transformation is conditional. Women may learn how to negotiate more successfully for safer sex; teachers may successfully challenge the prevailing social discourse about public education; but the power dynamics inherent to gender, class, language, race and governmentality endure. Transformation, in this sense, is not social revolution or a profound shift in social relations as much as it is the capacity of individuals and groups to learn how to exist and, in some cases, to improve upon their technical and political abilities to function within inherently inequitable power structures. Informal learning sometimes involves accommodation to new constraints. It can be a process whereby individuals take responsibility for regulating their conduct and re/making their identities to suit life in the new capitalist regime.

We have found these case studies rich – individually, as they were reshaped in conversation through interaction with one another – and collectively, as they stand in relation to each other. We hope that readers of this volume will find the common themes and contrasts as illuminating as we have. By juxtaposing our own informal learning processes as researchers with the learning of broader communities, we encourage our readers to understand the common, everyday nature of informal learning rather than see it as something engaged in only by exotic "others." We hope that this volume pushed the boundaries engendered by structures and discursive categories that may constrain all of our capacities to learn.

Endnotes

[1] Funding for the Network for New Approaches to Lifelong Learning came from the Social Sciences and Humanities Research Council of Canada (SSHRC#818-96-1033).

[2] Results of all these studies are reported in a series of working papers available on the NALL web site at *www.nall.ca* or its "sister" web site *www.wall.ca*

[3] This book also contains chapters from researchers who were members of Group Three, known as "Informal Learning Cultures." They were drawn into the book project after Group Five's process was complete.

[4] At the time when Percy and colleagues did this review, they found almost no published research or comparable discussion. With the exception of people such as Stephen Brookfield, British researchers have tended to focus on increasing participation rates in formal education.

[5] For more on this see Church, K. (2000) "The Communal "We": a conversation piece on the richness of being a network." Available on NALL's web site at *www.nall.ca*

References

Andresen, L., Boud, D. & Cohen, R., 1995, Experience-based learning, in: *Understanding Adult Education*, G. Foley (ed.), Allen & Unwin, Sydney.

Berger, N., 1990, *A Qualitative Study of the Process of Self-Directed Learning*, Doctoral dissertation, Virginia Commonwealth University, Division of Educational Studies, Richmond, VI.

Boud, D. & Middleton, H., 2003, Learning from others at work: communities of practice and informal learning, *Journal of Workplace Learning*, **15(5)**: 194–202.

Church, K., 2000, *The Communal "We"? A Conversation Piece on the Richness of Being a Network*, Available on the website for the Network for New Approaches to Lifelong Learning (NALL) at http://www.nall.ca

Colley, H., Hodkinson, P. & Malcolm, J., 2004, *Informality and Formality in Learning*, Learning and Skills Research Centre, Lifelong Learning Institute, University of Leeds, Leeds, UK.

Coombs, P.H., Prosser, R.C. & Ahmen, M., 1973, *New Paths to Learning for Rural Children and Youth*, UNICEF International Council for Educational Development, New York.

Foucault, M., 1980, *Power/Knowledge: Selected Interviews and Other Writings 1972–1977* (C. Gordon, trans.), Harvester Press, Brighton.

Garrick, J., 1996, Informal learning: some underlying philosophies, *Canadian Journal for the Study of Adult Education*, **19(1)**: 21–46.

Harrison, L., 2003, A case for the underestimated, informal side of lifelong learning, *Australian Journal of Adult Learning*, **43(1)**: 23–41.

Knowles, M., 1975, *Self-Directed Learning*, Cambridge Books, New York.

Leean, C. & Sisco, B., 1981, *Learning Projects and Self-Planned Learning Efforts among Under-educated Adults in Rural Vermont*, National Institute of Education, Washington, DC.

Livingstone, D., 1999, Exploring the icebergs of adult learning: findings of the first Canadian survey of informal learning practices, *Canadian Journal for the Study of Adult Education*, **3(2)**: 49–72.

Livingstone, D., 2005, Expanding conceptions of work and learning: recent research and policy implications, in: N. Bascia, A. Cumming, A. Datnow, K. Leithwood & D. Livingstone (Eds.), *International Handbook of Educational Policy*, Springer, Dordrecht, The Netherlands.

Longworth, N., 2003, *Lifelong Learning in Action: Transforming Education in the 21st Century*, Kogan Page, London/Sterling, VA.

Melville, N., 1987, Bubble and streak: an independent learning project, *Adult Education*, **59(4)**: 317–323.

Penland, P., 1979, Self-initiated learning, *Adult Education Quarterly*, **29(3)**: 170–179.

Percy, K., Burton, C. & Withnall, A., 1994, *Self-Directed Learning among Adults: The Challenge for Continuing Educators*, Association for Lifelong Learning, Lancaster.

Peterson, R.E., 1979, Present sources of education and learning, in *Lifelong Learning in America*, Josey-Bass, San Francisco, CA.

Polanyi, M., 1967, *The Tacit Dimension*, Doubleday, Garden City, NY.

Sennett, R., 1998, *The Corrosion of Character: The Personal Consequences of Work in the New Capitalism*, W.W. Norton, New York/London.

Spear, G. & Mocker, D.W., 1982, Lifelong Learning: formal, non-formal, informal and self-directed, Information Series No 241, ERIC Clearinghouse of Adult Career and Vocational education, Ohio State University National Centre for Research in Vocational Education, Columbus, OH.

Spear, G.E. & Mocker, D.W., 1984, The organizing circumstance: environmental determinants in self-directed learning, *Adult Education Quarterly*, **35(1)**: 1–10.

Tough, A., 1968, *Why Adults Learn: A Study of the Major Reasons for Beginning and Continuing a Learning Project*, Ontario Institute for Studies in Education, Toronto.

Tusting, K., 2003, A review of theories of informal learning, *Working Paper No. 2*, Lancaster Literacy Research Centre, Lancaster, UK.

Watkins, K.E. & Marsick, V.J., 1992, Celebrating informal learning, *Adults Learning*, **2(4)**: 102–104.

Chapter 2
Participation and Learning in Turbulent Times: Negotiations Between the Community and the Personal

Stephen Billett

Introduction

The collection of studies that comprises this volume extends existing boundaries and sets new parameters for the scholarly consideration of adults' lifelong learning. It achieves this through capturing the experiences of individuals and communities who can be seen to be "on the margins" in some ways. It reconceptualizes the scope for, purposes of and spaces where lifelong learning occurs and in ways that are worthwhile for individuals and their communities. The chapters collected in this volume do not sit comfortably with some orthodoxies of lifelong learning. Yet, in some, there is a particular freshness and cogency, and a sensitive but scholarly treatment of topics that would often be seen as "out of bounds" or just too difficult for much mainstream academic work about lifelong learning. Hence, rather than treading lightly, the contributors sharply draw attention to issues that are not effectively addressed within existing scholarly work. Moreover, in doing so, they represent experiences that reflect the contemporary era of turbulent social and economic change, and articulate their impact upon communities and groups of individuals who are marginalized or in peril of being so. Indeed, the freshest and most helpful chapters are those that identify and discuss the particular purposes of individuals' engagement in and learning through their communities in ways that highlight the complex and sometimes contradictory nature of their participation.

Indeed, well-rehearsed concerns about inequities based on gender, social class or occupation seem almost comfortable positions when we are asked to consider, as we are here, the participation and lifelong learning of sex workers, disenfranchised migrants, psychiatric survivors and retirees, to name some. These accounts hone in on the negotiated engagements in research projects, community partnerships and organizations, and the working life that constitutes their learning. As readers, we are often tempted to brush these processes aside. "Unnecessary detail," we argue, or "too difficult to do anything about." And we feel a restless desire to move on. Yet, such an act should generate dissatisfaction. Understanding the theoretical and practical premises and processes of lifelong learning would remain incomplete unless we consider and account for those on-the-margins and their communities. While attention has been given elsewhere to more mainstream adult

21

K. Church et al. (eds.), *Learning through Community: Exploring Participatory Practices*.
© Springer Science+Business Media B.V. 2008

cohorts, the people/groups here remind us that other lifelong needs, purposes and process exist beyond the mainstream. Hence, the contributions to this volume flesh out some of the compelling realities of the messy and complex process of engagement in and learning through social practices.

Consequently, the chapters in this volume engage with and test comfortable and already well-rehearsed concerns as well as, perhaps, the personal biases of readers. In this way they achieve their goal: to consider something of the scope of participation and learning through engaging in communities of different kinds and through different means. This task includes elaborating and illuminating the needs of individuals who are categorised in ways that fail to adequately account for their personal stories, needs and aspirations and approaches to learning. So, the contributions within this volume offer relief from texts about lifelong learning which have become increasingly associated with a one-dimensional view of it as securing economic goals for individuals and those enterprises that employ them. The contributions here remind the reader about the broader project for adult lifelong learning and how it proceeds in different ways in different communities. Against the backdrop of a globalized economic agenda for personal, workplace and national imperatives now pragmatically adopted in many Western economies (Cohn and Addison, 1998), this collection suggests that the boundaries and scope of adult learning are not so easily constrained. Nor are they rendered comprehensive by the kinds of instrumental views and policies that currently constitute the goals for and worth of lifelong learning by global agencies (Organization of Economic and Cultural Development, 1996) and national governments.

However, more than merely capturing and rehearsing the essence of the contributions herein, my intention is to engage with them and consolidate their cases within a conception of lifelong learning premised on participation in communities: participatory practices. There are at least two purposes for doing this. Firstly, to overcome the kinds of marginalization articulated in these contributions, it is necessary to align them to existing and robust conceptions of learning and development, thereby legitimating these accounts of lifelong learning and placing them in a more mainstream discourse. Also, as the editors suggest, the idea of collectively conducted learning needs to be carefully elaborated. Secondly, throughout this volume, the issue of how to describe and capture this process of learning and its outcomes remains contentious and slightly awkward. The moniker of "informal learning" is used throughout, and in different ways and combinations. Yet, such a moniker is ultimately unhelpful in describing the kind of learning processes that are reported here. It denies the ways in which the affordances provided by the communities (albeit in ways which are encouraging or resisting) shape learning, and de-emphasises the agentic engagement of humans in learning processes (Billett, 2002a). Authors Stratton and Jackson report that they did not use the terms "formal", "non-formal" and informal" at all. "The boundaries between non-formal and informal learning … seemed problematic and blurred," they note. My chapter responds to an invitation from the editors to profile the ways that informal learning is a contested concept across all chapters in this volume. In that way, it attempts a conceptual reconciliation.

All of the chapters in this volume reference processes of learning through engagement in communities. I suggest that this process might be understood best not as "informal learning," but as participatory practices (Billett, 2002b). This conception reflects a duality between what is offered to invite the learner to engage and learn (i.e. "affordances" such as direct support, activities and interactions), and how individuals respond to community activities and interactions, albeit at different levels and in different ways. In this view, learning arises through participation in social practices (Sfard, 1998). Quite deliberately, other kinds of settings (e.g. workplaces) become reference points for both individual development and societal continuity and transformation. So, rather than being on-the-margin, less potent or less legitimate than other ways of learning, learning through participation in communities stands as "legitimate," purposeful, and, in many ways, not so distinct from learning which occurs in other kinds of settings.

I make my case in the following way. First, I propose that adult learning be viewed as the engagement of people in communities through practices of participation. Central to this concept is the duality between the affordances of the social world (i.e. the communities in which individuals participate) and how individuals elect to engage in those practices. This duality is negotiated in ways perhaps best characterized as being between the social and personal. I then consider the cases presented in this volume in terms of both affordances and engagement. Emerging through this analysis are patterns of negotiations between affordances and differential engagement by participants. That is, there are relational elements to these negotiations that render inadequate simple prescriptions such as learning being "informal". Finally, I advance some links between what is proposed here and more legitimated approaches to learning, as well as some concluding comments about the contributions of the collected work of this volume.

Participatory Practices

There is a tendency in much of the educational literature to distinguish between teaching/instruction and learning, with the latter being shaped by the former. However, most contemporary accounts of learning support the view that learning arises through individuals" active and ongoing construction of meaning from what they experience, particularly from the social world. In other words, learning is not dependent upon teaching. Further, the presence of intentional arrangements to support learning – such as those in educational institutions – is not required for the promotion and securing of rich and purposeful learning (Scribner, 1984). Instead, it seems that our very conscious engagement with the world is a continual process of learning. This learning is necessary for us to make sense, make decisions and evaluate our actions and conceptions. In short, there is no separation between the process of thinking and acting, and learning (Lave, 1993; Pelissier, 1991). The world we engage with can be seen as shaping learning through its contributions of both brute and institutional fact (Searle, 1995). That is, the brute world with its physicality, its demands and, for adults in particular the process of ageing, shapes how we construe and construct what we experience and how we engage in thinking and acting.

As humans, we have a long heritage of knowledge from which we derive concepts and actions. Over time, we have also generated institutional "facts," such as the conceptual and procedural knowledge to conduct effective work performance. Such facts arise in response to cultural demands (Scribner, 1985) and are manifested situationally (Billett, 2001). They shape what we experience, and what and how we learn. In order for individuals to achieve their purposes for doing and learning, they need to participate in social practices. This participation is negotiated, on the one hand, between what the social world and the brute contributions afford us, and on the other, by how we engage with what is afforded us. Consequently, it is necessary to consider human learning and development in terms of the legacies that arise from these negotiations. The concept of participatory practices (Billett, 2002b), then, acknowledges *both* the factors which afford participation by the social world *and* the bases by which individuals engage with what is afforded them.

There is, however, another legacy of these negotiations between the personal and the social that takes us beyond a dualistic view of human learning and development. We encounter it in societal or cultural practices such as those that characterize the communities featured in this volume. In these settings, individuals do not simply reproduce existing social practices. They constantly remake, revise and transform them, in a process of negotiation between the personal and social and brute world. Hence, parallel processes of ontogenetic development (i.e. across the lifespan) and societal contributions are enacted through participatory practices. Importantly, there are dualities between the social and personal relational. What constitutes an invitation to participate in a social practice for one individual might be seen as restrictive, inappropriate or unhelpful for another. So, beyond either invitations to social participation or individuals' bases for responding, we must understand the relations between the two (Billett, 2006b). Specifically, we must consider how the negotiations between affordances and engagements play out in the communities that are represented in the studies that constitute this volume. Indeed, as the editors pointed out in their introductory chapter, the groups profiled here are "not simple aggregates of individuals."

While these propositions are intended to be consistent with those exercised throughout this collection, I offer another way of capturing these accounts, namely, that they describe learning as participatory practices. For instance, the first case study critically appraises the orthodox focus of adult learning and concept of "informal" learning and seeks a conceptual platform that is more able to account for the gamut of practices and communities wherein individuals participate and learn. The subsequent chapters do much to expand the parameters of what is taken as adult learning, yet the phrase "informal" learning persists throughout in ways that are, in some cases, both redundant and awkward. All contributors to this volume agree that the lives (and learning) of their study participants are powerfully shaped by circumstances, by institutional facts of different sorts, not the least being the different kinds of collectives that are represented. To describe these activities as being "informal" is an unnecessary and not always helpful label.

Affordances and Engagements

In this section, I highlight instances of affordances, engagements and the relationships between the two that characterize, elaborate and in some ways legitimate the learning reported in the communities referenced throughout this volume.

Affordances

The concept of affordances or invitational qualities refers to the degree by which individuals are invited into the social practices in which they participate, and how that participation and subsequent learning is supported. Importantly, the invitational qualities can be positive or negative, and also selective. These affordances can be seen as what comprises the invitational qualities of the social experience (Valsiner, 2000). So whereas a social experience comprises what is expressed by the social world in terms of societal and situational norms and practices, the invitational qualities are how these norms and practices serve the needs and interests of individuals and cohorts. These invitational qualities or affordances are expressed at a cultural, societal and situational level. For instance, Stratton and Jackson (2007) refer to the way that the affordances associated with family and work life are often distributed in distinct and uneven ways across genders, and issues of class provide instances of the distribution of societal affordances. Other contributors refer to societal status as shaping the invitation to participate in a particular community. These instances reflect the distribution of affordances on societal and cultural bases. Moreover, the chapters reference a range of instances that describe how these invitational qualities are enacted and distributed in ways that particularly reflect how these contributions to learning are constituted at the situational level.

Take, for example, the editors' description of how their research cluster developed. In Chapter 1, they provide an account of the changing affordances and bases of engagement within this collective endeavour (Church et al., 2007a). Overall, the process was one of forming a community within a larger project that was enacted using a research paradigm and disciplinary bases that were not accommodating. In the context of that community, the "Group Five" projects represented purposeful affordances to what might otherwise have been a wholly marginalizing experience. The affordances provided support for the members and permitted a level of engagement that, ultimately, resulted in this publication. To maximize those affordances, the group moved its meeting site from the university, a setting which was seen as uninviting, to an environment that was more invitational and prompted more open participation. However, the invitational qualities in this new space were transformed again through different levels of participation and also by the occasional presence of the manager of the research network.

Similarly, Meaghan's (2007) account of learning safe sex practices among Canadian prostitutes presents a complex instance of the enactment of affordances. Those outside the sex work community see the work, variously, as deviant, undesirable and illegal. The workers are portrayed, quite erroneously, as a health threat. Hence, the kind of societal support or affordances for learning safe sex practices are likely to be restricted to whatever can be afforded within the sex work community. Moreover, this societal sentiment about sex workers leaves open the invitation for others to victimize, take advantage of or other-wise abuse prostitutes, which may in turn cause them difficulty in protecting themselves against physical and sexual violence. Such is the exercise of this sentiment that these workers cannot always rely on police protection; police may be unsympathetic or even exploitive. So the societal affordances are low and represent threats to the safety of these workers.

Yet, Meaghan proposes that within the community of sex workers, particularly those engaged in collective practices, experienced co-workers do extend significant support: from specific sexual techniques to a range of practices and behaviours that make the work less risky. These affordances are characterized as mentoring, apprenticeship and peer education, all terms that we generally find associated with more socially sanctioned forms of work. Moreover, and in consideration of trans-forming a social practice, Meaghan reports that the power of collective action by sex workers has afforded a level of legitimacy, legal standing and societal tolerance in New Zealand. In this way, the sex-worker community is engaged in transforming the societal sentiment about sex work. Yet, those workers who operate on the streets are denied some of the affordances of the worker community that can be found in brothels. The concerns for safe work and affordances to assist people to work safely in this occupation are serious. Meaghan claims the mortality rate for female prostitutes is 40 times higher than that for the general population. This rate would spark public outcry if it pertained to employment that is socially sanctioned. Consider the occupational health and safety regimes that are enacted to protect min-ers, fishing boat operatives and forest workers in countries such as Canada. The point here is that societal affordances are central to the kinds of risks that sex workers face and it is the affordances of the community that stand to protect these workers against this risk.

Curiously analogous here are the studies done by Bascia (2007), and Dehli and Fumia's (2007) which provide accounts of how the societal portrayal of teachers also renders them open to public criticism and lower levels of support within the community. Portrayals of these workers as militant, unprofessional and lazy leave them open to public criticism and constrains how they can act (Dehli and Fumia, 2007). So, again, societal sentiment acts as an affordance that constrains teachers' capacity to engage with the community and inhibits the activities of those representing their interests.

In their study of the Healthy Cities project, Schugurensky and Miles describe a range of affordances that enable senior citizens to advise their local government about generating a better environment for older residents. Many had been invited to participate in this project through existing community organizations or affiliations. Processes, spaces and mechanisms for taking up positions were established to make it possible for participants' contributions to be accepted. However, those affordances were not equally distributed. It was noted that the majority of participants were Anglo, and had levels of education that did not represent the senior population of Toronto. Others, feeling excluded from a process that seems to be more invitational to these particular kinds of individuals, banned themselves from participation. Importantly, as one individual reported, the very views that were not represented were the ones that were most dire and required to be a priority for improving the health and welfare of Toronto citizens.

Conversely, other communities afforded opportunities for those on the margin. A good example is the courier service run by psychiatric survivors that is described by Church et al. (2007b). It afforded its members not only employment, but also a capacity to engage in organizational and decision-making roles in a community organized service. So, more than a scheme that afforded employment, this community-based business offered a base of support and engagement to these survivors of psychiatric treatment. Through their work, they learned about providing a service, building a capacity to organize and also to assist others. In a similar way, Church and her colleagues report on the activities of a community organization that supports the learning of English for migrant women. Indirectly, it also provides them with garment making skills as it provides them with the opportunity to engage with and observe other women employed in the garment making industry. But beyond these language and skill development opportunities, it offered the affordance of social contact to women who might otherwise be isolated in conducting work that is often home based. Again, the learning arising here was more than technical; it also secured shared understanding and subjectivity through the development of a collective identity for these women. These examples are noteworthy for the way they highlight the salience, necessity and approach by community organizations to provide affordances to those who are marginalized by societal sentiments and, accordingly, experience little in the way of a welcoming invitation to participate. So, here these organizations afforded bulwarks against weak societal affordances.

Yet, as if to emphasize the turbulent nature of contemporary times and relations between communities and their participants, Church et al. (2007b) note that perceptions of being positively invitational can quickly change and inhibit participation. For instance, despite a long history of serving the needs of the marginalized in the provision of food and training to prepare food, some community groups perceived Resto Pop, the community restaurant, as being less invitational when it engaged with a government department to secure continuity of its funding. As Church et al. (2007b) note, from being seen as reflecting particular community needs, the restaurant came to be seen as a pariah by certain affinity groups who felt it had violated their interests through engaging with government to secure these funds. Hence, perceptions of its affordances and bases for participation rapidly changed. In these ways the degree by which individuals were invited to participate and learn in their communities stands as a consistent theme across the studies.

Engagement

In this section, I shift my attention to consider the bases by which individuals elect to participate in socially derived practices, such as work activities or community-organized activities. While these practices and communities will afford different levels of invitational qualities, including direct guidance and support for learning, ultimately the bases of individuals" engagement with these practices will be salient in shaping their learning, and how they conduct those practices. For instance, individual researchers within the Group Five research project exercised different bases for engagement in the project, which included the frequency and level of their participation in meetings and interactions associated with this group (Church et al., 2007a). Hence, the kind of engagement and learning was not uniformly experienced across this group of researchers. This had consequences for the continuity of the community of researchers and also affected their opportunities to share their interests with others. The important point here is that tagging a group of individuals as teachers, psychiatric survivors, migrants, older residents, etc. is not sufficient to understand their participation and lifelong learning. Instead, it seems that individual's perceptions about and ways of participating in communities and socially derived practices are shaped by personal factors as much as collective attributes.

Note, for instance, that Church and her colleagues perceived garment workers as agentic in their participation and learning (Church et al., 2007b). These workers engaged with others in their community, observed practices and were able to develop shared understanding by participating in activities which otherwise might not have been available to them as isolated and often home-based workers. The same could be said of the couriers and the restaurant workers. However, what is most important in these examples is the quality of their engagement with and learning about the collective discourse that was being enacted in the restaurant and the courier company. In a similar way, the practices of sex workers require them to be agentic in participating in their work (Meaghan, 2007). This includes the negotiation of sexual acts to avoid disease and unwanted pregnancies, but also to protect themselves against physical and sexual assault. The bases for participating in sex work were quite distinct, thereby exposing these workers to greater or lower levels of risk. Yet, it was suggested that solo workers, who were usually young or desperate because of an addiction, were less likely to engage in the kinds of safe work practices that were promoted by more experienced and, perhaps "in control," sex workers. So here, elements of social and brute fact played out in particular ways that shaped the women's engagement in their paid work. Consequently, the bases by which they engage with other workers is premised on important imperatives for them which include being able to control the situation and negotiate their potentially perilous work. The brute fact of addiction and social sentiments about sex work afford little comfort to these individuals.

Similarly, in the Healthy Cities project it was important for older Toronto residents to engage in order to shape local government policy (Schugurensky and Myers, 2007). The project offered a basis for individuals to express the concerns about and needs for their communities. Yet, again, the bases for individuals' engagement were quite diverse. A number of participants in the task force had previously been involved in local government; some earlier had been aldermen. Some of these claimed or feigned reluctance to be involved, but went ahead because it was their duty to do so. Yet, others struggled to engage and participate fully and viewed their engagement as being compromised by the activities and capacities of others. They resented the character of other participants from higher social and economic status, suggesting that the perspectives they brought did not reflect the reality for the most disadvantaged senior citizens in Toronto – those, for example, who were unable to provide themselves with adequate food and pharmaceuticals. A few individuals had sponsored themselves to participate in the project and were keen and agentic to do so (Schugurensky and Myers, 2007). In this way, all participants demonstrate agency but the direction and intent of exercising it can be seen as being distinct.

So the bases of individuals' engagement with what is afforded them as directed by their agency, personal histories and circumstances shaped how they participated and learned in these communities. That learning is likely shaped by the direction, intensity and focus of their engagement with their capacities to shape their construal and construction of what they experience (Billett et al., 2005). Yet individuals' capacity to negotiate is shaped by both brute and social facts of the kinds outlined above. Hence, participation and learning through these practices is not uniform. Instead, it is shaped by relations between what is afforded individuals and how they take up what is afforded them.

Relational Participation

So far I have emphasized two contributing elements: the personal (i.e. engagement) and the social (i.e. affordances). Rather than separate them as irreconcilable dualisms, I would argue that these elements should be understood as dualities, in other words, as concepts which are interlinked. So, beyond a consideration of the elements of the duality between the social and personal, the relations between them are central in understanding how individuals engage and learn through their participation. Writing elsewhere I have stressed that learning is shaped in different ways by the degree of press that the social world can enact upon the individual, and also the degree by which individuals construe, engage with and can negotiate what they experience (Billett, 2006b). The important point here is this relational quality. The negotiation between the personal and social is not uniform, even within the same circumstance. The kinds of learning that are illuminated by the contributions to this volume are subject to the negotiation between the press of the social world, including the community which individuals participate, on the one hand, and on the other hand the degree by which the individual recognizes this press, and engages and appropriates what they encounter.

For instance, in Stratton and Jackson's study (2007), practitioners of community economic development viewed the insights of many academics as unrealistic and not related to practice. Consequently, what the field calls for is individuals who can understand the requirements of both perspectives, those "bridge people" who can effectively span the two fields of endeavour. Indeed, they claim, these bridge-builders are a particular kind of academic. So, whereas perhaps the majority of academics are drawn to focus within their own field, some elect to engage with communities outside universities, responding to the press of their social world in ways that are quite distinct from the majority of academics. For the community development practitioners in this study, the academic community is seen as offering particular kinds of affordances which are generally held to be unhelpful. All the same, these practitioners require the activities of academics with a particular orientation to engage with and assist them.

Indeed, the bases for participation in the Network for New Approaches to Lifelong Learning as discussed by the editors in Chapter 1 were clearly relational. They were situated and took root in a community comprised of the Group Five projects (Church et al., 2007a). Academics leading the Network's mainstream projects appear to have experienced a different level of affordances and bases for participation in NALL overall. By contrast, those in the "fringe" projects construed what was afforded them as comprising a lower level of invitation. Moreover, even within the Group Five grouping there were distinct bases of participation.

As noted, there are likely to be quite distinct bases for sex workers to negotiate between the personal and social. As Meaghan (2007) reports, some women are particularly well positioned to work safely and be in control through regular and wealthy clients – a well-protected environment and careful client communication. However, through circumstances, others are pressed into more risky practices which highlight the relational bases for negotiating work, working life and lifelong learning. The contrast is perhaps most starkly represented in the comparison between the experienced sex worker's operation in the Niagara area and the indigenous woman in Winnipeg. With a regular clientele and efforts to tailor her services to meet their needs, the former is far more in control than the latter, who engages in street prostitution to feed a drug habit, is open to physical and sexual violence and, according to Meaghan, even exploitation by law enforcement officers.

Similarly, the participatory processes which underpinned the Healthy Cities project (Schugurensky and Myers, 2007) were quite distinct and relational. Some citizens were selected for their participation because of their experience with community groups and participatory processes, such as local government. These individuals have particular forms of social capital which may have made it easier to engage in the process of contributing to this project. Others, however, referred to feeling distanced and marginalized by language and race. So, while some learned that their previous work in local government was valued and situated them well to make further contributions, others learned that because of their language, race or social origins that they were treated in a different and inferior way. Therefore, despite the efforts of an effective chairwoman, affordances and opportunities to learn were unequally distributed.

The point here is that beyond the affordance and bases of engagement are the particular ways in which the enactment of both is relational. This can be seen as complicating and rendering the processes of lifelong learning as personally unique in some ways, and thus difficult to order from government or societal perspectives. However, it reflects the reality of the learning. Hence, there is a need to consider both the array of personal, social and brute factors that shape this learning.

Legitimating Learning Through Community Practice

The conception and enactment of participatory practices as detailed in the contributions of this volume have pedagogic and curricular qualities. The pedagogy of practice is evident in these contributions as is the organization and enactment of practice curricula. Evident in the activities of sex workers, migrant women learning about garment making, and psychiatric survivors were the enactment of curricula generated by the community-based activities in which individuals engaged. In addition to the specific pedagogic practices such as apprenticeship, mentoring and support that were afforded by these workplaces, there was also the agentic engagement of the participants. Observation, engagement in discussion and community activities were enacted by the participants as learners. Thus, aspects of practice-based pedagogies were referred to throughout with their intentional purposes of developing capacities and also sustaining and remaking the communities in which these study participants were situated. There was also evidence of learners being agentic, with subjects playing active roles not only in developing their own capacities but also actively remaking the practices in which they engaged. Moreover, some of these communities provided structured opportunities for learning which are analogous to the organization of curricula within educational institutions. They are consistent with concepts such as "the learning curriculum" (Lave, 1990), which are helpful in understanding and legitimating learning through participation in social practice. For instance, at A-Way Express Couriers, there was a learning pathway which engaged psychiatric survivors not only in the task of being a courier, but also in the organization and administration of the courier service.

Moreover, there was evidence not only of the intended learning outcomes from participation in these communities, but also unintended outcomes. For instance, some participants learned activism through participating in practice. Others, through participating in communities for social purposes, also learned more about their paid work (e.g. garment workers). The identification of these curricular and pedagogic dimensions serve to reinforce the inadequacy of the use of the term "informal" to describe how learning experiences are organized and enacted in social practices such as those featured in this volume. Therefore, just as many of the qualities that characterize and legitimate the intended, enacted and experienced curricula in educational institutions can be identified in workplace settings (Billett, 2006a), the same qualities are identifiable in the instances of community and social practices discussed here. As with workplace settings, it seems that the intentional bases for participation, learning and sustaining the communities referred to here stand as purposeful and legitimate instances of curricula that are not well characterized by the moniker of being "informal."

Participation in Learning Through Engagement in Communities in Turbulent Times

Several elements stand out as clear objectives for this volume: the need for a broader set of purposes that would legitimate adult learning; a more nuanced understanding of the processes and practices that comprise adults' lifelong learning; and the requirement to understand how these practices impact communities and individuals in these turbulent times. These objectives are rehearsed by all contributors and illuminated powerfully in the cases that they present.

In summary, I see here a fourfold contribution. Firstly, the contributors identify, elaborate and illuminate processes and circumstances of lifelong learning that go beyond those that have traditionally been given attention (i.e. schools, colleges and universities) and those that have received much recent attention (i.e. in large workplaces). To these highly researched and discussed learning spaces, they have added participation in community or collaborative programmes for migrants, sex workers, psychiatric survivors, home workers, senior citizens, union workers and teachers' classrooms and staff rooms.

Secondly, the collection captures something of the contestation of learning through the process and project of researching adult learning. Beginning with the initial misalignment between the core thrust of the NALL project and the work of Group Five, the processes of the research work are made transparent and presented as informative instances of social action. Through their process, the researchers themselves rehearse themes that occur amongst the researched throughout this volume. The explicitness of the research story and its perceived misalignment with mainstream programme goals provides a useful contribution about another kind of work: research. This is effectively elaborated through the rich associations between the researchers and those whom they research and write about, and becomes thematic for this volume. There is a sense of engagement that sustains and directs the writing of these chapters that provides helpful insights and promotes empathy. Detachment is not part of understanding the needs of migrant women, sex workers, senior citizens, those who have survived psychiatric experiences, and those marginalized through life experiences. There is also the exploration of teachers' roles as they struggle with their identities and the public (governmental) portrayal of those identities, as well as community education development practitioners' work which informs premises for their agency and learning. So, collectively, this work presents a compelling case for why research into adults' goals and learning should be engaged and embodied, not detached and disembodied. In engaging those on the margins, this volume brings to the table perspectives that urge considerations beyond the current orthodoxy of lifelong learning for boosting individuals' enterprises productivity.

Thirdly, the collective contributions emphasize the complexity of the practices that social institutions serve to support and/or regulate individuals' participation and learning. Whether it be senior citizens' involvement in local government; sex workers need for supportive and educative practices; community-run restaurants that are perceived to have "sold out" for having secured government support; the contradictory discourses that teachers are subject to; home workers negotiating with their support agency; or female migrants addressing issues of immigration law, the studies highlight the fractious, contested, and necessarily contradictory practices that are inherent in these engagements. Easy conceptualizations, such as these being the "hidden" curriculum, are rendered inadequate by the complexities of the interdependence between individuals and social institutions, and among the social institutions involved as exemplified here. The salient conceptual contribution is to emphasize the interweaving of both social and individual contributions to individuals' learning.

Finally, although these studies focus on marginalized individuals and cohorts, the lessons they afford have a broader implication. These studies are highly amplified accounts of individuals' struggle for self development and stability in changing circumstances and these turbulent times that are characterized by increasing instability. Even at the personal level, the brute fact of ageing and the social facts of participating in working life exposes individuals to the need for learning, the often compensatory learning, sometimes critical learning, sometimes socially critical learning as adults work through their lives.

Yet, and in conclusion, to do justice to this rich body of work requires going beyond unhelpful monikers such as "informal learning." Instead, it is necessary to understand the actions of the individuals as participants in social life through engagement with particular kinds of communities, and conversely, the ways in which these communities afford opportunities for learning. Together, these comprise the participatory practices through which lifelong learning progresses. However, such participatory practices are not solely the domain of marginalized individuals and communities. They are played out as well in educational institutions, large and small workplaces, in the home, and in research projects, and the other kinds of communities and social practices as represented within this volume. Clearly, the overall project of adult lifelong learning has progressed from focusing simply on individuals' personal and cultural development outside the workplace and then throughout working life. These chapters take us beyond the current theoretical preoccupation with learning linked to the maintenance and development of national economies. Indeed, they offer something of the scope of the adult learning project throughout life itself.

References

Bascia, N., 2007, How Alberta Teachers' Association maintains an even keel, in K. Church, N. Bascia & E. Shragge (Eds.), *Learning through Community: Exploring Participatory Practices*, Springer, Dordrecht, The Netherlands.

Billett, S., 2001, Knowing in practice: re-conceptualising vocational expertise, *Learning and Instruction*, **11(6)**: 431–452.

Billett, S., 2002a, Critiquing workplace learning discourses: participation and continuity at work, *Studies in the Education of Adults*, **34(1)**: 56–67.

Billett, S., 2002b, Workplace pedagogic practices: co-participation and learning, *British Journal of Educational Studies*, **50(4)**: 457–481.

Billett, S., 2006a, Constituting the workplace curriculum, *Journal of Curriculum Studies*, **38(1)**: 31–48.

Billett, S., 2006b, Relational interdependence between social and individual agency in work and working life, *Mind, Culture and Activity*, **13(1)**: 53–69.

Billett, S., Smith, R. & Barker, M., 2005, Understanding work, learning and the remaking of cultural practices, *Studies in Continuing Education*, **27(3)**: 219–237.

Church, K., Bascia, N. & Shragge, E., 2007a, Informal learning: the turbulence of Academic Collaboration, in K. Church, N. Bascia & E. Shragge (Eds.), *Learning through Community*, Springer, Dordrecht, The Netherlands.

Church, K., Shragge, E., Fontan, J.M. & Ng, R., 2007b, While no one in watching: learning in social action among people who are excluded from the labour market, in K. Church, N. Bascia & E. Shragge (Eds.), *Learning through Community*, Springer, Dordrecht, The Netherlands.

Cohn, E. & Addison, J.T., 1998, The economic returns to lifelong learning in OECD countries, *Education Economics*, **6(3)**: 253–307.

Dehli, K. & Fumia, D., 2007, Teachers' informal learning, identity and contemporary education reform, in K. Church, N. Bascia & E. Shragge (Eds.), *Learning through Community*, Springer, Dordrecht, The Netherlands.

Lave, J., 1990, The culture of acquisition and the practice of understanding, in J.W. Stigler, R.A. Shweder & G. Herdt (Eds.), *Cultural Psychology*, Cambridge University Press, Cambridge.

Lave, J., 1993, The practice of learning, in S. Chaiklin & J. Lave (Eds.), *Understanding Practice: Perspectives on Activity and Context*, Cambridge University Press, Cambridge.

Meaghan, D., 2007, Stigma to sage: learning and teaching safer sex practices among Canadian sex trade workers, in Church, K., Bascia, N. & Shragge, E. (Eds.), *Learning through Community*, Springer, Dordrecht, The Netherlands.

Organisation of Economic and Cultural Development (OECD), 1996, *Lifelong Learning for All*, OECD, Paris.

Pelissier, C., 1991, The anthropology of teaching and learning, *Annual Review of Anthropology*, **20**: 75–95.

Schugurensky, D. & Myers, J.P., 2007, Informal civic learning through engagement in local democracy: the case of the Seniors" Task Force of Healthy City Project, in K. Church, N. Bascia & E. Shragge (Eds.), *Learning through Community*, Springer, Dordrecht, The Netherlands.

Scribner, S., 1984, Studying working intelligence, in B. Rogoff & J. Lave (Eds.), *Everyday Cognition: Its Development in Social Context*, Harvard University Press, Cambridge.

Scribner, S., 1985, Vygostky''s use of history, in Wertsch, J.V. (ed.), *Culture, Communication and Cognition: Vygotskian Perspectives*, Cambridge University Press, Cambridge.

Searle, J.R., 1995, *The Construction of Social Reality*. Penguin, London.

Sfard, A., 1998, On two metaphors for learning and the dangers of choosing just one, *Educational Researcher*, **27(2)**: 4–13.

Stratton, M. & Jackson, E.T., 2007, Knowledge collisions: perspectives from CED practitioners working with women, in K. Church, N. Bascia & E. Shragge (Eds.), *Learning through Community*, Springer, Dordrecht, The Netherlands.

Valsiner, J., 2000, *Culture and Human Development*, Sage, London.

Part II
From the "Margins": Case Studies

Chapter 3
Women, Violence and Informal Learning

Shahrzad Mojab and Susan McDonald

Introduction

This chapter is based on a comparative study recently conducted among immigrant women of two distinct communities in the Greater Toronto Area: the Spanish-speaking community and the Kurds. The purpose of the study was to contribute to our understanding of the impact of violence on immigrant women's learning. What is the relationship between patriarchal, political, social and economical power structures of violence and the experience of immigrant women's learning in the diaspora? How do women who have experienced violence either in domestic or war situations best learn about their rights, the law and strategies for resistance? What features are similar or different between these types of learning? We argue that the experience of violence does impact learning. It should not, however, be seen as a delimiter or as an impediment to learning, but rather as an accepted fact that should be taken into account in any learning effort.

Each author worked closely with one of two communities. Our division of labour was based on general familiarity as well as particular knowledge of either the Spanish or Kurdish languages. Estimates on the size of the Spanish-speaking population in Toronto vary depending upon definitions and measurement methods used; an accepted number is 145,000. The Kurds constitute a much smaller number and are more recent arrivals to Canada. According to the 1996 Statistics Canada survey, there are 4,225 Kurds living in Canada.

An in-depth, non-structured, conversational interview was used in order to document the life histories of these women as these were told, perceived and created by them. The Spanish-speaking women also participated in a workshop wherein they focused on learning about the law. Fourteen women from each community participated in the research. These women represented a cross section of socio-economic and educational backgrounds within their communities. Nevertheless, they shared many similarities as "immigrant" women in Canada; in particular, their labour force participation manifested the racialized and genderized nature of the Canadian job market (Mojab, 2000).

The distinctiveness of the two communities has provided us with rich data by which to understand the impact of trauma caused by violence against immigrant women. In

K. Church et al. (eds.), *Learning through Community: Exploring Participatory Practices.*
© Springer Science + Business Media B.V. 2008

this study, the concept of "violence" against women was used broadly. We included women who were in situations of domestic violence as well as women who experienced political violence or violence as a result of war. The Spanish-speaking women had especially experienced domestic violence, while the Kurdish women either participated directly in the Kurdish nationalist movements or lived in a family where a close member (often a male member, i.e. a husband, father or brother) was a political activist.

In reporting and analysing our data in this chapter, we try to maintain the distinct voices of the women of each community in order to avoid hasty generalizations. Consideration of the particularities of each case can enhance our understanding of some of the hidden elements of violence and the subtleties of women's ways of knowing and learning.

Violence and Informal Learning

Although learning has been studied for a long time, as a highly complex and contingent human undertaking it remains inadequately theorized. In modern(ist) educational practice and discourse, the focus is on formal learning in schools and institutions; however, *informal* learning has always and at all times been equal to or even more significant than formalized learning as it continues throughout the life of an individual. We are just beginning to pay attention to people's informal, ongoing learning that is crucial for living in an ever-changing world (Garrick, 1996; Hake, 1999; Tobias, 1999). There has been no significant theorization on the learning of uprooted, war-stricken women in the process of re-rooting in Western countries. Our study aims at contributing to the debate on issues of informal learning and begins from a premise that learning is a socially constructed phenomenon and, as such, is "genderized," "racialized" and shaped by other social formations including class or immigrant status.

Our collective knowledge about violence against women has improved considerably. The academic journal *Violence Against Women* is now in its sixth year of publishing. In the area of action, too, there has been some progress, although one in three women around the world was "beaten, coerced into sex or abused in some way" at the turn of the twenty-first century (See Carey, 2000:A22). Under the pressure of women's and feminist movements, ending violence has become a target of public policy. For example, the federal and some provincial governments in Canada have run television advertisements to raise public awareness about the need to end violence against women. For the first time, the 1999 General Social Survey by Statistics Canada collected data on spousal violence. In 1993, Statistics Canada released the results of the *Violence against Women Survey*, which was the first of its kind with 12,300 women interviewed across Canada. The study found that 29% of married women (including those in common–law relationships) have been subjected to violence at the hands of a marital partner at some point in the relationship (Statistics Canada, 1993). However, one of the criticisms of the Statistics Canada study was that it reached women who speak one of the official languages (French or English). Therefore, the results do not reflect the prevalence of violence against women who speak other languages (Davis-Barron, 1993:A16; See also Bannerji, 1999) such as the women who have participated in this study. For instance, there are no statistically accurate studies on the prevalence of domestic abuse in either of the communities that we studied (McDonald, 1999a).

There is however, a small, but growing body of literature looking at immigrant women who have experienced domestic abuse and their unique social, legal and economic problems (see, e.g., Orloff et al., 1995; Jang, 1994; Roy, 1995; Martin and Mosher, 1995). There are also some studies (MacLeod and Shin, 1994; Godin, 1994; Law Courts, 1995; McDonald, 1999b) that focus on their needs, including the specific legal needs of immigrant women in Canada. Crenshaw (1991), Richie (1985) and Richie and Kanuha (1993) all examine the issue of domestic violence in immigrant and visible minority communities challenging feminist writing. Ammons (1995), Wang (1996) and Dasgupta (1998) address the harm of cultural stereotypes within the domestic abuse context.

It is essential to understand and acknowledge the impact of violence on learning for women. For every woman, the duration, nature and intensity of the violence varies and, consequently, the severity of the trauma experienced also varies. Judith Herman (1992:33) provides the following definition of trauma:

> Traumatic events overwhelm the ordinary systems of care that give people a sense of control, connection and meaning. Traumatic events are extraordinary, not because they occur rarely, but because they overwhelm the ordinary human adaptations to life. They confront human beings with the extremities of helplessness and terror and evoke the responses of catastrophe.

As Herman's definition suggests, when an individual experiences trauma she loses her sense of control, connection and meaning. The complexities of beginning a new life in the diaspora and learning about the new country's legal system (whether criminal, family or immigration law) can only compound this loss. The woman must be able to regain control, connection and meaning in order to live a healthier, fuller life.

The severity of the effects of trauma depends upon the quality and duration of the event, the availability and timing of appropriate treatment and conditions for recovery, or access to a safe place to resettle into and the personality and coping strategies of the individual (Rathus and Jeffrey, 1980). In their work on violence, women and education, Rundle and Ysabet-Scott (1995:8) outline the effects of trauma. A fear of being punished, humiliated or rejected for making mistakes can contribute to a difficulty in beginning new things or taking risks. As well, one's sleep patterns are often disturbed and the resulting exhaustion may cause individuals to find learning draining and tiring.

Trauma erodes one's sense of self, one's self-esteem and confidence; there are feelings of blame, guilt and responsibility for the traumatic event. All these feelings can work to prevent an individual from becoming a successful learner. Indeed, the pressure to learn or to make decisions, as in a custody battle or dealing with settlement issues, can augment the feelings of guilt, shame and low self-esteem. These feelings manifest themselves in many ways. One of these is through disassociation or a sense of detachment – spacing out, feeling numb, being unaware of what is going on.

A further effect is the inability to concentrate, which may be manifested by difficulty listening, distraction or preoccupation. An individual may experience panic attacks, including faintness, dizziness, shaking or feeling out of control and flashbacks to the trauma itself or to the feelings that the trauma caused. Given the nature of domestic abuse or the condition of war, there may be a concern for safety: in the learning place, travelling, in the home. Finally, there may be health problems, such as depression or physical ailments. Perhaps the most serious of these effects is the inability to trust. Trust opens one up to vulnerability and alters power positions (Baier, 1986:240 and Shay, 1995). It can create dependency, feeling vulnerable to disappointment or betrayal, and risking self-harm. Any of these conditions can create difficulties in the learning process.

There has been some research on trauma and its implications for learning. For example, Gowen and Bartlett (1997) look at women in abusive situations and the resulting impact on literacy learning. Horsman's latest work, *Too Scared to Learn* (1999), is a comprehensive text detailing her research across Canada with women around issues of literacy and violence. Horsman asked two questions of literacy workers and participants. What impacts of abuse do you see in your literacy programme? How can/should literacy programmes address the impact of violence? Horsman found that both workers and learners were overwhelmingly frustrated. Learners felt that their failure to learn must prove that they are "stupid" and workers in turn felt incompetent. She argues that the link between violence and illiteracy is crucial and the silence must be broken in order to address how learning can be effectively carried out under these conditions. We share Horsman's concerns. We, too, see learners' sense of failure and suggest ways of overcoming traumatic impediments to learning.

Informal learning – how individuals learn at work and through daily interactions – can occur anywhere along a continuum of intentionality and consciousness. Watkins and Marsick (1992) have proposed a theory of informal learning that, while focused on learning in organizational settings, is useful for this study. One of the seven elements they identify is "delimiters," or the limitations of the learning context. These delimiters can be viewed as the framing problem, or the naming of the things to which we will attend, or the placing of limitations on our context. The delimiters in a given situation can limit learning to a narrower context. Various delimiters were evident in the women's situations: language, access to resources, lack of information, trauma and crises, as well as other survival needs. An understanding of such delimiters can assist us in facilitating learning. As English notes in her study, adults are "capable of sorting out the priorities that have meaning and practical benefit to their lives" (1999:392). Recognizing these priorities and respecting them will go a long way to providing a meaningful learning experience.

Susan, Shahrzad and the Communities of Women

Accessing traumatized women's learning and learning styles requires a special methodology of sensitivity. We utilized a feminist-anti-racist participatory methodology to facilitate the participation of the women in the definition of their learning process, legal needs and in the design and implementation of solutions. This method enables the researcher to establish a relationship of trust and respect with participants in the research. Feminist methodology advocates an integrative and interdisciplinary approach to knowledge, with an emphasis on beginning with embodied people and their location in social space.

We used feminist research methods such as oral history and testimony to collect different types of data; multiple sources of information lead to better qualitative studies as compared to those based on a single source (Green-Powell, 1997). The use of testimony as an interview technique helped women who witnessed and/or experienced violence to alleviate their pain in remembering the events (Agger, 1992). The feminist oral narratives enabled us to examine the Kurdish and Spanish-speaking communities as a whole while locating the individual woman within her community; as Reinharz suggests, through the individual we can understand culture, and culture can help us to understand the individual (Reinharz, 1992). In other words, feminist oral narratives and life history methods permitted us to participate in the social systems in which Kurdish and Spanish-speaking women were implicated (Clandinin and Connelly, 1994; Freeman, 1993; Okley and Callaway, 1992; Thomson, 1995).

Susan and Women in the Spanish-Speaking Community

The Women's Program of the Centre for Spanish-Speaking Peoples, Toronto, offers information, counseling and support to women who have experienced abuse. While staff members offer assistance in numerous areas, they themselves are not legally trained and there is no lawyer at the Centre who practices family or criminal law. As a result, the legal needs, both representation and information, of the clients are immense. Through consultation with the staff and based upon my own work (McDonald, 1998, 1999a, b), two goals for the initial phase of this research were established. The first was to identify the legal education and information needs of Spanish-speaking immigrant women who have experienced domestic abuse. The second was to determine how best to address these needs with consideration for particular factors which could impede or enhance learning: the social location of the women, pedagogy and the impact of trauma on learning. The final phase of the research was intended to develop and implement the participants' learning and action ideas.

Drawing upon my relevant work in Chile, I conceptualized the research process as one that would move from individual interaction and data collection (one-to-one, researcher and participant) to collective interaction and data collection (the group of participants and the researcher) (McDonald, 1998). This process was important in facilitating the development of trusting relationships between the researcher, participants and community partners, and among participants themselves.

The staff of the Women's Program believed that a traditional focus group would not be an adequate method for the collective inquiry. Given the experiences of the women, the staff believed that they would need a longer time period to become acquainted and trust one another in order to talk openly and work well together in a group setting. A retreat and workshop were designed to address this need, and the research was divided into two phases.

During the summer of 1999, 14 women were interviewed in their own homes. The majority of the interviews were in Spanish, with some in English if the woman so chose. Many but not all of the women were clients or former clients of the Women's Program. Their ages ranged from mid-twenties to mid-sixties. All but one was married and all but one had children; some had grandchildren. Most had permanent residency or citizenship status in Canada. Their education and class backgrounds varied widely. Most were in receipt of social assistance, although some were working. The group was clearly socially diverse.

The retreat and workshop took place at a farm outside of the city. The first day was spent getting to know one another, swimming in the pond and enjoying the outdoors. This was their first time out of the city for many woman and their children.

The workshop took place on the second day. A variety of participatory activities were used which allowed the women to design a legal education and information programme to address their needs. The workshop and activities were developed to reflect identified needs while maintaining the confidentiality of the data collected during the individual interviews. Hence, after introductions and the opportunity to talk about expectations, a group agreement based on respect, trust and confidentiality was developed to use for the day. The women were then led through an exercise designed to understand differences and similarities, as well as privilege and discrimination. The next activity identified barriers in accessing the legal system both in theory and in practice. After a break for lunch, there were two more exercises, the first to identify the women's legal information and education needs, and the second to design a programme that would address these needs. All the activities were grounded in the women's experiences. There was enough time for women to share and learn from one another.

Data were gathered to specifically identify the legal education and information needs of Spanish-speaking immigrant women who have experienced domestic abuse and to determine how best to address these needs. The individual and collective inquiry also produced a significant amount of data on several other themes: power in domestic relationships, the nature and forms of abuse, the women's experiences with the legal system, and their learning strategies during crises and at other times.

Shahrzad and Kurdish Women

The Kurdish nationalist movement is among the most persistent ones in modern history. Since the end of the Second World War, it has involved four nation-states (Iran, Iraq, Turkey and Syria), major western and eastern powers (in particular, the United States, Britain, France and the former Soviet Union), and multiple local actors. The latter include various political organizations and different classes such as landowners, peasants, workers and urban bourgeoisie. Women's involvement in the movement has varied, from a marginal non-presence to a more active involvement in the conduct of politics and war. In the last two decades of the twentieth century, women joined the ranks of guerillas fighting against Turkey and Iran, entered parliamentary politics, published journals and created women's organizations. However, the patriarchal nationalist movement continues to depict women as heroes of the nation, reproducers of the nation, protectors of the "motherland," the "honour" of the nation and as guardians of Kurdish culture, heritage and language.

Although women are participants in the nationalist movements, they are subjected to the gender violence of both their own nation and the nation-states they are fighting. While the literature on Kurdish nationalism is growing in quality and quantity, research has ignored the gender dimension of the war in which women are targets of both internal and external violence. This study was an effort to bring to the fore some of the hidden consequences of the war on Kurdish women. What happens to the wife of a political activist who remains behind, in enemy territory, while the husband is fighting or seeking refuge in remote mountain areas? How is the wife treated by her family, her in-laws and the security forces? What happens to her children? How does she support herself and her children financially? How is life after reunion with the husband? What is the impact of years of separation on the marriage and children? What is the impact of dislocation to a new locale or in the diaspora in the West?

Kurdish women's responses to these questions have illuminated, in more detail, women's ways of strategizing for survival, ways of learning how to resist "organized" violence, and how to transfer that knowledge into other spheres of life such as meeting the challenges of new life in exile.

During the months of July and August 1999, nine Kurdish women in Ontario were interviewed. The women were recruited through the researcher's contacts in the community. The Kurdish community in Ontario is fairly small, though it is among the largest in Canada. In-depth, non-structured interviews were conducted in the participant's language of choice, either Kurdish or Persian. Interviews were taped at the woman's home. The interviews were scheduled for 2 hours but they went much longer. The shortest interview was about four hours and the longest one was about 12 hours. The desire to narrate one's life history through the medium of the interview was very strong among the Kurdish women. This study suggests that learning to *survive* completes the circle of Kurdish women's history in which struggle, resistance and desire to live abound.

Women's Informal Learning About Legal Rights

The Spanish women were asked during the interviews about how they wanted to learn or how best they learned. For many women, this was a difficult question, perhaps because they had never been asked such a question before. The effectiveness of the workshop, which took place after the individual interviews, was clearly demonstrated in this area of data collection. Through the interview, the women had become familiar with the question and most had expressed their ideas about how they wanted to learn and how they learned best. These ideas were affirmed and this may have assisted the women in speaking out during the workshop discussion. Several hours were dedicated to brainstorming on this issue and women were asked to develop a programme to address their learning needs. Working together, they did just that and were aware that the strategies they generated were theirs. The collective inquiry helped them to develop group ownership of information and solutions to problems.

During the interviews, the majority of the women spoke about circumstances when learning was difficult for them. Learning was most difficult at a time of separation, which for the women meant a decision to leave their spouses or that their spouses had been arrested. In abusive relationships, the time of separation is a time of danger, insecurity, and great loss. Tita (names of all study participants have been changed) described her inability to concentrate at this time:

> Now I am more calm. … When I separated, I had many problems. I had many doubts, so that nothing else fit in my head. I was going to school and I was not able to concentrate. I could not pay attention to the teacher.

Natalia, who was in an extreme crisis state at the time of separation, noted:

> To learn something like the laws and your rights, you must be very focused. This is not possible during these first days. As soon as the woman is sure about the future of her children, at this moment, she will begin to calm down a little. That is the most important thing. And afterwards, when she realizes that they are not going to deport her.

She further noted that:

> Groups are good, but at these moments, no. When one feels more safe, comfortable with what has happened.

The women expressed how they felt at the time of separation and how it affected their ability to concentrate. Ana Maria echoed their thoughts:

> It's very difficult because it is a crisis. You don't feel well and you feel very isolated. The head is full and you can't focus very well. So participating in a group would be very difficult. All the adrenalin was inside. I would not have been able to sit and talk with a group of women. I felt crazy and acted as if I were crazy.

As Herman describes (1999:33), the women lost their sense of safety and control. Because of this loss, Natalia and others indicated that learning or working in a group would not be appropriate. Their ability to trust had been challenged and individual support for learning would be necessary.

The women also talked about the content of the information they received at the time of separation:

> I want a paper that says that I have custody of my child. I don't want to hear that the system is going to judge if I am a good mother, if he is a good father, and what is best for the child. Agh!! No, no I don't want to hear that. But she called me and explained everything to me.

Unfortunately, the legal system cannot provide desired guarantees in many situations, particularly around issues like custody and immigration status. As well, the lawyer is required to present the client with their options and the client is to instruct the lawyer on the appropriate action to take.

Issues in family law often raise complex emotions. A few of the women expressed their feelings about their relationships, as in the following instances:

> This was very, very hard for me because it was like actually acknowledging that my marriage failed and I'm like the only one in the family that has that. And everybody looks down on that.

These emotions form part of the experience of marital breakdown for women and there should be space to include such feelings in any learning about the law.

At the time of the separation, the women wanted individual assistance, straightforward information and advice about their legal options. Too many options are confusing, and the lack of sure outcomes only contributes to their sense of instability, fear, and lack of control. Crucially, there must be room to express their feelings in a non-judgmental, safe environment.

For the majority of the women, an intermediary (a counsellor or friend) was involved throughout their contact with lawyers. The intermediary became involved in several ways. First, English was a second language for all of the women in the study. Even women who had arrived in Canada as children and thus had achieved fluency in English expressed confusion over the legalese used in their contacts with lawyers. The intermediary played the role of translator, not just for English to Spanish and back, but also from legalese to simple terms. In many cases, the women spoke to their lawyers exclusively through their counsellors or friends. Second, the intermediary assisted with access to lawyers or to the legal system in general. The Women's Program has developed considerable experience with the various rules and procedures in both family and criminal proceedings. All of the women spoke about learning from their friends, a process which facilitated their ability to access legal assistance. Finally, the intermediary was often the one person the woman trusted. The intermediary may have been the first person the woman approached about an abusive relationship. The intermediary played a strong supportive role for the woman and allowed her to talk openly about her experiences. The intermediary fulfilled the three functions of providing translation, access, and support for the woman and became indispensable to her in her daily life. A relationship of dependency was often created in which the women looked to their intermediaries for assistance with all aspects of their legal cases; the women developed the strategy of utilizing peer supporters to address their needs at the critical time of separation.

Learning in Spanish or learning in a bilingual setting was important to all the women, as many of them realized that the legal vocabulary that they would need is in English. Women also spoke at some length about factors that would enhance their learning. Gabriela noted:

> I would like to learn in my language, I understand more that way. I would like to participate. There are personal things, my experiences that I don't want others to know about, but I would like to help. Also visiting the court and having written materials. The use of skits would be good also.

Learning by seeing and doing was also important to the women:

> I liked the Victim Witness Program because it actually let me see the place where I was going to be. I had a guided tour. I would have liked to have seen a trial, 'cause I only ever seen a trial on TV. So I would have liked to have seen one and learned about it.

Celeste talked about the importance of not feeling overwhelmed, especially when the topic is complicated:

> I find that one session is not enough. It's too overwhelming. I find that it's too much infor-
> mation at one time and if it were cut in half—one session, some written stuff to take home
> and read, then the second session, you could move on and understand it a bit more.

Written materials, again in Spanish or in both Spanish and English, were important to all the women.

> Reading is important. When I need to learn something or understand it, I will read it
> through very well. Also some practice papers. Working through the documents would be
> really helpful. Like if you have a document, a fake one, but a real one, then you could go
> over it and actually write on it and understand what it meant. So when you see it in court,
> it's not as scary.

While Community Legal Education Ontario does produce written materials, few are in Spanish and few are on family law issues. A study on the legal information needs of low-income women regarding the Child Support Guidelines (McDonald, 1999b) demonstrated the overwhelming need for basic materials in family law. Cossman and Rogerson, in their submission to the McCamus Report on family law and legal aid, call for a "greater emphasis on and availability of educational materi- als" (1997:910). Given the complicated nature of many legal issues, Ana com- mented that written materials, while good, are not enough: "People read, but they don't understand."

Women consistently emphasized the importance of learning from the experiences of other women. Given that much of the information women obtain is from their friends or other women, this is not surprising. Maria noted that "The adult carries her experi- ences – the experience is very important." Wendy, who had had negative experiences when she sought assistance, summarized her thoughts in this way: "We learn a great deal through our friends. For example, there are many women who have poor concepts of the shelters. It's better to unite together, I say." Wendy had a clear understanding of how negative images of shelters and other social service agencies or individuals are developed through her own experiences and that of many friends. She believed, how- ever, that through positive reinforcement from friends, women could access the resources that are there to help them. In a similar manner, Cynthia talked about the importance of confidence that you gain when you are not alone: "You are going to be much more confident because it's a friend who has experienced the same thing."

These thoughts have been echoed in the poverty law scholarship. In the traditional model of lawyering, issues are dealt with as distinct, unrelated disputes, without refer- ence to the larger contexts, whether of gender, class or race. Alfieri (1988:683) calls this "dependent individualization." Despite changes in lawyering, the isolation inher- ent in a lawyer/client relationship based upon individual casework cannot lead to empowerment. Lopez (1992:52) notes that "existing practices too often isolate lawyer and client from other problem-solvers." Thus, the clients see their problems as only their problems, as if they exist in a vacuum, which reinforces the alienation, isolation and shame that they may already feel. They are denied the opportunity for, and the potential empowerment that lies within, the collective force of the community. The women who participated in this study recognized this.

Celia reflected on her experiences with the legal system. While talking about how alone she felt, she noted: "I would have liked to have had the experience of other women." Tita confirmed her thoughts: "I think it would have helped me a great deal to have the opportunity to hear the experiences of other women with the legal system." Cynthia beautifully described the emotional and intellectual learning that can occur when one uses the experiences of other women as a foundation: "One learns a lot with the experience of other women. It's an interchange of ideas, an interchange of emotions, an interchange of problems." Popular knowledge, or common-sense knowledge, is a key feature of participatory research (Maguire, 1987:38). It is that knowledge belonging to the participants at the grassroots level. Informal learning assumes that ordinary people have a rich knowledge base and are also capable of generating the knowledge necessary to engage in activities for their own and others' benefit. The women interviewed here clearly believed in their own knowledge and that it should be valued and part of any learning experience.

At the same time, during the workshop and the interviews, the women emphasized a role for professionals, for people who had experience with the legal system. The women acknowledged that they lacked information and that they need to begin to understand the implications of the law as it applies to them and to their situation:

> I would like to hear from professionals because they have the experience. I think it's important to hear from friends too, but they don't always have the answers—they know only what they went through.

> I would like to learn through a person or persons who would explain to me what the law is about.

We know that people often lack information, skills and experience to critically understand and analyse the social structures and relations that shape them. The women themselves recognized this and decided that they wanted professionals to be involved to address this problem.

A structured learning environment seemed to be important to the women: "It would be better to attend a course, or classes, because I always learn better [there]. Ms. Ruth has given talks and I like those." Similarly, Gabriela believed that a teacher, a facilitator, helps her learn. She also highlighted the importance of participation to reinforce any individual learning through reading:

> I learn better when someone teaches me, orients me, gives me information. Participation is very important. One's rights and the rights that the court has—you have to read these, but I learn more participating.

Margarita noted that for her:

> Participation really, really helps as well. I don't like it when one person is talking and talking 'cause I find when they do all the talking that I stop paying attention. But some talking and lots of questions.

While learning together in a group is important, individual attention is critical during times of crisis:

> I believe that discussions and workshops are good ways to learn. That helps a lot—working with other women with the same problems in groups. And with the necessary information—because ignorance is the worst—one feels completely lost

The size of the group does matter as Margarita noted: "I think a small group is better than a large group 'cause then you get everyone talking and everyone's ideas."

The women were clear about their needs. Regardless of the level of formal education each had completed, they were very aware of how they learned best. Working together, the women combined their collective desires and wisdom and recommend a programme that would address their needs. Thus, a partly structured learning environment emphasizing a facilitated participatory approach was crucial for building upon the rich knowledge that the women already possessed.

Women and Informal Learning About Survival

When I approached the Kurdish women about participating in this research, they were all very modest about their role and contribution. A typical response was that "you know everything, how can I help you?" or "What is in my life that could be of any interest to you, or has any value to others?" This sense of "uselessness" was further aggravated by a sense of "aging." Before getting to know these women better through the interviews, I overestimated their age. They appeared older than their actual age. Years of war has worn these women down and has affected their learning pace and purpose, especially when it is put in the context of the diaspora and learning to live a new life. Nahid says:

> It takes me long to learn something. I've become forgetful, I even do not remember some of the events in my life any more. I don't know if this is good or bad. But, I study hard for my English vocabularies, then I go to my class, I don't remember them. I feel sorry for the teacher, she is nice. Sometimes, learning the meaning of a word takes me to the distant past and all the horror of life during the war, then I forget the meaning of it again.

Hewa is also preoccupied with her age but she is determined to learn:

> I only wished that I was younger so I could continue my education in order to be more helpful and help people. I have written poems about this. The reason that I could not get my grade twelve diploma was because of continuous harassment. My dream was to finish university, and to be a teacher, and I am working towards that goal. Wherever I went they required ECE [Early Childhood Education]. So, I decided to go after getting my degree. A woman who is even older than me attends school, so I decided to push myself and begin learning the language and apply for ECE. I got advice from a good teacher who told me to go to a college. I was so interested that I stayed up until 3:00 or 4:00 in the morning to study. But the day after I could hardly remember what I had studied. This was very troublesome and I could not understand why I did not learn much. I had depression as well. I was very sleepy all the time, I often fell asleep in the class. But I decided to continue

Hewa received her ECE certificate on June 29, 1999.

The Kurdish women showed a strong desire for having control over their lives and especially the future of their children. This desire was combined with a stronger sense of "motherhood," that is, sacrificing their own happiness and well being for the sake of their children. Below is my conversation with Gilan who expressed this need so clearly:

I worked for several months, full-time, distributing flyers. I wanted to buy a car. [I interrupted her and said, "But Gilan, you just said you can't read or write in any languages, how can you get your driver's license?" She continued:] I need to be independent, I want to live like a normal mother. I have suffered so much that I want to make sure that my children will have all they want. You know that distributing flyers is very bad for my back, Pasdarans [Khomeini's security guards] kicked me so much that now I have a defected lower back. But, I needed a car so that I could drive my kids to McDonalds and do my shopping. I begged friends to teach me to drive and now I can drive. [Again in astonishment, I said "But you don't have a driver's license and you can't read." She replied:] I'm careful, and I found out about a place where you can pay $25.00 to someone and they will take the written test for you. [I again insisted, and asked her: "But what about following an address, names of the street, stores, etc.?" She said:] If you write it clearly I see it as a drawing and can read it. I always go to the store with my kids and they help me with reading the labels.

Gilan's strong desire to build a better life for her children is an impetus to learn; like many people, she is a visual learner who reads labels and signs pictorially.

Years of experience with injustice and oppression have incited Kurdish women to seek justice and to help others. This is best manifested in their interaction with authorities as they try to resettle in their new environment. Hewa recalled her interaction with an immigration officer:

After arriving in Canada, one day I went to the immigration office, all by myself for the first time. A woman officer asked me if I spoke Arabic. I said no, but she said I was lying because she has seen me the other day speaking in Arabic with another woman. I was shocked to hear her say that and I began to cry. At that moment, I begged God to give me the necessary knowledge to help the people who come to Canada and do not know the language. That is how I got involved with volunteering in a settlement office. I was offended by her comments. I was surrounded by some Kurdish and Iranian men who were wondering why I was crying so hard. Another officer came and asked me for my name so that they could find the officer who was in charge of my file. He was Mike and was a very nice person. I told him to tell her that not everybody who comes to Canada are criminals and thieves, we were somebody before coming to Canada.

The process of understanding the "informal" mechanisms of learning among the Kurdish women in the diaspora raised other issue midway through the research that I had to incorporate into our study. I found out that I had to record the women's lives in great detail if I was going to make any sense of what was going on. In fact, I had to revisit my methodological approach, and combine feminist participatory research with oral history, memory, and testimony in order to capture their learning experiences. The reason for this was the ever-present stories of "past," "home," "war," "motherhood," "martyrdom," "enemies," "land," "national pride," "heroes" and "leaders" in the women's lives. These notions were tightly woven into the fabric of their lives. This means that the understanding of "informal learning" mechanisms and strategies should be contextualized within the historical, social and cultural life experiences of participants. In this contextualization, understanding and identifying relations and structures of power are fundamental. The importance of this was brought home to me during my recent visit to Iraqi Kurdistan. There I "informally" interviewed women in positions of power, including ministerial positions, about their process of learning – learning to come down from the mountains and putting down their arms, now managing the affairs of a nation which is in the process of creating itself. At the beginning, they gave me a blank look and were surprised with the naivete of my questions. They often answered by saying, "You know, you should know our history," or made a specific reference to significant historical events such as the 1991 uprising. The integrated connection that they made between their learning process and their lives made me conclude that the need for contextualization goes beyond the diaspora experience itself (which includes personal experiences of trauma in the homeland).

There are many obstacles in engaging Kurdish immigrant women in a collective "informal" learning network. Whether the learning is formal or informal, the motivation to learn, or understanding what needs to be learned, depends on consciousness. A relevant question, emanating from the experience of Kurdish women, is how we can link social justice issues and the questions of race, gender, class and all other bases of marginalization to the processes of "informal" learning.

Furthering our Understanding

These parallel studies acknowledged from the beginning that trauma as a result of violence has an impact on learning. During the individual interviews, the women spoke at length about fear, uncertainty, anxiety, stress, self-doubt, lack of confidence and more. They spoke about their learning needs and they wanted simple, clear and direct information. Our research suggests that traumatized women need individual, one-on-one support. They seek uncomplicated information and simple advice: too many options are confusing, and the lack of sure outcomes only contributes to their sense of instability, fear, and lack of control. We also realized that it is essential to focus on more than just outcomes in any programme for learning about something as complex as the law. Learning occurs as women begin to connect, to trust, and to share again. Learning occurs when the critical elements of action, or attending to the experience, and reflection are present (English, 1999; Merriam and Clark, 1993). This learning must be acknowledged and valued.

Factors that limited the women's learning include the lack of connection between the content of learning and the social and political consciousness of the women. They include their lack of personal or active involvement in their legal experiences and the impact of trauma on learning. Finally, they include the traditional model of legal services that does not emphasize client learning. Rather than seeing delimiters in a way that limits learning, they must be viewed as critical tools in framing an appropriate context. If the learners' delimiters are respected, then greater learning will occur in the long run. If learners have a positive but limited learning experience, they will be more likely to widen their vision to include the larger context at another instance. We realized the degree to which the impact of trauma can be seen as a delimiter; this, in particular, has not been previously recognized in public legal education (McDonald, 2000). Trauma is a terrible impediment to learning; women cannot learn when they have been horribly damaged by their experiences. Recognition of the limitations is necessary to ensure a positive learning experience for those involved. However, it is equally important to consider the experience of violence as a new source of learning, its basis, a learning that can transform social, sexual and political relations of power.

Finally, we believe that the distinctions between formal, non-formal and informal learning are important in that they allow us to better understand the dynamics of learning. We need to be aware of the complex relations between these forms of learning, and we need to know especially their social and historical contexts. It is no accident of history that formal education began to displace informal learning with the rise of industrial capitalism. There was then a much more complex division of labour in industry and agriculture that created highly specialized skills and jobs to an extent that informal learning was not able to transmit requisite skills. For example, considering our project, we know that the legal profession is extremely complex; its language is formidable even for the well educated. Few of us understand the full implications of a lease we sign with our landlord. Even in campuses, law libraries are separate, with their special collections and organization. How can anyone understand this complex system through informal learning? Complex division of labour and overspecialization create conditions that demand formal learning. Understanding this relationship between learning and social and economic imperatives allows us to understand the policy implications of learning. This raises the issue of the role of the state and the market in the provision of training, the creation of skills, and the structuring of the job market, and the place of "informal" learning in this complex set of relations. Such policy implications must include recognition of the special needs and abilities of diasporic women who have been traumatized by experiences of violence either in their homeland or their new nation.

References

Agger, I., 1992, *The Blue Room: Trauma and Testimony among Refugee Women: A Psycho-Social Exploration*, Zed Books, London.

Alfieri, A., 1988, The antinomies of poverty law and a theory of dialogic empowerment, *New York University Review of Law and Social Change*, **16**: 659–712.

Ammons, L., 1995, Mules, madonnas, babies, bathwater, racial imagery and stereotypes: the African-American woman and the battered woman syndrome, *Wisconsin Law Review*, **5**: 1003–1080.

Baier, A, 1986, Trust and antitrust, *Ethics*, **96**: 231–260.

Bannerji, H., 1999, A question of silence: reflections on violence against women in communities of colour, in E. Dua & A. Robertson (Eds.), *Scratching the Surface: Canadian Anti-Racist Feminist Thought*, Women's Press, Toronto, pp. 261–277.

Carey, E., 2000, One in Three Women Abused, UN Report Shows, *Toronto Star*, 20 September, A22.

Clandinin, D.J. & Connelly, F.M., 1994, Personal experience method, in N.K. Denzin & Y.S. Lincoln (Eds.), *Handbook of Qualitative Research*, Sage, Thousand Oaks, CA,, pp. 413-427.

Cossman, B. & Rogerson, C., 1997, Case study in the provision of legal aid: family law, in *A Blueprint for Publicly Funded Legal Services*, Ministry of the Attorney General, Toronto, pp. 773–912.

Crenshaw, K., 1991, Mapping the margins: intersectionality, identity politics, and violence against women of color, *Stanford Law Review*, **43**: 1241–1299.

Dasgupta, D.S., 1998, Women's realities: defining violence against women by immigration, race, and class, in R.K. Bergen (Ed.), *Issues in Intimate Violence*, Sage, London, pp. 209–219.

Davis-Barron, S., 1993, Survey Hailed as Best Ever on Violence Against Women, *Toronto Star*, 18 November, A16.

English, L., 1999, Learning from changes in religious leadership: a study of informal and incidental learning at the parish level, *International Journal of Lifelong Education*, **18(5)**: 385–394.

Freeman, M.P., 1993, *Rewriting the Self: History, Memory, and Narrative*, Routledge, New York.

Garrick, J., 1996, Informal learning: some underlying philosophies, *Canadian Journal of Studies in Adult Education*, **10(1)**: 21–46.

Godin, J., 1994, *More than a Crime: A Report on the Lack of Public Legal Information Materials for Immigrant Women who are Subject to Wife Assault*, Working Document, Department of Justice, Ottawa.

Gowen, S.G. & Barlett, C., 1997, Friends in the kitchen: lessons from survivors, in G. Hull (Ed.), *Changing Workers: Critical Perspectives on Language, Literacy and Skills*, State University of New York Press, New York.

Green-Powell, P., 1997, Methodological considerations in field research: six case studies, in K.M. Vaz (Ed.), *Oral Narrative Research with Black Women*, Sage, Thousand Oaks, CA, pp. 197–222.

Hake, B., 1999, Lifelong learning in late modernity: the challenges to society, organizations and individuals, *Adult Education Quarterly*, **49(2)**: 79–90.

Herman, J., 1992, *Trauma and Recovery: The Aftermath of Violence – From Domestic Abuse to Political Terror*, Basic, New York.

Horsman, J., 1999, *Too Scared to Learn: Women, Violence and Education*. McGilligan Books, Toronto.

Jang, D., 1994, Caught in a web: immigrant women and domestic violence, *Clearinghouse Review*, **28**: 397–405.

Law Courts Education Society of British Columbia, 1995, *Domestic Violence and the Courts: Immigrants and Visible Minority Perceptions*, Vancouver, British Columbia.

Lopez, G., 1992, *Rebellious Lawyering: One Chicano's Vision of Progressive Law Practice*, Westview Press, Boulder, CO.

MacLeod, L. & Shin, M., 1994, *Like a Wingless Bird: A Tribute to the Survival and Courage of Women Who are Abused and Who Speak Neither English nor French*, National Clearinghouse on Family Violence, Ottawa.

Maguire, P., 1987, *Doing Participatory Research: A Feminist Approach*, Center for International Education, School of Education, University of Massachusetts, Amherst, MA.

Martin, D. & Mosher, J., 1995, Unkept promises: experiences of immigrant women with the neo-criminalization of wife abuse, *Canadian Journal of Women and the Law*, **8**: 3–44.

Merriam, S.B. & Clark, M.C., 1993, Learning from life experience: what makes it significant? *International Journal of Lifelong Education*, **12(2)**: 129–138.

McDonald, S., 1998, Popular legal education in downtown Santiago, *Convergence*, **31**: 147–155.

McDonald, S., 1999a, Not in the numbers – immigrant women and domestic violence, *Canadian Woman Studies*, **19(3)**: 163–167.

McDonald, S., 1999b, *Phase II: Legal Information Needs of Low-Income Women in Ontario*, The Child Support Guidelines Department of Justice/CLEO, Toronto.

McDonald, S., 2000, *The Right to Know: Women, Ethnicity, Violence and Learning About the Law*, Ph.D. thesis, Ontario Institute for Studies in Education of the University of Toronto, Toronto.

Mojab, S., 2000, The power of economic globalization: deskilling immigrant women through training, in R.M. Cervero & A.L. Wilson (Eds.), *Power in Practice: Adult Education and Struggle for Knowledge and Power in Society*, Jossey-Bass, New York, pp. 23–41.

Okley, J. & Callaway, H. (Eds.), 1992, *Anthropology and Autobiography*. Routledge, London.

Rathus, S.A. & Jeffrey, S.N., 1980, *Adjustment and Growth – The Challenges of Life*, Holt, Rinehart and Winston, New York.

Orloff, L., Jang, D. & Klein, C., 1995, With no place to turn: improving legal advocacy for battered immigrant women, *Family Law Quarterly*, **29(2)**: 313–329.

Rundle, L.B. & Ysabet-Scott, N., 1995, Violence: a barrier to our education, *Women's Education*, **11**: 5–10.

Reinharz, S., 1992, *Feminist Methods in Social Research*, Oxford University Press, New York.

Statistics Canada, 1993, *Violence Against Women Survey*, Ministry of Industry, Ottawa.

Richie, B., 1985, Battered black women: a challenge for the black community. *The Black Scholar*, **16**: 40–45.

Richie, B. & Kanuha, V., 1993, Women of color in public health care systems: racism, sexism and violence, in B. Bair & S. Czleff (Eds.), *Wings of Gauze: Women of Color and the Experience of Health and Illness*, Wayne Statue University Press, Detroit, MI.

Roy, S., 1995, Restoring hope or tolerating abuse? Responses to domestic violence against immigrant women. *Georgetown Immigration Law Journal*, **9**: 263–290.

Shay, J., 1995, *Achilles in Vietnam: Combat Trauma and the Undoing of Character*, Simon & Schuster, New York.

Thomson, A., 1995, Life histories, adult learning and identity, in J. Swindells (Ed.), *The Uses of Autobiography*, Taylor & Francis, London.

Tobias, R., 1999, Lifelong learning under a comprehensive national qualifications framework: rhetoric and reality, *International Journal of Lifelong Education*, **12(2)**: 85–99.

Wang, K., 1996, Battered Asian American women: community response from the battered women's movement and the Asian American community, *Asian Law Journal*, **3**: 151–184.

Watkins, K.E. & Marsick, V.J., 1992, Towards a theory of informal and incidental learning in organizations, *International Journal of Lifelong Education*, **11(4)**: 282–300.

Chapter 4
Stigma to Sage: Learning and Teaching Safer Sex Practices Among Canadian Sex Trade Workers

Diane Meaghan

Introduction

A broad definition of safer sex including physical, sexual and emotional dimensions was used in this work to investigate how Canadian prostitutes acquire a working knowledge of safer sex practices and what that knowledge constitutes by way of specific practices (Hanson et al., 1995). Utilizing feminist standpoint theory that takes women's experiences to be an entry point for investigation and places a high value on women's strengths and capabilities, the practices of sex workers were viewed as sites of investigation of political struggle and a possible source of social change (Smith, 1974, 1987). The body of literature on feminist theory and critical feminist pedagogies suggests the importance of understanding the politics of knowledge production and dissemination within considering the effects of gender privilege and oppression in the learning environment (Tisdell, 1995). With an emphasis on women's experiences, feminist pedagogy encompasses teacher–learner collaboration, cooperative communication styles and holistic approaches to learning as well as theory building linked to projects of action. By establishing a meaning of difference in addressing the specific interests of various women, divergence based on gender, race and class draws on women's experiences in ways that illustrate that "woman" is not a homogeneous category (Ng, 1986; hooks, 1990).

Feminist standpoint theory was linked with popular adult education theory to explain how sex workers learn as part of an active, cooperative and social process and to what extent they practice safer sex; whether it was possible for sex workers to function as pedagogical models in the transfer of skills and knowledge; and if practicing safer sex engenders agency and empowerment that could redefine the dominant discourse from disease and deviance to knowledgeable, sexual service work. Popular adult education is based on the assumption that learning is most effective with active participation, different learning styles are employed, content is relevant to the learners' lives and learners are treated as equals (Bates, 1996). The goal is to develop the individual's capacity for social change through a collective, problem-solving approach by emphasizing participation, reflection and a critical analysis of social problems (Bates, 1996:226). Such non-formal learning is characterized by voluntary participation and learning opportunities that are constructed in

K. Church et al. (eds.), *Learning through Community: Exploring Participatory Practices.*

a manner to support social change. Key characteristics include people's experiences as the focal point, leadership that is shared, highly participatory processes, creation of new knowledge, connections between the local and the global and an emphasis on collective action for change (Menzie, 1993).

Interviews were conducted with 37 female and 2 transsexual (male to female) sex workers in 4 cities in Canada. Ethnographic data were obtained in semi-structured interviews, open-ended discussions and supplemented with the researcher's observations and interviews with other participants in sex work culture, medical personnel, community workers and policy experts. Experienced women as well as those new to the industry were questioned within a variety of genres including street work, brothels, massage parlours and incall/outcall escort services. Individual sex workers and representatives of sex workers' collectives served as consultants to provide information, to critique the analysis and to assist in formulating recommendations.

Historical Framing of Sex Work

At the turn of the century, religious groups who viewed prostitution as "sin" and feminists who constructed prostitutes as victims suffering from venereal diseases both focused the attention of the state on sex work (Hart, 1977; Meaghan, 2000). Legislation was implemented to control working conditions and to protect the interests of clients, often scapegoating sex workers in the process. In what Max Weber refers to as a "rational" approach of bureaucracy, the state's culturally conservative framing employed an administrative discourse that emphasized infection and recommended community and religious interventions to counteract "deviance". In an effort to rehabilitate individuals and to respond to the moral panic in the culture, the prostitute was classified, managed and treated (Bell, 1994). Although the concept of "sin" was later replaced with a medical model of disease, a particularly persistent connection was established between infection and sex work that pathologized prostitution as a social problem. The problem of sex work was the problem of the sex worker, typically viewed as a victim of sexual abuse, disease and drug addiction and rendered personally problematic and politically passive (Lerum, 1999).

Western government policies and practices constituting prostitution were structured around elements of fear and danger that reinforced a negative view of sexuality and did not encourage sexual autonomy and pleasure (Pheterson, 1989; Overall, 1992; Anthony, 1992). The focus was on the stigmatization of those who performed this kind of work as well as health issues concerned with prostitution. Viewed as "reservoirs of infection", sex workers were blamed for disease and disorder in society; rarely were they seen as individuals possessing a specialized knowledge that could be shared with others to promote safer sex practices and sexual agency. Casting sex workers in medical, scientific and popular discourses as the focus of a social predicament resulted in their alienation from mainstream society. A lack of access to conventional cultural ways of contributing to the production of forms of knowledge restricted the sex worker's experiences and curtailed the introduction of a sex worker discourse to compete with scientific and professional ideologies (Delacoste and Alexander, 1987). As a result, sex workers viewed policy makers and social service agencies with distrust that discouraged a collaboration approach which might foster a more complete understanding of safer sex practices.

By the late 1980s, Canadian health officials became concerned that the proportion of AIDS cases among adult women was increasing over time (Health and Welfare Canada, 1991). The Human Immunodeficiency Virus (HIV) and the Acquired Immune Deficiency Syndrome (AIDS) as well as other Sexually Transmitted Diseases (STD), were determined to be associated with risk behaviours. UNAIDS reported that AIDS was the leading cause of death among women of childbearing age in many cities in Europe and North America (Wilton, 1994). Women were seen to be in danger of contracting HIV infections through unprotected sexual intercourse and infected blood (Panos Institutes, 1990). By the year 2000, the rate of AIDS cases among women matched that of men, affecting some 6–8 million women worldwide (Schneider and Stoller, 1995; United Nations/World Health Organization, 1999). By adopting the World Health Organization Global AIDS Strategy, Health and Welfare Canada instituted preventive, educational, supportive and treatment initiatives for the women and children who were increasingly at risk (Health and Welfare Canada, 1996).

Dominant in policy and planning concerning HIV/AIDS was a heterosexual male "norm" that constituted the male body as the recipient of a disease, as well as conceptualized seroprevalence initially in gay men and later in female sex workers (Patton, 1994). A stigmatized lifestyle characterized by excessive sex and drugs was seen as the etiological basis of sexually transmitted diseases (Oskamp and Thompson, 1996). The notion that people who acquired HIV/AIDS had been intemperate provided heterosexual women engaged in non-commercial sexual activities with a false sense of security. A risk-based, intervention approach was adopted that stereotypically blamed deviant subcultures consisting of "high risk" individuals while correspondingly insisting on their invisibility in society (Davis and Shaffer, 1994). Concerns about sex workers as a source of infection surfaced particularly for heterosexual men, masking the real risks posed to sex workers by clients (Brock, 1989). The simultaneous blaming of sex workers, dismissing women's health needs and failing to acknowledge that opportunistic infections differ in women from men obscured the rapid increase in female rates of sexually related infection.

Commercial Sex Work and Safer Sex Practices

Studies in Western nations including Denmark, Switzerland, Great Britain, Australia, New Zealand and the United States have found that female sex workers engage in remarkably high levels of condom use and experience low levels of

HIV/AIDS infection (Darrow, 1992; Morgan Thomas, 1992;). Seroprevalence HIV rates were found in a United Kingdom study to be 5.7% among sex workers and 5.8% among non-sex workers; in both groups infection was associated with injection drug use or among women who had ongoing relationships with men who injected drugs (Cohen et al., 1989). Canadian sex workers have similarly been found to more consistently use condoms than other populations comparable in age, race and sex (Bastow, 1995). The US Department of Health (2001) has invariably reported that 3–5% of sexually transmitted diseases are related to sex trade work, compared with 30–35% among teenagers. In the largest epidemiological study conducted by the Centers for Disease Control and Prevention (1993), it was found that HIV infection rates were low among female sex workers with no proven cases of HIV transmission from sex workers to clients (Blackfield Cohen and Alexander, 1996).

These and other studies confirm that female sex workers are not the major source of HIV/AIDS in the West, due to the fact that they are more likely to adopt preventive measures such as using a condom for vaginal sex and not engaging in kissing activities thought to be a health risk for hepatitis A, glandular fever, herpes and meningitis. Female sex workers also perform fellatio, widely considered to be a low-risk activity rather than exclusively engaging in intercourse, and they rarely engage in anal intercourse (Patton, 1994). Elieson (1992) observed that male clients of female sex workers had twice the rate of condom use of clients who had sex with male sex workers. Day (1993) reported that, among men in London, England who had sex with female prostitutes, 43% also had sex with men, 18% did not consistently use condoms and 2% had injected drugs. Unlike female sex workers, however, male clients rarely acquire a negative social identity, nor are they condemned for the spread of diseases, targeted with STD prevention initiatives and confronted with legal restraints. Given the significantly lower rate of female-to-male transmission of HIV/AIDS and their eagerness to use prophylactics, female sex workers' risk to clients has been found to be negligible (Padian et al., 1991).

In contrast to the repressive/censorship position that dominated the sex debates during the past two centuries, research that focuses on female sex workers' understandings of their activities reveal that they value diversity, choice and the primacy of pleasure (Rubin, 1984; Valverde, 1998). To be successful in their occupation, they develop techniques which minimize danger and promote safer sex practices (Meaghan, 1989; Hanson et al., 1995). Since sexual self-assurance and control are key considerations, the majority of sex workers learn safer sex alternatives such as frottage ("body slides") and masturbation ("hand relief") through mentoring, apprenticeship and peer education (Hanson, 1997a). A study conducted in the United Kingdom found that one third of clients reported learning about STD risks and safer sex practices through association with prostitutes (Panos Institutes, 1990:91).

Professional sex workers with expertise, a commitment to long-term work and an ability to persuade clients to accept condom use are less likely to be HIV-infected than novices; both groups may be at greater risk of STDs, however, if they are street workers (Cohen, 1992, p. 76-7). The ratio of on-street to off-street, sex workers varies with geographic location, laws and customs but usually accounts for approximately 10–20% of the female sex workers in North American cities (Shaver, 1993). Sex workers make distinctions between work and personal relations; generally they do not perceive that they are at risk in the latter relationships and they are no more likely than other women, therefore, to use protection in their personal relationships. Recent studies indicate that they are also more likely to be subjected to domestic violence (United States Department of Health, 2001).

Police surveillance and apprehension impedes the development of safer sex practices and increases the danger particularly for street workers, since working safely cannot be established in an atmosphere of fear and stigmatization. Legal restrictions render women more vulnerable to client pressure for unprotected sex in exchange for additional remuneration (Alexander, 1990). Criminalizing sex work results in women being driven into poorly lit and deserted areas of work and makes them less able to report and seek prosecution if they are subject to abuse by their customers. A sex worker's fear of arrest may be paramount compared to issues of health and safety; women who must negotiate quickly are less able to evaluate the health status of their clients. Stigmatization also interferes with promoting safe sex by driving sex workers underground without legal recourse if they are physically assaulted or robbed. Marginalization increases the likelihood that impoverished women (the homeless, those injecting drugs or heavy users of alcohol) will be pressured into "barebacking" as a form of survival sex (Briesman, 1999, p. 8).

Commercial sex work with an emphasis on autonomy and consent need not be risky; coercion and abuse are components of specific human relations generally in a context of illegality. Some sex workers describe verbal abuse, assault and coercive sex that restrict their ability to protect their health and safety (Bernard, 1993:684). The US Department of Health (2001:2) reports that among street sex workers, 80% have been physically assaulted. The study indicates that 60% of abuse was perpetrated by clients, 20% by the police and 20% in domestic relations. The mortality rate for females in prostitution is 40 times that of the population of women at large (Davis and Shaffer, 1994). Further, men who are HIV positive and those who have committed date rape are less likely to practice safe sex (Gorna, 1996). Increased penalties and the establishment of criminal records render women more vulnerable and further reduce employment opportunities for those who leave the industry.

Learning to Work Safely in the Canadian Sex Industry

In the research that is the focus of this chapter, subjects ranged from 18–38 years of age (with a median age of 26 years). Most were unmarried, predominantly educated at the high school level and had been engaged previously in sales, clerical and factory work. The majority had worked for 5 years or less in the business, with 82% employed in brothels, escort agencies and as independents. Slightly more than half had children and approximately one third were living with a spouse or co-vivant. A very significant number (93%) reported routine, voluntary health assessments for sexually transmitted diseases. Eight percent reported contracting gonorrhoea, 6% reported contracting chlamydia, 7% reported contracting genital warts, 6% reported contracting hepatitis B and 4% reported contracting pelvic inflammatory disease (rates consistent with the general population). Approximately half of the sample had been charged with prostitution-related offences and 38% reported being physically or sexually assaulted in the course of their work.

There was a range of knowledge and skills among the women interviewed concerning safer sex practices. One young woman who was working in an Edmonton park suggested that HIV/AIDS was a genetically inherited disease. At the other end of the continuum, a very savvy and sophisticated woman working out of a luxury hotel in Toronto boasted that she was able to put a condom on a client with her mouth and without the man's knowledge. Typical of the women in this survey, Sandra, a middle-age, Caucasian woman working for 6 years with an out-call escort service in Hamilton, remarked that unlike women in the population at large "prostitutes screen clients and set limits concerning the acts they will perform."

The vast majority of women in this study exhibited high levels of knowledge and efficacy regarding safer sex practices. Every woman surveyed was knowledgeable about the risks of venereal diseases, how to use condoms, the need to utilize non-penetrative sexual techniques, the necessity of negotiating with clients and the desire of self-control with respect to the use of drugs and alcohol. A common sexual activity they engaged in was oral sex and a least common activity was anal intercourse, relating these activities as least and most unsafe. With the exception of one woman, all were aware that the HIV/AIDS virus was concentrated in bodily fluids, people can transmit STDs who do not appear ill, washing prior to sex does not significantly reduce the risk of STDs and people at risk of contracting STDs may have unprotected intercourse with an infected partner.

While working in a brothel, Jenny learned how to use latex condoms, combining them with water-based lubricants such as K-Y jelly and spermicides (containing nonoxynol-9) while maintaining spontaneity and sexual arousal. Servicing five to six clients a day in a 5-day, work week, she is comfortable in demanding a safe sex norm in her workplace. At times, she will diplomatically inquire about a client's past and initiate discussions concerning risk reduction in ways that do not cast aspirations on the client's behaviour. The negative aspects of condom use are overcome by demonstrating "caring and concern" for both parties and making the condom into a fetish object as part of foreplay. Following ejaculation, she will hold the rim of a condom carefully while withdrawing a flaccid penis. Her negotiation skills and communication abilities help her to resist the pressure to engage in unprotected sex, use drugs recreationally or engage in anal intercourse. Stating that she has instructed other sex workers and clients who do not attend health clinics about safer sex practices, she stresses the importance of clarifying her position with clients, refusing to comply if pressured for sex without a condom and seeking agreement when suggesting alternative, safer sex behaviours. Questioned as to whether she had ever been approached by health officials in her area to serve as a community sex educator, she laughingly replies that "you are dreaming in colour if you think medical people would work with us."

Women in the study reported that vaginal sex formed 63% of the service to clients, oral sex 21%, masturbation 13% and anal sex was not reported. All the women described using male latex condoms (although not with 100% consistency), together with water-based lubricants. A few reported using female condoms (Femidom) with a variety of lubricants. Variance in condom usage ranged from 89% among street workers to 95% for women in brothels and escort services. Most women recounted successful condom use with few incidents of breakage. They described a 92% rate of condom use for vaginal sex, 87% for fellatio and 17% for masturbation.

Tanya, a young Black woman working in a Toronto massage parlour, suggests that the best way for her to be protected is to quickly take the lead in an encounter. She establishes authority by controlling the conversation and maintaining eye contact. Emphatically stating that she is paid for specific acts and not the general use of her body, she encourages the client to name the sexual services desired. She sets boundaries by insisting on negotiating specific acts and she retains the right of veto over acts she is unwilling to perform. Relying on her intuitive skills, she makes a series of quick decisions relating to issues of health, ability to pay and safety in her initial encounter with a potential client. Clients who have poor personal hygiene are enticed to engage in a sexual fantasy that includes a shower. Utilizing a preliminary massage as an "ice breaker" allows her to check the client's body for ulcers or warts around the genitals, penal discharge and "nits" (crabs) in the pubic hair. The detection of such problems will prompt her to engage in "trick sex" (involving the use of her hand or the space between her legs), creating the impression that the client's penis has been inserted in her vagina. Nor does her attentiveness cease when business is concluded; each step of the encounter is scrutinized and if danger seems imminent she will terminate service.

Most of the women in this survey demonstrated confidence, self-efficacy and excellent negotiating skills, traits essential to successful interactions with clients who want to have safe sex as well as affecting the client's behavioural choices. Ninety percent of those working in massage parlours, escort services and independently (most of the women in this survey except those involved in street work) made comments such as sex trade work led to "liking myself better", "feeling more confident" and "having higher self-esteem", than they experienced prior to taking up such work. One woman expressed the notion that "thinking in good ways about myself" helps to establish a psychological climate in which she is able to avoid risky sexual situations.

Sarah exemplifies how sex education utilizes processes of adult learning and transformative education as defined by Mezirow (1991). As an independent sex worker and founding member of the Sex Workers Alliance of Niagara (SWAN), she shared the attention to detail she devotes to establishing personal relations and attending to the psychological needs of her clients. This very personable and experienced woman has a number of apprentices who wish to win her approval to work in the Niagara region as they become proficient at their craft. Mentoring of this nature supports much of what is currently known about how individuals learn, including the socially constructed nature of knowledge and the importance of experiential and socially situated, learning experiences. Sarah views change as a process of questioning assumptions and reflecting on beliefs and goals results from variance in the individual woman's work environment. As a change agent, she assists sex workers to engage in learning, to be proactive and to think of themselves as individuals capable of taking action and controlling the conditions of their work.

As a "spiritual prostitute," her relationships with clients are complex; some have assisted her to move her household, been invited to dinner in her home and acted as role models for her young son. To avoid entrapment by the police, she establishes client contacts through elaborate cellular telephone ruses or through email communiqués prior to meeting. By inquiring about favourite lingerie, wine and music, Sarah creates the expectation that the client will have a unique and rewarding experience. In anticipation of spending quality time with her (characterized as a "great treat"), she informs her clients that encounters are only affordable on an occasional basis. Through polite and courteous behaviour, she sets the tone concerning self-affirming activities that nullify risk-taking behaviours. Understanding that most men are intrigued by her very physically fit physique, she concentrates on assisting clients to define and verbalize their sexual interests. On occasion she pretends to be a stranger who is picked up in a restaurant; in another instant she redecorates her bedroom in a harem motif to cater to a client's fantasy. She reports that flirtation and continuous "small talk" of a friendly nature go a long way in setting boundaries that last year netting Sarah a US$250,000 income.

In order to ensure safe contacts, most women in this survey exert control over the sexual encounter by securing payment prior to services being rendered, and they attempt to elicit client compliance by using an assertive, business-like stance that communicates the terms of the encounter in explicit detail. The degree of control individual woman were able to exert during sexual encounters appears to vary with age, experience, self-confidence and location of work. A commonly employed strategy while working on the street was to ask another woman to note a client's license plate, to use a cellular phone to "report" their whereabouts in the customer's presence and to carry a nail file or sharp object in their purse.

Most of the women in this study reported that they avoid drinking and using drugs because these activities encourage risky sexual behaviours that can lead to the transmission of diseases, unintended pregnancy and violence. Young street workers were more likely to engage in high-risk activities with clients when offered extra money for sex without condoms. Arlene, a young Aboriginal woman who began working the streets of Winnipeg to sustain her habit of "shooting coke with friends," was more at risk than most sex workers in this survey. She admits to not practicing safe sex periodically when desperate to raise money for drug consumption. As a result of using drugs over the course of 6 years, she has also on occasion shared injection equipment.

Without translating the dangers of street work into a discourse on victimhood, Arlene tries to "remain aware of what is happening around me", especially when taking clients to her home. A number of her clients and the police have made disparaging remarks about sex with a "drunken Indian", highlighting the manner in which gender inequality is eroticized and racialized. She takes for granted that she will be periodically "hassled by the cops", and that she will be required to "pay money or give free sex to them to keep working" as part of the conditions of her occupation. Her omnipresent concern is not about contracting an infection, but rather that she will be beaten by a client or arrested again "because the cops always crackdown on us Natives." Having been arrested close to a dozen times and having been incarcerated on three occasions, she is persecuted in ways that uphold racialized and gender hierarchies of class power. Each arrest puts her closer to relinquishing custody of her son and daughter to the Children's Aid Society.

Condoms serve both as a physical and symbolic barrier in sex workers' professional lives. Thus, the majority of women do not apply the same safer sex standards in their private as in their professional lives. Some 92% indicate that they consistently used condoms for vaginal sex with occasional clients. These women negotiate differently, however, and use less or no prevention among partners (with regular clients falling mid way between the other two groups). These findings are similar to other studies that suggest the rare use of condoms by sex workers with a primary partner due to issues of intimacy and trust (Bailey et al., 1992; Murray et al., 1996).

The key debate appears to hinge on the rationale for policies of discrimination that control and regulate sex workers, driving them underground and putting them further at risk. Continued marginalization and stigmatization make it more difficult and dangerous for sex workers to engage in prevention work. Although little attention has been paid to the behavioural aspects of sex work, this field study found that sex workers take the initiative to obtain information and engage in safer sex practices. Within the sex worker community, educational messages are advanced by peer group educators rather than through traditional health education systems. Accessing information, services and skills training as well as enhancing self-respect provides important lessons of empowerment. Although these influential educators are an invaluable source of safer sex, educational practice, they appear to be ignored in mainstream policy making, research and educational programmes.

The New Zealand Prostitutes Collective: Promoting Safer Sex and Social Change in the Sex Industry

This study parallels findings which emerged from a New Zealand study that found sex workers viewed sexuality as an interactive and negotiated social transaction concerning partner choice, kinds of sexual experiences, contraceptive use and disease prevention (Hanson et al., 1996b, Hanson, 1997b). In the course of their daily work, most women acquired skills to deal with issues of intimacy, decision making, communication, negotiation and assertiveness (Hanson et al., 1995). Inasmuch as self-assurance and control are key considerations, the majority of women quickly learned from each other regarding the occupational health and safety issue of "no condom, no sex" as a non-negotiable practice (Hanson, 1997b). To some extent, contact with clients and reading trade magazines supplemented their repertoire of skills. Hanson (1996a) suggests a number of lessons that non-industry women could learn, such as taking control of sexual situations and introducing condoms, using water-based lubricants to minimize breakage and informing someone regarding their destination when leaving with a new acquaintance.

The New Zealand research demonstrates how sex workers' understanding of community, shared knowledge and a sense of empowerment can lead to organized political action that challenges the dominant discourse concerning prostitution. Sex workers were mostly involved in direct relations with clients; many parlour workers and those working for escort agencies exhibited a high degree of independence from owners. Their lack of experience with exploitation as compared with sex workers in other parts of the world may have contributed to the eagerness with which they took responsibility for their own health and engaged in peer education. With the advent of the HIV/AIDS "crisis" in New Zealand in 1987, the impetus for establishing the New Zealand Prostitutes Collective (NZPC) came from sex workers. Health professionals primarily concerned to prevent the spread of infection within the general population invited the Collective to work with the government in the promotion of safer sex practices (Barwood, 1998).

Although Western studies suggest that sex workers have no greater likelihood of being HIV positive than the general population, clients were fearful of contracting AIDS (Barwood, 1998, p. 8). Catherine Healy, National Coordinator of the NZPC, and World Health Organization consultant, remarked that since the publicity drive against AIDS began there was a general downturn in the industry. Several studies conducted between 1983 and 1998 in four New Zealand cities discovered "no discernible infection among New Zealand born, female sex workers" (Lichtenstein, 1999, p. 57). Serological findings gave credibility to the notion that sex workers were leading proponents of disease prevention. The fact that sex workers were at personal risk and perceived a threat to their business may explain their willingness to form a partnership with various departments of the Ministry of Health in order to prevent the spread of sexually transmitted diseases. Members of the NZPC recognized the benefit of working in a government-endorsed organization that utilized state funding, infrastructure and support services for sex workers, clients and the public.

The New Zealand Collective was staffed by workers who were currently or formerly part of the industry, thus ensuring that workplace culture was understood and the concerns of sex workers were paramount. Healy remarks that "there are so many things you don't understand if you haven't worked in the industry" (Barwood, 1998, p. 8). Since most women were self-employed and worked outside of the law, the information provided by the NZPC focused on health and safety issues. In regional drop-in centres such as Wellington, Christchurch, Auckland, Tauranga and New Plymouth, advice and counselling were offered together with HIV/AIDS testing, health support services, self-defence instruction, needle exchanges and legal services. The NZPC's motto of "No Joe No Go" (which stressed the need for clients to wear a condom in each sexual encounter) reflected actual safety conscious practices that exceeded those in the population at large (Healy and Reed, 1994).

Catherine Healy and Anna Reed (1994) suggest that sex workers were perceived to be reservoirs of HIV/AIDS infection for the general population and this distorted view whipped up public hysteria. They cautioned that men who refused to wear condoms, engaged in high-risk sexual practices and used commercial sexual services (when traveling to countries with high rates of HIV/AIDS infections) were more at risk of spreading disease in the community than sex workers. NZPC staff distributed a publication of *Siren* (Sex Industry Rights and Education Network) that contained a column which discussed disease prevention. A frequently appearing article entitled "Sexual Health Update" suggested specific ways that sex workers should exercise precaution against acquiring infection from clients (Siren, 2000:16). An "Ugly Mugs" list that warned of uncooperative or dangerous clients was also available in NZPC offices.

The NZPC had an objective beyond issues of health and safety; they wanted to create an organization that would empower sex workers to advance their political and legal rights. The approach by the health department accelerated informal discussions previously undertaken by sex workers to establish a support group. The Collective was determined to counter negative public images of the sex industry and to decriminalize prostitution by actively working to repeal existing laws concerned with soliciting [Summary Offenses Act, 1991], brothel keeping, living off the earnings of prostitution, procuring sexual intercourse [Crimes Act, 1961] and offences associated with the Massage Parlours Act, 1978 (Prostitution Law Reform, 2000). Founded in part to foster pride among sex workers and to combat the scapegoating of sex workers by the Wellington police in particular, the Collective threatened the government with discontinuing its safer sex work and exposing acts of persecution to the media if a discussion of decriminalization was not placed on the agenda.

Prior to the establishment of the Collective, sex workers had made several unsuccessful submissions to parliament to establish decriminalization. Based on the demand for full recognition of women's human rights (discussed at the First World Whores Congress in 1995, held in Amsterdam), the work of Catherine Healy and Catherine O'Regan helped to draft a 1997 bill that began the process of decriminalization. Tim Barnett, Labour MP and author of the bill, remarked that the "dangers in the sex industry relate to health and the abuse of power. ... I contend that the current law creates victims and protects perpetrators. It is unenforceable and it is implemented inconsistently" (Prostitution Law Reform, 2001, p. 1). In recognition that stigmatization and legal prosecution prohibit harm reduction and disease prevention, the Select Committee of the parliament moved to decriminalize prostitution (in a vote of 87 to 21) through the introduction of a bill that passed into law in May 2001.

Reframing Sex Work Pedagogy as a Model for Safer Sex Education

Recognizing that sexual ignorance gives rise to inappropriate behaviour and sexual knowledge is acquired continually through formal and informal learning processes, safer sex prevention programmes are moving away from information-based strategies to a more holistic approach (that deal with multiple determinants of behaviour and reflect varied learning styles) adapted to different patterns of sexual activity (di Mauro, 1995). Altering social perception and motivating behavioural change is a complex task that must incorporate a variety of conflicting messages that cannot be abstracted from a larger social environment (Karka, 1994). Some recently developed preventative health programmes are comprehensive, multifaceted and integrated into a wide variety of community services. Effective campaigns depend upon knowing what motivates sexual behaviour as well as the factors that encourage risk taking. Such programmes emphasize an educational approach that takes into account individual decision making within a specific cultural context. These programmes require changing the social climate to optimize learning that will facilitate behavioural modifications.

Traditional health education programmes have generally been counterproductive because they fail to connect sexual behaviour with deep-seated feelings and to engage in active and interactive learning that will enhance confidence-building and social skills (Beatie, 1990). Conventional education discourses are either insipid, equating sex with reproductive biology or they are based on fear arousal and attempt to dissuade sexual activity. Both approaches are individual in orientation, utilize prescriptive "top-down" methods and overlook the social environment (Marland, 1990). Normative sex education programmes often lack a discussion of women's sexual needs, alienate women from their bodies, omit discussions of male control over female sexuality and reproduction and fail to suggest how men's behaviour puts women at risk (Kitzinger, 1994). For women in particular, programmes of low-intensity intervention that do not provide for discussion of risk and individualized practice around condom negotiation are likely to be ineffective in terms of translating knowledge into behaviour (O'Leary and Jemmott, 1995).

Power relations embedded in sexual relations of compulsory heterosexual practices have made it difficult for women to assert their sexual and health interests. Despite the fact that socio-economic and gender inequality limits women's power to negotiate sexual practices with partners, women have been disproportionately charged with the responsibility of behavioural change within relationships (Panos Institutes, 1990). Two centuries of public policy have produced and maintained gender appropriate sexual behaviour (including the notion of sex as vaginal intercourse), which has accorded primacy to male desire, given men an assumed "right" of sexual access to women and socially controlled women's sexuality (Ehrenreich and English, 1973). Dominant discourses reflected in and promoted by state documents have constructed female sexuality as passive and banal while male sexuality is depicted as active and novel. The media encourages gender boundaries by presenting women as sexual purists engaged in heterosexual monogamy and in need of protection, or correspondingly as deviant women engaged in illicit activities (Lupton, 1994:122). The hierarchical nature and the ideological agenda of the medical profession has contributed to the social construction of gender that has led to women having little choice about whether or not they will engage in sexual activities with men. Public health authorities have also targeted sex workers as sources of infection and instituted mandatory testing and coercive approaches to close businesses engaged in commercial sexual activity (Gostin and Webber, 1998; Meaghan, 2000).

Interventions must address the power imbalance that can restrict a woman's ability to exercise control and express desire in sexual situations. No attempt to deal with safer sex for women will be successful unless issues of structural discrimination and inequality are taken into account. Labour market segregation by gender, the feminization of poverty and unpaid labour within the family increasingly cause women to use sex as currency in the formal and informal economy. Women's ability to practice safer sex is constrained by dominant cultural constructs of acceptable female sexuality and the social and economic marginalization which presents limited alternatives. Freely consenting to sexual acts and experiencing sexuality devoid of physical and emotional coercion may be of greater concern for some women than the long-term risk of infection. It is currently recognized that the best approach to establishing safer sex practices is to educate and motivate people to make low-risk choices based on the realities of their lives, and by acknowledging, as sex workers suggest that sexuality can be explicit, erotic and safe.

A cooperative alliance between "pro-sex" feminists and "choice" sex workers could go a long way to providing sex workers with access to resources, to recognizing their skills as educational resource agents and to confronting poverty, discrimination and marginalization for many women. Sex workers who are vulnerable, exploited and politically disenfranchised are unlikely to have the highest health status; women who are autonomous and able to take charge of their lives are most likely to be at the forefront of social change. Feminist support for decriminalizing sex work could assist to deconstruct the negative images of sex workers, end the social stigmatization arising out of the separate spheres of "madonna" and "whore" and afford these women dignity, human, labour and legal rights of protection against assault and police harassment.

In discrediting myths of prostitutes as irresponsible practitioners of unsafe sex, New Zealand sex workers repositioned themselves as health care specialists. Demonstrated skills and knowledge, together with epidemiological reports that found no reported cases of infection among these sex workers gave legitimacy to their claims as safer sex professionals. Approaches of adult education were utilized that drew upon workers' previous experiences, linked safer sex concepts with practices, required group members to develop new knowledge and redefined their roles in order to produce a desired outcome. Through contact with medical personnel, government officials, politicians, academics and the media, members of the New Zealand prostitutes' rights organization gained confidence and organizational skills that helped them link the goals of public health agencies with that of sex workers. Aligned with government personnel in a campaign to protect public health, attention became focused on the behaviour of clients and the police. Sex work discourse was not only employed to ensure safer sex practices but also served as an instrument of empowerment to create a supportive environment for political advocacy. Challenging and undermining hegemonic discourse reversed public opinion and resulted in the inclusion of a formerly marginalized group in public policy formation. By offering specialized services for sex workers, conducting surveys with academics and addressing the government's concerns with respect to health issues, the NZPC was able to make the case for the establishment of the political and legal rights of sex workers through decriminalization.

The Canadian government might profit from the lessons learned through the successful partnership established between the NZPC and the New Zealand government to recruit sex workers as peer educators. Traditional approaches of policy makers in Canada, however, continue to target sex workers as disease bearing and to exclude the contributions they could make to learning safer sex practices. Recently proposed in a working paper entitled "Dealing with Prostitution in Canada", the Canadian government indicated that it intends to enact more rigorous laws with tougher penalties for prostitution (Davis and Shaffer, 1994; Bastow, 1995). Removing criminal penalties would empower those who sell sexual services, provides safer working conditions, prevent the acquisition of a criminal record and eradicate the double standard between sex workers and clients. The manner in which Canadian sex workers challenge the formation of notions about sexuality and create autonomy for themselves, demonstrates high sexual literacy. Their ability to learn to work safely suggests the potential for expanding the definition of adult educators to include this group in policy construction and programme planning. A paradigm shift that views Canadian sex workers as transmitters of sexual diseases to one that sees them as sexual experts provides a way for sex workers to become an essential part of a public campaign to establish safer sex practices.

Focusing on the knowledge of sex workers raises questions about the possibility of developing a prostitute-centred pedagogy of safer sex practices. In contrast to dominant discourses that stigmatize and ignore the experiences of sex workers, prostitute pedagogy affirms the right of women to control the conditions of work and further recognizes the skills and knowledge of their work (Meaghan, 1999). It also raises issues about whether sex work practices constitute an alternative body of knowledge that could be utilized as a community resource concerning safer sex interactions in informal and formal educational settings. Providing sex workers with an opportunity to have input into public policy and the design and delivery of prevention programmes would be a useful way to transmit their skills and knowledge to other sectors of the community including clients, health and social service workers and adult populations at large. Such knowledge might not only serve in transformational learning to generate innovative social sexual practices but could also provide sexual self-determination that might result in greater desire, knowledge, resistance, agency and empowerment in other aspects of women's lives.

References

Alexander, P., 1990, Mandatory testing of prostitutes will not prevent AIDS, in C.C. Abt & K.M. Hardy (Eds.), *AIDS and the Courts*, Abt Books, Cambridge, MA.
American Civil Liberties Union Foundation, 1990, Mandatory HIV testing of female prostitutes: policy statement of the American Civil Liberties Union, in M. Blumberg (Ed.), *AIDS: The Impact on the Criminal Justice System*, Merrill Publishing, Columbus, OH.

Anthony, J., 1992, Prostitution as choice, *Ms. Magazine*, May–June: 86–89.

Bailey, F., Fox, L. & Oliver, R., 1992, Heterogeneity among Commercial Sex Workers and Commonalities of Condom Use, *Eighth International Conference on AIDS*, Amsterdam.

Barwood, G., 1998, Why was the New Zealand Prostitutes Collective established? *Between the Sheets*, **2(3)**: 1–2.

Bastow, K., 1995, Prostitution and HIV/AIDS, *HIV/AIDS Policy and Law Newsletter*, **2(2)**: 2–5.

Bates, R., 1996, Popular theatre: a useful process for adult educators, *Adult Education Quarterly*, **46(4)**: 224–236.

Beatie, A., 1990, Partners in prevention? AIDS, sex education and the National Curriculum, in D. Morgan (Ed.), *AIDS: A Challenge in Education*, Routledge, New York.

Bell, S., 1994, *Reading, Writing and Rewriting the Prostitute Body*, Indiana University Press, Bloomington, IN.

Bernard, M.A., 1993, Violence and vulnerability: conditions of work for street-working prostitutes, *Sociology of Health and Illness*, **15**: 683–705.

Blackfield Cohen, J. & Alexander, P., 1996, Female sex workers, scapegoats in the AIDS epidemic, *Women at Risk: Issues in the Primary Prevention of AIDS*, Plenum Press, New York.

Briesman, R., 1999, Clinic for sex workers, in *The Evening Post*, Wellington Newspapers Limited, Wellington, July 7, p. 8.

Brock, D., 1989, Prostitutes are scapegoats in the AIDS panic, *RFD/DFR*, **18(2)**: 13–16.

Centres for Disease Control and Prevention, 1993, *HIV/AIDS Surveillance Report*, **5(3)**: 7–17.

Cohen, J., 1992, Different Types of Prostitution Show Wide Variation in HIV and Other Sexually Transmitted Disease Risk, Paper presented at the *Eight International Conference on AIDS*, Amsterdam.

Cohen, J.B., Lyons, C.A., Lockter, G.J., McConnell, P.A., Sanchez, L.R. & Wofsy, C.B., 1989, Emerging Patterns of Drug Use, Sexual Behaviour, HIV Infection and STDs in High Risk San Francisco Areas from 1986-1989, *Fifth International Conference on AIDS*, Montreal, Canada.

Darrow, W.W., 1992, Assessing targeted AIDS prevention in male and female prostitutes and their clients, in F. Paccaud, J.P. Vader & F. Gutzwiler (Eds.), *Assessing AIDS Prevention*, Birkhauser Verlag, Germany.

Davis, S. & Shaffer, M., 1994, Prostitution in Canada: The Invisible Menace or the Menace of Invisibility? http://www.walnet.org/csis/papers/sdavis.htm, pp. 1–56.

Day, S., 1993, Prostitution and risk of HIV: male partners of female prostitutes, *British Medical Journal*, **307**: 359–361.

Delacoste, F. & Alexander, P., 1987, Sex at work, in F. Delacoste & P. Alexander (Eds.), *Sex Work: Writings by Women in the Sex Industry*, Cleis Press, San Francisco, CA.

di Mauro, D., 1995, *Sexuality Research in the United States: An Assessment of Social and Behavioral Sciences*, The Social Research Council, New York.

Ehrenreich & English, 1973, *The Sexual Politics of Sickness*, 1st edn., Feminist Press, New York.

Elieson, K., 1992, HIV Seroprevalence and Risk Factors among Clients of Male and Female Prostitutes, Paper presented at the *Eighth International Conference on AIDS*, Amsterdam.

Gostin, L. & Webber, D., 1998, The AIDS Litigation Project, part 1: HIV/AIDS in the courts in the 1990s, *AIDS and Public Policy Journal*, **13(1)**: 74–87.

Gorna, R., 1996, *Vamps, Virgins, and Victims*, Cassel Publications, London.

Hanson, J., Sutton, T. & Bell, T., July 1995, The Sex Industry: Services, Empowerment and Education, Paper Presented to the Department of Education Studies, Waikato University, New Zealand.

Hanson, J., 1996a, Learning to be a prostitute: education and training in the New Zealand Sex Industry, *Women's Studies Journal*, **2(1)**: 77–85.

Hanson, J., Sutton, T. & Brown, F., 1996b, Researching the Sex Industry, Paper presented to the Adult Community Education Association, Hamilton, New Zealand.

Hanson, J., 1997a, Pros and Prejudices: The Sex Industry, Media Sensation and the researcher, Paper presented to the *Canadian Sociology and Anthropology Annual Conference, Learned Societies of Canada*, University of Newfoundland, St. John's NFLD.

Hanson, J., 1997b, Sex tourism as work: a discussion with New Zealand prostitutes, in M. Opperman (Ed.), *Sex Tourism and Prostitution: Place, Players, Power and Politics*, Verso Books, New York.

Hart, G., 1977, *Sexual Maladjustment and Disease: An Introduction to Modern Vererology*, Nelson Hall, Chicago, IL.
Health and Welfare Canada, 1991, *Canadian Communicable Disease Surveillance System*, Vol.17S3, Queen's Printer, Ottawa.
Health and Welfare Canada, 1996, *Women and AIDS: A Challenge for Canada in the Nineties*, Queen's Printer, Ottawa.
Healy, C. & Reed, A, 1994, The healthy hooker, *The New Internationalist*, **252**: 16–17.
Hooks, B., 1990, *Yearning, Race, Gender and Cultural Politics*, Between the Lines, Toronto.
Karka, S., 1994, *Self-Directed Learning: Myths and Realities*, ERIC clearinghouse on Adult Education, Columbus, OH.
Kitzinger, J., 1994, Visible and invisible women in AIDS discourses, in L. Doyal, J. Naidoo & T. Wilton (Eds.), *AIDS: Setting a Feminist Agenda*, Taylor & Francis, London.
Lupton, D., 1994, *Moral Threats and Dangerous Desires: AIDS in the News Media*, Taylor & Francis, London.
Lerum, K., 1999, Twelve-step feminism makes sex workers sick: how the state and the recovery movement turn radical women into '"useless citizens,"' in B. Dank & R. Refinetti (Eds.), *Sex Work and Sex Workers: Sexuality and Culture*, Vol. 2, Transaction Publishers, London.
Lichtenstein, B., 1999, Reframing '"Eve"' in the AIDS era: the pursuit of legitimacy by New Zealand sex workers, in B. Dank & R. Refinetti (Eds.), *Sex Work and Sex Workers: Sexuality and Culture*, Vol. 2, Transaction Publishers, London.
Marland, M., 1990, HIV and AIDS: towards a coherent approach to schools, in D. Morgan (Ed.), *AIDS: A Challenge in Education*, Routledge, New York.
Meaghan, D., 1999, Women in Black: The Political Economy of Prostitution in Cuba under Market Socialism, Paper presented at the *Canadian Sociology and Anthropology Association, Learned Societies of Canada*, University of Sherbrooke/Bishop University, Sherbrooke, Quebec.
Meaghan, D., 2000, *The Political Economy of Stripping: The Social Construction of Sex Trade Work*, Unpublished Ph.D. dissertation, Ontario Institute for Studies in Education/University of Toronto, Toronto.
Menzie, J., 1993, *Unruly Practices: Power, Discourse and Gender in Contemporary Social Theory*, Polity Press, Cambridge.
Mezirow, J., 1991, *Transformative Dimensions of Adult Education*, Jossey-Bass, San Francisco, CA.
Morgan Thomas, R., 1992, HIV in the sex industry, in J. Bury, V. Morrison & S. McLachian (Eds.), *Working with Women and AIDS: Medical, Social and Counseling Issues*, Routledge, NT.
Murray, R., Alison, J., Robinson, P. & Tess, K., 1996, Minding your peers and queers: female sex workers in the AIDS discourse in Australia and South-East Asia, *Gender, Place and Culture*, **3(1)**: 43–59.
New Zealand Prostitutes Collective, 2000, *Prostitution Reform Bill 2000*, Wellington, New Zealand.
Ng, R., 1986, The social construction of immigrant women in Canada, in R. Hamilton & M. Barrett (Eds.), *The Politics of Diversity, feminism, Marxism, and Nationalism*, Book Centre, Montreal, Canada.
O'Leary, A. & Jemott, L.S. (Eds.), 1995, *Women at Risk: Issues in the Primary Prevention of AIDS*, Plenum Press, New York.
Oskamp, S. & Thompson, S., 1996, *Understanding and Preventing HIV Risk Behaviour*, Sage, Newbury Park, CA.
Overall, C., 1992, What's wrong with prostitution? Evaluating sex work, *Signs*, **17**: 705–724.
Padian, N.S., Shiboski, S.C. & Jewell, N.P., 1991, Male-to-Female transmission of Human Immunodeficiency Virus, *JAMA*, **266**: 1664–1667.
Patton, P.K., 1994, HIV and female sex workers, *Bulletin of the World Health Organization*, **71, 3(4)**: 397–412.
Panos Institutes, 1990, *Triple Jeopardy: Women and AIDS*, Panos Dossier Publications, Paris.
Pheterson, G., 1989, *A Vindication of the Rights of Whores*, Seal Press, Seattle, WA.
Rubin, G., 1984, Thinking sex: notes for a radical theory of the politics of sexuality, in Abelove, M. Aina & D. Halperin (Eds.), *The Lesbian and Gay Studies Reader*, Routledge, New York.

Schneider, B. & Stoller, N. (Eds.), 1995, *Women Resisting AIDS: Feminist Strategies of Empowerment*, Temple University Press, Philadelphia, PA.

Shaver, F., 1993, Prostitution: a female crime? In E. Alderberg & C. Currie (Eds.), *In Conflict with the Law: Women and the Canadian Justice System*, Press Gang Publishers, Vancouver.

Siren, 2000, Sexual Health Update, **17**: 16–17.

Smith, D., 1974, Women's perspective as a radical critique of sociology, *Atlantis*, Fall, **14(1)**: 82–88.

Smith, D., 1987, *The Everyday World as Problematic: A Feminist Sociology*, Northeastern University Press, Boston, MA.

Tisdell, E., 1995, *Creating Inclusive Adult Learning Environments: Insights from Multicultural Education and Feminist Pedagogy*, ERIC, Office of Educational Research and Improvement, Columbus, OH.

United Nations/World Health Organization, December 1999, The AIDS Epidemic and its Demographic Consequences. *Conference on Modeling the Demographic Impact of the AIDS Epidemic in Pattern 11 Countries*, New York, pp. 13–15.

United States Department of Health, 2001, Prostitution in the United States – The Statistics, http://www.bayswan.org/stats.html

Valverde, M., 1998, Beyond gender dangers and private pleasures: theory and ethics in the sex debates, *Feminist Studies*, **15(2)**: 237–254.

Wilton, T., 1994, Silences, Absences and Fragmentation, in L. Doyal, J. Naidoo & T. Wilton (Eds.), *AIDS: Setting a Feminist Agenda*, Taylor & Francis, London.

Chapter 5
Informal Civic Learning Through Engagement in Local Democracy: The Case of the Seniors' Task Force of Healthy City Toronto

Daniel Schugurensky and John P. Myers

Introduction

This chapter explores the dimensions of informal civic learning of a local democracy initiative known as Healthy City Toronto (HCT). It examines one of the programmes of HCT, the Seniors' Task Force, particularly the content and process of the participants' learning.

This study is part of an international research project that explores the pedagogical dimension of participatory democracy, with a focus on the informal learning acquired by citizens in programmes of shared decision making at the level of municipal government. It attempts to shed light on these issues by addressing three areas that are relatively underrepresented in the research on citizenship education: adult populations, informal learning and local democracy.

First, a cursory literature review suggests that most large-scale research on citizenship education, from the pioneering work by Almond and Verba (1963) to the recent international study coordinated by Judith Torney-Purta (2001), has concentrated heavily on K-12 schooling, and particularly on secondary school programmes. These studies range from curriculum analysis to observation of teaching practices to surveys of students' civic knowledge and attitudes. Moreover, the field of adult citizenship education, at least in countries with high immigration rates like Canada, tends to be understood almost exclusively as courses for the naturalization test, and is sometimes conflated with English as a second language (ESL).

Second, research on citizenship education seldom pays attention to the area of informal learning. The low attention given to informal learning in the field of citizenship education is not an anomaly, as it reflects an overall neglect for this area in educational research and policy (Livingstone, 1999; Eraut, 1999a, b). Since citizenship education focuses on school settings, most references to informal learning tend to be limited to the discrepancies between the formal curriculum and the hidden curriculum, such as the assessment of the democratic or anti-democratic nature of the classroom environment. Informal civic learning outside of educational institutions is rarely addressed.

K. Church et al. (eds.), *Learning through Community: Exploring Participatory Practices.*
© Springer Science + Business Media B.V. 2008

Third, research on citizenship education has not given enough emphasis to the organizational structures that could promote or inhibit the civic engagement (and consequently the civic learning) of ordinary citizens. When these "enabling structures" for democratic participation are considered in the analysis, they rarely go beyond the classroom environment or the institutional school setting. Although there is an important body of practice and research within citizenship education that goes beyond the school boundaries (such as the "in-service learning" movement), these contributions do not tend to explore the learning that occurs through participation in larger channels for citizens' involvement in spaces of deliberation and decision making. Scholars from disciplines like political science and urban planning have examined these spaces of local governance, but, with a few exceptions, the studies have not paid enough attention to the pedagogical dimension of these processes.

Having said that, educators and non-educators alike are increasingly interested in these topics. This attention, expressed in concepts like "pedagogy of the city" or "pedagogy of public participation," goes hand-in-hand with the growing scholarship on informal learning (of which the New Approaches for Lifelong Learning, or NALL, constitutes a paradigmatic example), and the recent proliferation of mediation spaces between the state and civil society, particularly for shared urban governance. This space of co-determination is neither part of the state apparatus, nor can it be located exclusively in civil society. Rather, it can be conceptualized as a public sphere where the state and civil society intersect.

Healthy City Toronto, the site of this study, is a project of public participation in municipal affairs that started in 1989. Since its inception, one of the main purposes of HCT has been the democratization and decentralization of decision making, which is sought through increasing public involvement in local governance (City of Toronto, 1997–1999). Among the different projects undertaken by HCT, the Seniors' Task Force was chosen for this study because, according to HCT officials, it has been one of the most successful projects in terms of democratic process and active participation.

The data for this study were gathered over 4 months during the summer of 2000. Interviews were conducted with 15 of the 18 Seniors' Task Force members (nine female and six male), the chair of the Task Force (a city councilor), 3 community organizers of HCT, and several participants of the citywide consultation process. The interviews were conducted in English and Portuguese, and lasted between 45 min and 2 hours. The interviewees were asked to make judgments, evaluate features, and express opinions about their involvement with the Seniors' Task Force, focusing on their perceived learning about municipal government, citizenship, and democracy, as well as on their educational background and their history of civic participation. At the end of each interview, Task Force members completed a questionnaire in which they assessed their changes in knowledge, skills and attitudes associated with their democratic participation in the Seniors' Task Force.

This chapter is organized into five sections. The first one briefly discusses the literature on informal learning, citizenship education and local democracy. The second discusses the role of enabling structures for participatory democracy. The third section introduces the case study, the Seniors' Task Force of Healthy City Toronto. The fourth section describes the informal learning acquired by Task Force members. The fifth section raises several conclusions and recommendations.

Beyond the Civics Classroom: Informal Learning, Citizenship Education and Local Democracy

Informal Learning

Following Vygotsky (1978) and Bandura (1977), learning can be characterized as a social process, the result of a constant interaction between the self and the context. For the purpose of this study, informal learning refers to the body of knowledge, skills, attitudes, perspectives and values acquired outside of the curricula of educational institutions (formal education) and outside of the programmes and workshops offered by a variety of social agencies (non-formal education). Considering the variables of consciousness and intentionality, informal learning can be organized in three main areas. The first area, known as "self-directed" learning (Tough, 1971) or "explicit informal learning" (Livingstone, 1999), is the result of deliberate learning projects. This type of learning is intentional and conscious. The second area is incidental informal learning, which is unintentional because it was not deliberately pursued in the first place but is conscious in retrospect. The importance of this area for the exploration of informal learning is evident in a study by Gear et al. (1994) who report that, in spite of using Tough's concept of "learning projects" to ask about informal learning, 80% of the learning episodes mentioned by their interviewees were not intentionally sought. The third area, known as "tacit informal learning," relates to the learning acquired through socialization which is usually unplanned and unconscious. This is what Polanyi (1966) described in a book entitled precisely *The Tacit Dimension*, which can be characterized as "that which we know but cannot tell."

Citizenship Education

Broadly speaking, citizenship education can be defined as "the contribution of education to the development of those characteristics of being a citizen" (Cogan and Derricott, 2000). Despite this broad definition and the shared notion that citizenship learning is a lifelong process, most research on citizenship education focuses on secondary schools, particularly on classroom processes, teaching and curricula (Cogan and Derricott, 2000; Frazer, 1999; Hahn, 1998; Niemi and Junn, 1998; Torney-Purta et al., 1999).

Traditionally, school-based civics courses have been concerned with the teaching of national history, national laws, and the structure and functions of government institutions. Even today, civic education in many countries of the world still focuses on the legal and formal aspects of politics, fostering compliance and neglecting real and controversial political issues (Ichilov, 1998). This constitutes a passive and normative approach to democratic politics that emphasizes the cognitive domain (particularly, the transmission of information and memorization of facts) and the affective one (the promotion of patriotism and allegiance to the nation-state), without addressing sufficiently the reality of political processes, the ability to critically analyse the economic, political and cultural relationships of society and the basic knowledge, skills and attitudes required for active participation in democratic institutions. The instructional methods are usually teacher-centred and textbook-centred, with emphasis on lectures and multiple-choice tests that focus on names and dates.

Participatory Democracy

Co-determination in city governance is not the only way through which ordinary citizens can participate in democratic politics and influence decision making. Opportunities for political participation include a wide range of activities such as voting, campaigning in electoral politics, involvement in social movements such as labour unions or protest groups, advocacy, running for office, writing letters, serving on a committee or advisory board, engaging in civil disobedience, etc. However, self-governance through local participatory democracy is particularly relevant for the development of a culture of participation and political activism, largely because the city is the closest level of government for most citizens. Moreover, as Carole Pateman (1970) pointed out, of the available contemporary systems of governance, participatory democracy is arguably the most educative one.

Indeed, the educational potential of participatory democracy is impressive. A case in point is the Participatory Budget (PB) of Porto Alegre (Brazil), which after 12 years of operation has become a massive school of active citizenship in which civil society actors, government officials and citizens learn a variety of knowledge, attitudes and skills relevant to democratic co-governance. By engaging actively in deliberation and decision-making processes, individuals and communities learn and adopt basic democratic competencies and values. They learn to listen carefully and respectfully to others, to request the opportunity to speak and to wait for their turn, to argue and to persuade, to respect the time agreed upon for individual interventions and for ending the meeting, to advance the needs of their neighbourhoods while considering the city as a whole. They also learn about the needs of other groups and to exercise solidarity with them. In summary, ordinary citizens develop self-confidence, political capital (capacity to influence political decisions), concern for the common good and an overall democratic spirit (Abers, 1998, 2000; Fedozzi, 1997; Pontual, 1999; Schugurensky, 2001a, b).

Enabling Structures and Local Politics

Participatory democracy does not flourish in a vacuum. Likewise, citizen participation in local governance seldom occurs spontaneously. It usually requires enabling structures, including a strong commitment on the part of government officials, the availability of public spaces for deliberation, and the existence of open and fluid mechanisms of shared decision making between city hall and civil society. Enabling structures aim to decentralize decision making by giving citizens input into resource allocation criteria or into the formation of local policies, a process that is sometimes organized around city-wide issues that affect everyone such as transportation or pollution. More often, however, the process is organized around the needs of a particular neighbourhood or a specific population group such as seniors, the case of this study.

However, enabling structures by themselves are not "silver bullets" that solve all the difficulties of achieving good participatory democracy processes. Enabling structures are a necessary but insufficient condition for an inclusive and active civic participation in local governance. The success or failure of enabling structures for participatory democracy is largely contingent upon local contexts, as those structures interact with many other economic, social, cultural and political factors that can facilitate or inhibit participation, such as the political culture, the historical traditions, the norms, the expectations and the power relations of a particular society. Thus, the existence of opportunities for political participation does not mean that all citizens will participate on an equal basis or that the internal decision-making processes are fair to everyone. A common critique of participatory democracy is that it has limited capacity to counteract existing social inequalities, and that sometimes can even reinforce those inequalities by encouraging those with higher social and political capital to participate, creating material and psychological barriers for those with lower social and political capital. In his latest work on the concept of "political field," Bourdieu (2000) observes that social constructions of class, race and gender have built-in cultural mechanisms of exclusion from political participation. This is not just the result of the unequal distribution of political abilities or competencies, but also an issue of expectations for political participation placed on different social groups. Nevertheless, this does not mean that these challenges are insurmountable. The case of the participatory budget of Porto Alegre, for instance, has managed to overcome the three main challenges of participatory democracy: the challenge of inequality, the challenge of co-optation and the challenge of inequality.

Indeed, a variety of co-determination experiences around the world (from Kerala to Porto Alegre to Toronto) suggest that, despite the aforementioned limitations, local politics and neighbourhood participatory systems have great potential to promote citizens' political engagement and civic partnerships between government and communities. Enabling structures for participatory democracy create greater opportunities for citizen involvement in policymaking than exist through electoral politics and generate a variety of benefits for municipal governments, neighbourhood associations and social movements, such as decreases in violent conflict, increases in efficacy and transparency, improvements in policy responsiveness, a new sense of solidarity and civic responsibility, and the development of democratic attitudes among citizens and government staff (Berry et al., 1993). Moreover, active involvement in local governance can help to counteract the belief that politics is a zero-sum game in which the "winner takes all" and the loser drops out. This is important because mainstream citizenship education courses fail to teach one of the main lessons of political history: persistent civic engagement (the slow, patient building of coalitions and majorities) can generate social change (Carter and Elshtain, 1997). It is also important because this involvement can bring back the feeling that in democratic politics there is always another chance to be heard, to persuade and, eventually, to influence policy. If civic education is about the development of an informed and active citizenship, it is evident that lessons on history and government are important but not enough. For most people, active engagement starts at the local level. As Putnam (1995) remarks, civic education is not merely about knowledge of the number of houses of Congress, but also about how can we get the streetlights on our block fixed.

At the same time, local politics should not be excessively glorified. In discussing local democracy with Toronto as a background, Jack Layton (1990) claims that the reality of city government falls somewhere in between two common myths. The first is that local politics is unimportant because it offers only mundane services, and the second is that democracy is practiced more vigorously at the city government level. Among the undemocratic elements of local government are the high level of apathy and alienation among voters, the influence and power wielded by special interest groups (especially business and developers), the fact that elected politicians do not represent very well the socio-economic composition of the urban areas, and the reality that many local politicians are appointed to their positions rather than elected (Layton, 1990). Layton claims that the promotion of citizen participation by municipal governments in Canada is not due to a belief in the democratization of decision-making power with the public, but an attempt to appease the public by appearing to listen to them.

Indeed, public participation can easily be manipulated as a mechanism for legitimacy building and co-optation, a process well described decades ago by Sheryl Arnstein (1969) in her pioneering piece on citizen power as tokenism. In examining past efforts to engage citizens in decisions about health in Canada, Church (2001, p. 1) contends that "the usual scenario has government orchestrating a process in which citizens speak but are not heard; the object of the exercise is to legitimate government policy decisions." This is difficult to surmount, notes Church, due to the imbalance of power between citizens (especially those with lower socio-economic status) and major stakeholders. Likewise, Layton (1990) contends that municipal governments in Canada have been sites of political patronage that have moved away from public accountability and involvement, distancing citizens from political processes and decision making. All this suggests that enabling structures are a necessary but inadequate condition for genuine participation. A structure that allows participation, even if designed with the best of intentions, is useless if not used properly.

   The perspective that we take in this study is that the state is not only an actor in policymaking with purposeful and relatively autonomous action, or a mere instrument of the dominant groups in a given society. It is also, and fundamentally, an arena of struggle among different interests; it is a terrain of negotiation and confrontation, of conflict and consensus, between social actors over public policy (Barker, 1999; Morrow and Torres, 1995; Offe and Ronge, 1975). Whereas we do not idealize local politics, we believe that municipal governance is a privileged space for promoting citizen participation in public policy because it is the closest to where people live and work and because decisions made at this level affect people's everyday lives in a noticeable way. For instance, through the Seniors' Task Force of Healthy City Toronto, the municipal government provided enabling structures for seniors to actively participate in deliberation and decision making with city officials on issues relevant to them.

The Setting: The Seniors' Task Force of Healthy City Toronto: An Overview

Healthy City Toronto is an innovative model of holistic community health that was created in 1989 under the auspices of the municipal government. Its conception of health emphasizes the socio-environmental aspects at the individual and community levels, derived from the nineteenth century public health movement, such as the Health of Towns Association in Britain, as well as health initiatives held in Canada (City of Toronto, 1997). During the last two decades, several important initiatives have strengthened Canada's involvement with innovative community health programmes. In 1984, a 1-day workshop was held in Toronto, entitled "Healthy Toronto 2000," which was followed in 1986 by the Ottawa Charter of the World Health Organization. These events influenced the World Health Organization to create the European Healthy Cities Project in 21 cities, and later to establish the first North American Healthy City Projects in Rouyn-Noranda, Quebec in 1987 and in Toronto in 1989 (1993 Interim report, in City of Toronto, 1997). Once established, the Healthy City model was expanded to rural areas under the name of "Healthy Communities."
   Healthy City Toronto is a decentralized model of municipal government that devolves decision making by creating interdepartmental and community partnerships, such as with citizen groups and the private sector, as opposed to a top-down organizational approach (City of Toronto, 1997). To this end, the Healthy City model supports programmes of public participation in city decision making in order to develop structures and processes for genuine citizen participation in local governance, to promote public accountability and to reduce barriers to participation. These programmes can be initiated either by citizen groups or by the City of Toronto. In both cases, Healthy City Toronto provides educational training, information and resource databases on civic participation, media relations and electronic networking, and acts as a liaison between these initiatives and community

organizations. Besides the cases already mentioned, Healthy City Toronto has identified other forms of municipal citizen participation that it supports, including Town Hall meetings, issue focused area meetings, neighbourhood citizen representatives, deputations to council or committees of council, citizens as consultants to the City, joint working groups, roundtables in which the city is one of the stakeholders, advisory programmes, and feedback/input from citizens to councilors (City of Toronto, 1997).

The Seniors' Task Force

In January 1998, the Toronto City Council formed the Task Force to Develop a Strategy for Issues of Concern to the Elderly in order to identify the salient issues and needs concerning the 350,000 seniors living in Toronto. The formation of this initiative was recommended by the Toronto Transition Team Report, "New City, New Directions," and was later renamed the Seniors' Task Force. This initiative was a response to growing evidence in Toronto that seniors' issues were being ignored by the municipal government despite the increasing proportion of seniors in Toronto's population, as well as to international initiatives such as the United Nations International Plan of Action on Aging and its designation of 1999 as the International Year of Older Persons (Raphael et al., 2000; Statistics Canada, 1999, National Advisory Committee on Aging, 1999).

According to the perception of HCT staff, the Seniors' Task Force has been one of the most successful projects at addressing barriers to participation. This relative success can be attributed to several factors, such as the provision of interpreters for non-English speakers, the Task Force's issue-oriented approach and direct link to policy formulation, the participants' availability to prepare for and attend meetings (relative to other age groups), a participation-friendly process that encouraged everyone to express their concerns and voice their opinions (through a combination of large and small group meetings), and the strong commitment and participation of city councillors. Particularly important in this regard was the involvement of the Chair of the Task Force, Anne Johnston (the most veteran councillor in City Hall and a senior herself), who believes both in improving the living conditions of seniors and in providing opportunities for ordinary citizens to learn the mechanisms of power.

The Terms of Reference of the Seniors' Task Force outlined five main goals, which were adopted in March 1998: (1) to develop structures to advise City Council on issues affecting seniors and to involve seniors in this process; (2) to ensure that policies, programmes and services developed and delivered by the municipality meet the needs of seniors; (3) to value the involvement of seniors in the life of the city; (4) to identify a role for the City in the International Year of Older Persons 1999; and (5) to provide a process for rationalization of all previous municipal Seniors' committees (City of Toronto, 1999). The Vision Statement of the Seniors' Task Force, adopted in June 1999, further clarified its goals:

> By 2005, the City of Toronto will be a leader in supporting quality of life for seniors by providing reasonable access to services, a safe physical environment, choices in work and social opportunities, and a voice in local government decisions which affect their lives. (City of Toronto, 1999, p. 4)

The Task Force, which held monthly meetings from January 1998 to October 1999 (the final report was adopted by City Council on October 26), had 25 regular members representing the different areas of the city, of which 7 were city councillors and 18 were senior citizens. Other than geographical distribution, 3 criteria were used for the selection of the senior citizen members. They had to be "1) active in seniors' organizations and associations; 2) able to reflect their own views and experiences as well as those of their members; and 3) able to consult others within their communities" (City of Toronto, 1999, p. 10).

In order to collect input from a broad representation of seniors in the process, the Task Force organized 39 consultations with 1,064 seniors, representatives of senior organizations, and representatives of agencies that serve seniors. These consultations were held in local communities, in the native languages of the participating groups, and in small and large group discussions. These consultations were organized around three questions: (1) what are the major issues and priorities for seniors living in the new city of Toronto? (2) what citizen participation models should be adopted to advise City Council on seniors issues? and (3) what suggestions did they have for marketing 1999 as the International Year for Older Persons in Toronto? (City of Toronto, 1999, p. 12). Information resulting from this process was disseminated in community newspapers and a newsletter, The Seniors' Task Force News, and was used at the monthly Senior Task Force meetings to guide the discussions. The five most common issues that were identified by seniors in the consultations were access to information, health and health services, housing, transportation and services. Seniors were also able to provide input to the consultation process through a staffed telephone line and by email, fax or postal service.

Profile of the STF Participants and Representation

The 15 seniors of the STF that were interviewed (60% are female and 40% are male) had an average age of 73 years, with a range from 59 to 84 years. The majority of them (73%) were born in Canada, and one of them is an Aboriginal Canadian. Although the composition of the STF was not supposed to be a perfect sample of Toronto's multicultural population, it is noticeable that some groups with a significant demographic presence in the city (such as Blacks and Latinos) were not represented on the Task Force.

The educational level of the members is above the national mean. All have completed secondary education, and over half of them (60%) have completed post-secondary education, including two masters' degrees. All of the members have a long history of participation in civic or community organizations, and all but one were involved with an organization before joining the Task Force. About 60% were active in their local communities (via neighbourhood centres, committees or associations), and the remaining 40% were involved in other volunteer, advocacy and religious organizations.

Almost half of the interviewees (43%) were already familiar with the dynamics of the Toronto municipal government before their participation in the Seniors' Task Force. Among them, a few had been city employees in the past, and others had volunteered in other Task Forces or had been involved with city departments and city officials in the course of their jobs. For these members, involvement in municipal government was not an entirely new situation; furthermore, some of them had extensive experience on these matters, from occupying elected positions (e.g. alderpersons) to heading a variety of committees.

The remaining 57% of the members did not have any direct experience with the Toronto municipal government prior to the Seniors' Task Force, and were presumably less familiar with its functions.

This information suggests that, although Task Force members collectively had high levels of political capital compared to the average citizen, there were internal differences in specific political capital regarding municipal politics. It is unclear from the data collected in this study (and a subject for future research) whether this imbalance created a situation of unequal opportunity, in the sense that the more "experienced" members had more leverage than the "inexperienced" ones in influencing the agenda.

Members of the Task Force also had high levels of community and civic participation, which is not surprising due to the strategies used to recruit and select them. The selection method specifically targeted experienced community leaders by inviting individuals who were already known to city councilors and staff. At the time of joining the Task Force, 93% of the members interviewed were either affiliated with a particular community organization or had recently been active in an organization, and 87% were personally invited by a city councillor or city agency to serve on the Seniors' Task Force. The interview data likewise supported that organizational affiliation was a strong determinant in the selection process of the Task Force members.

> [I was invited] because councillor [X] knew me. I wrote a lot of letters to her because of my position in the community centre, and met her a few times. The councillors eventually come to the community centre events. I had to send in my resume, and got a letter from her confirming.

Sometimes, prospective Task Force members previously knew a city councilor and were contacted directly by the councillor to participate. For instance, one member who had volunteered for a councillor's electoral campaigns felt compelled to participate in the Task Force when approached by the councillor, "I didn't want to [participate] but you know how you get roped in."

Occasionally, as the following quote indicates, seniors were appointed by their own organization at the request of the city:

> Someone from [an ethnic-based center] asked me to serve on the STF. They told me to go and so I went.

> The staff of the HC office contacted the staff at City Hall involved with disability and accessibility for a recommendation. I was recommended by the people from "access."

Only two of the interviewees reported that they applied independently to serve on the Seniors' Task Force as opposed to being invited to participate. These seniors applied to participate on the Task Force on their own initiative and felt that they were subjected to slightly different rules of selection than those invited:

> I think there has to be a better or fairer way of identifying citizen participants. I contacted City Hall to say I was interested in participation on the Seniors' Task Force. They said, "Contact your local councillor". They asked me to submit a CV. My understanding is that others didn't have to apply.

This is a relevant issue because it reflects the difficulties of the Healthy City Staff in generating a selection process that ensures expertise, representation and openness at the same time. In attempting to achieve "expertise," the process allowed for the city to appoint most members of the Task Force, the assumption being that councillors and city officials could identify "good participants" based on their background and past civic activities. In attempting to achieve "representation," some organizations were asked to select delegates to the Task Force, although it was understood that members were participating there on individual capacity and had no official mandate expressed by their organizations. In order to achieve "openness," the process allowed for independent applications of any senior in the city who was interested in participating. Regarding this particular group, it is not clear how many of these at-large applications for a membership position in the Seniors' Task Force were submitted, how many were refused, and the criteria for accepting or refusing them.

The data indicates that participation in the STF is more representative along constructs of gender and ethnicity than of class, although broader representation was achieved through speaking with seniors in the consultation process. In terms of gender, the Task Force was composed of 10 female and 8 male members. Internally, the Task Force did not have a formal hierarchical organization that might have restricted the participation and voice of certain members. In the interviews, seniors did not indicate any feeling of being excluded from the process. However, some of them suggested that certain members manipulated power and shared it unequally. Several complained of the aggressiveness of a few individuals who dominated the discussion sessions. This circumstance recalls Bourdieu's observation that language and the ability to communicate are unequally distributed in society and that they play an important role in public participation (Bourdieu, 1984). In classroom settings and group dynamics in general, teachers and facilitators can reinforce those inequalities (consciously or unconsciously) through their interaction with participants, for instance, encouraging the participation of some members and inhibiting the participation of others. However, the facilitator can also work to equalize opportunities for participation. In this regards, several STF participants observed that dominating members were restrained effectively by healthy city staff and by councillor Ann Johnston, the chair of the Task Force. As one member remarked, "Ann Johnston was terrific. She knew how to get people to be quiet after a while. She knew how to make it more equal and I found her to be very fair."

There was a conscious effort to include a range of ethnic groups on the Task Force, although several members criticized that the representation was insufficient in respect to the diversity of the population of Toronto. Prominent advocacy/community groups were asked to send an unofficial member to serve on the Task Force, which include an Aboriginal association, a disabilities division of the city government and an Italian association; as well, individual advocates of certain ethnic groups were invited to join the Task Force. The majority of the Task Force members was contacted due to their affiliation with an advocacy or community group, and was thus targeted to represent, albeit unofficially, a particular minority population. Despite these conditions, several members reiterated that they believed the Task Force did not go far enough, as one member remarked, "I've been disappointed because there have been too many WASPs and not enough representation."

Privilege was evident in the small number of low-income seniors selected for the Task Force. The homogeneous socio-economic representation is due, at least in part, to the built-in class bias of targeting community leaders, who are likely to have higher socio-economic status (SES), to serve on the Task Force. However, despite the low representation of working class seniors, issues of class, specifically concerning disadvantaged seniors, were at least raised during the monthly meetings. The presence of dissent and conflict, although tentative, suggests that the deliberative process was not entirely consensual and, as some have charged, a clear practice of appeasement:

> I'm not happy with the new Toronto Seniors Council because it's middle class. I'm more interested in health care and housing. We're not zeroing in on it.

> The recommendations are all airy-fairy. I haven't seen anything acted on. Depends if they will be acted on. I told my councillor I need to get back into it (seniors' issues) because I think I have a slant on it. They think all seniors have a phone, TV, etc., and most don't. This whole thing was political, who you know. I keep talking about the income of people who can't go to the meetings because they can't afford transportation. I keep bringing this up. I'd let them know about the reality of seniors on low income; some can't afford food or drugs.

Representation of the broader population of seniors was expected to occur through the consultations, and the interviews indicated that there was some success in this regard. The role of the Task Force members was to implement the issues that were raised at the consultations, rather than to express their own interests or the interests of their organization. Seniors and coordinators who participated in the consultations (but not on the Task Force) stated that the consultations were "genuine" in the sense that they were very open and that seniors were asked about their needs and were listened to. They recounted that it was easy to speak out because there were small group discussions. However, some seniors noted that the consultations were not inclusive enough to provide the Task Force with a sufficient diversity of input. In their view, the consultations should have reached a wider public:

> In the Seniors' Task Force who do we talk to? The people who want to come out to meetings. We're not reaching people in the guts of the community. There's a whole deep water that we're not sounding. There's a large community that needs to be reached, largely ethnic.

> We got a lot of information. I wanted to address all of the issues but they said, "That's not your mandate." We were supposed to sort priorities in order, which we received from the consultations.

Because the Task Force members were supposed to be in contact with individuals in their community and as community leaders to better understand the issues and views that exist, it can be argued that non-active seniors (i.e. who did not attend the consultations) were "virtually" represented, although this argument masks ethnic and class inequalities and questions of the distribution of power in political participation.

Citizenship Learning Among Members of the Seniors' Task Force

During the interviews, participants were asked about their informal learning experiences pertaining to citizenship and democracy. In order to contextualize their informal learning with previous learning experiences, they were also asked about their civic learning in the formal and non-formal educational systems.

Citizenship Learning Prior to Participation in the STF

The majority of participants (80%) did not take any courses on citizenship or politics in the formal school system, or at least could not remember if they had. The few interviewees who recalled taking courses on some aspect of citizenship or government mentioned civics lessons from secondary school that were integrated into history lessons and university courses on political sciences:

> There was a course called civics. In French in Quebec and in English in Ontario. They were darned good books. They weren't separate courses but parts of others.

> I've taken courses every year- philosophy, literature- but not related to government. When I went through high school there weren't these types of courses. There should be a course for each cultural group. I get the feeling that there are more opportunities for the cultural groups than they are aware of.

Only one person mentioned informal civic learning in a school setting, which occurred through participation in the school council. Although unsurprising, this is nonetheless a frustrating finding for those who believe, like Dewey (1927), that education for democracy works at its best in democratic schools where people learn democracy by doing it:

> I haven't had any courses, but I've been to a lot of conferences. In high school, I was president of the students' league, and got into politics in high school being elected on the student council.

When asked if they had taken courses or workshops on citizenship or government as adults, outside of the formal school system, only three interviewees responded positively. One of them took a course concerning local politics (specifically on how to run an electoral campaign) and the remaining two took courses as part of their involvement with labour unions:

> I've taken endless courses, 22 years of courses. Of course, they were useful to my understanding of politics. We learned 22 years ago that there would be fewer jobs and the majority would be service jobs. And now it's a fact.

> Yes, I was president of a union at [name of a company] for 12 years. So we were always taking courses on things the government did, like wage and price control. Lots of stuff about government. With me being in the union, it made me see who was looking after themselves. This happened also in the union. You have to be able to read between the lines. No courses in school because I went to commerce and it was more business and it was during the war.

In summary, by the time they joined the Seniors' Task Force, only one third of participants had taken some type of prior course on citizenship, politics or government either in the formal system during their youth or in the non-formal system as adults. The subjects of the formal courses were civics/government (secondary) and political science (undergraduate). Non-formal courses dealt with issues such as campaigning, economy, employment, government and wage negotiations, and most of them were offered by unions.

Informal Citizenship Learning Through the STF

The primary type of learning that occurred during the Seniors' Task Force was informal, usually acquired by doing, talking, listening and observing during the activities performed on the Task Force. The informal learning was unintentional and largely unconscious because the Seniors' Task Force was not conceived of as an opportunity for structured learning for the participants, but as a way for citizens to engage in the political process of their city, community and peer group. However, this informal learning was not complemented by non-formal learning (planned and intentional), as sometimes occurs in these types of initiatives. Indeed, as seniors did not attend pre-service or in-service courses or workshops designed to prepare them in advance for their future activities, or to improve their participation as members of the Task Force during their involvement, the non-formal dimension of learning was absent from this experience. Some members identified this circumstance as a missed opportunity to improve their participation. According to these seniors, Healthy City staff assumed that at the time of joining all members already possessed the specific competencies needed for successful performance in collective deliberation and policy formulation. As one member pointed out, "the Seniors' Task Force staff expected that you already know how to participate."

Some of the informal learning acquired by members of the Task Force was self-directed (when, for instance, a member consciously intended to learn something about a particular issue), and some was incidental (unintentional but eventually conscious), but the bulk of it fell into that gray area of "socialization" or "tacit learning," which includes all the learning that is unintended and unrecognized. The participants in the Seniors' Task Force did not intend to learn about democratic citizenship and politics, although in reflecting on their experience during the interviews they all revealed some level of awareness of their learning. For some of them, this awareness was arrived at independently, while most became aware of their learning as a consequence of the interview process.

When asked about the type and amount of learning that is a priori required to participate effectively in local governance, several seniors noted that formal schooling and even experience in politics are less important than being motivated and well informed. For these seniors, the most crucial requirement is that participants have an interest in the issues at stake and are aware of all their implications and of their broader societal context. The following two quotes illustrate this viewpoint:

> One part is that if you have no criteria then there is no preparation for their responsibilities. What our role was going to be was not defined. On the other hand, people without experience will be self-learners while they participate. Experience is less important than is interest. Some people with a lot of experience may not have done much work, such as facilitating meetings.

> It's useless for a person to go through school and think that they have it all. Knowledge is learned day-to-day. It's pointless to be on the Seniors' Task Force without knowing what's going on, being informed on issues, read two papers, and watch the CBC.

In their recollection of the most important learning experiences that occurred throughout their participation in the Task Force, members referred both to specific learning events ("episodic memory") and to generalized knowledge that transcends particular learning episodes ("semantic memory"). What was noticeably weak in their recollections was the recognition of particular competencies learned through participation in the Task Force. Indeed, members did not talk much about the acquisition (or the refinement) of political skills such as organizing, mobilizing, persuading, conflict solving, public speaking, listening, "working the system," decision making or strategizing. Their deepest self-perceived changes had less to do with the acquisition of specific competencies but with the acquisition of specific information about an issue or with the adoption of new insights about human nature or new attitudes towards a particular group or issue:

> When we went down to city hall, we found out a lot about things I really didn't know about – the inner workings of the city. I found out a lot of things that were a surprise, like dental care and that pools were free in Toronto and not in Scarborough.

> I learned one thing, people are people. Probably the greatest lesson I learned, you approach people carefully.

> As a result [of this] I learned patience and perseverance in dealing with politicians who I found are sincere, good people, but very busy. Anne Johnston is very bright and I admire her a lot.

The first quote illustrates a particular type of incidental learning about a particular situation (in this case, the unevenness in the provision of municipal services across the city and the perceived unfairness in user fees structures) that relates to the gathering of public information not readily available to the public. The old adage that "information is power" seems to be at play here, in the sense that communities cannot challenge unfair policies unless they are aware of their existence. The second and third quotes are examples of attitudinal learning, particularly in relation to other people (be they politicians or other grassroots participants). The last quote in particular is consistent with other studies that found that in local democracy people may change their perceptions towards professional politicians (they tend to increase their trust in some local politicians who are involved in the process in a positive way) but do not necessarily increase their trust towards other politicians or towards the political system in general (Schugurensky, 2001b). Nor does it imply, as it is suggested in the second quote, a higher level of trust for people in general.

The results of the questionnaire on informal learning applied at the end of the interview were consistent with the trends identified during the dialogue with the Task Force members. Although overall the perceived changes (measured through pre- and post- scores) resulting from their participation were relatively moderate, there were some internal differences between changes in knowledge, skills and attitudes. Indeed, seniors declared that the most important learning was in the area of new knowledge and that the least significant changes occurred in the area of skills, with attitudinal changes falling somewhere in between.

Within the category of knowledge, the largest specific increases noted by seniors were on "city councilors," "city government" and "local issues and policies," which are areas with which the participants may have had little contact prior to their participation. In the attitudinal area, the most important change identified by the seniors was in terms of political efficacy ("confidence in your capacity to influence political decisions"). The greatest perceived increase in skills related to group working ("working with others"). There was not a significant difference in learning when the aggregate scores were controlled for education level and gender.

In terms of learning strategies, we pointed out above that the original questions on this topic (different variants of "How did you learn what you learned?") did not prove very helpful, as members had trouble in recalling the specifics of their learning process. Then, these questions were reformulated in terms of hypothetical scenarios (e.g. "If you move to another city and decide to get involved in a seniors' Task Force, how would you learn what you need to learn in order to participate?"). Given this scenario, the most frequently invoked strategy mentioned by participants was "talking to people," particularly people with some experience in the process or with expertise on the issues to be discussed. The majority stated that they would seek out people knowledgeable about seniors' issues or people affiliated with the municipal government. A few interviewees also noted that in order to find out what the main issues are they would read local newspapers and watch the local news:

> You have to have a sense of curiosity! I'd ask questions to whoever is organizing the Task Force and to the city. You'd largely want short, executive reports, not huge volumes of reports to read.

First I'd find out about their cultural ways, the whole economics of their country. Then I'd seek people out, read prior to going down. I'd say to them, "Lay your cards on the table."

Others said that they would join community or civic groups, such as a church, and meet other seniors at community centers. Interestingly, one fifth of the sample argued that seniors' issues and municipal governments are very similar anywhere in the world. For these interviewees, there was not a great need to learn much before participating, because the knowledge and skills already acquired through the STF would be sufficient to fully participate in a new environment.

Summary and Conclusions

In general terms, the informal learning accrued through participatory democracy in local governance tends to be isolated from explicit and intentional pedagogical efforts carried out by educational institutions and agents. Paraphrasing NALL, in spite of the universal recognition of the importance of citizenship education, we still have very limited understanding of the relations between the formal and non-formal citizenship education programmes, on the one hand, and people's informal citizenship learning, on the other. A better understanding of those connections and misconnections could equip urban planners, community developers, and citizenship educators alike with analytical and instrumental tools to more adequately integrate informal civic learning with organized civic education programmes.

As a result of their deliberation process, the seniors of the Task Force elaborated a Final Report with 55 recommendations, and the Toronto City Council adopted all of them by amendment in 1999. This was a considerable achievement of the seniors and the city officials who were part of this process. Nevertheless, 1½ years later, only a few of the recommendations have been enacted. Some of them, such as the restoration of rent control (13) and additional support for lifelong learning programmes (48), were derailed by widespread municipal budget cuts. Other recommendations were redundant in the sense that they called for the continuation of existing by-laws and policies, like the demands for support for equitable community health policies and practices (12) and the promotion of fire safety programmes (42). Some of the recommendations, however, have been implemented to varying degrees. Among the enacted recommendations are the funding of local public health programmes and services for seniors (10); better promotion of public and community meetings sponsored by the city to seniors (33); better clearing of snow from sidewalks (39); making awareness of elder abuse a criteria for awarding certain grants (51); improved street signage (53); and the creation of the Seniors' Assembly (55).

Of the recommendations that have been implemented by Council, the creation of the Seniors' Assembly is particularly important and innovative. The assembly's permanent body consists of 45 senior-related organizations, and it has been funded in the municipal budget for four annual meetings, which began in the fall of 2000. The Seniors' Assembly continues the work begun by the Seniors' Task Force by serving as a direct link between Council and senior advocates in Toronto.

Furthermore, it will maintain the pressure on Council to address senior issues and help to give a voice to organizations of seniors in the municipal government.

In terms of the learning acquired by the participants, the findings of this study raise six considerations:

- Spaces of participatory democracy are spaces of civic learning, although the amount of learning in the process seems to be inversely correlated with the members' previous political experiences.
- The quantity and quality of such learning depends on and can be mitigated by the type of activities carried out in the collective setting, the diversity of participants, and the extent of previous learning.
- The previous formal and non-formal civic learning of the participants was not perceived as useful to improve political performance in local democracy.
- The educative and empowering potential of participatory democracy, to be fully realized, requires innovative strategies to bring more "non-professional citizens" to the table.
- Engagement and feelings of collective efficacy are higher when the process is clearly defined, when actors have a clear understanding of the nature and implications of each stage of the process, and when they have control over the outcomes.
- Learning is largely tacit and unconscious and thus participants often have difficulties retrieving and articulating the learning acquired through their involvement.

The first consideration is that public spaces for democratic engagement can be sites of considerable civic learning, which brings us back to Pateman's assertion that participatory democracy has a high educative potential. However, this assertion can be qualified by the proposition that the amount of learning in the process seems to be inversely correlated with the members' previous political experiences. Although STF members reported increases in political and institutional knowledge, gained some political skills, and experienced some changes in attitudes and values, the extent of these changes were considerably lower than those reported by members of Porto Alegre's participatory budget who had little political experience prior to their participation in that process (Schugurensky, 2001).

Second, this study suggests that the quantity and quality of the learning depends on and can be mitigated by the type of activities carried out, the heterogeneity of participants, and the extent of their previous learning. The small changes in attitudes can be explained by the fact that the STF did not provide a space to meet and deliberate with people who were very different from them or had radically different ideas from their own. They all belonged to the same generational group, and were there together to advance the common interests of that group, not to debate controversial ideas in a diverse setting or to assess the merits and weaknesses of conflicting projects. When this type of situation occurs, there is a higher chance that some people discover a new approach to an issue and changes their attitudes toward it. In the case of the STF, the main attitudinal changes related to increasing levels of tolerance to other people and trust in local politicians who demonstrate a committed support to the process. The negligible change in political skills was probably due to the fact that most members already had well-developed skills from their long experience in political and civic life in their own communities, and to the fact that the exercise of the Task Force was mainly to draft a series of proposals and not so much to negotiate them with the political powers. The changes in knowledge were more noticeable, particularly in reference to new information acquired through interaction with the city machinery and its actors.

Third, most members of the STF did not recognize in their school or in their non-formal education any adequate preparation for the tasks that they faced in their deliberation and decision-making process. If there was a connection between the informal learning process on civics that occurred during participation and the participants' previous formal and non-formal educational experiences, it was not acknowledged by them. Although their school experience took place many years ago, there is not much evidence that current civics courses in schools make a significant contribution in preparing people as informed, critical and active citizens who become willing and able to participate in political lives in their communities. This observation is supported by two characteristics commonly held by the participants: that they have had extensive experience in civic and political engagement, and that the majority has had little previous citizenship education in both formal and non-formal educational settings. This implies that the bulk of their knowledge and experience in politics was gained through previous participation rather than through coursework and other formal learning experiences, and that it was acquired informally without the explicit recognition that learning was taking place. In any case, the fact that participants in local democracy view the formal and non-formal education courses they took in the past as largely irrelevant for enabling their effective participation in civic and community involvement constitutes another call for the reconceptualization of existing citizenship education programmes.

Fourth, the levels of learning and empowerment among participants are likely to increase if deliberative public spaces include more than "professional citizens" and bring more "non-professional citizens" to the table. Indeed, one of the challenges of participatory democracy programmes is to attract those who are not already active participants in politics and civil society (Nylen, 2002). For a variety of reasons, these programmes tend to attract the more educated and empowered citizens who in turn increase their political capital, while average citizens remain unequipped for and disengaged from local politics.

In the case of the STF, this challenge was partially overcome because "ordinary seniors" had the opportunity to provide input (and many of them took it) through short consultation sessions held in different areas of the city. However, in terms of civic learning and political empowerment, "novice" members experienced little growth, because the most relevant learning opportunities were open only for the politically veteran seniors.

Fifth, both levels of engagement and political efficacy increase when the rules of the game are clear and when participants feel they have an impact on the outcomes of the process. The STF succeeded in creating among actors a clear understanding of the nature and implications of each stage of the process, and the relationship between the phases of consultation, deliberation, decision making, policy recommendation and policy adoption. This is important because in many cases the initiators of these processes (usually government staff) fail to make explicit to the community what they expect to achieve together and what expectations they have of each other, creating unnecessary instances of frustration, resentment, disillusion and mistrust.

Finally, members had difficulties retrieving and articulating the informal learning acquired through their involvement in the process. This confirms the challenges of previous research to dig up informal learning (Eraut, 1999a, b; Livingstone, 1999). Most of the learning experienced by Task Force members was unconscious, and they were highly unaware of it until asked to reflect on the experience by somebody else. Indeed, one of the main tasks in researching informal learning is to find strategies to identify tacit knowledge and make it more explicit.

These considerations on informal learning through participatory democracy raise some issues for formal and non-formal citizenship education. To begin with, the fact that members of the Seniors' Task Force attributed little relevant civic learning to their formal school experiences could be attributed to the traditional civic curricula that prevailed several decades ago. However, in recent years significant changes are occurring in terms of the philosophy and the practice of formal civic education in a variety of countries, altering its content, its method and the social environment (Hahn, 1998). As schools shift from passive to active approaches, and begin to include elements of dimensions of participatory democracy in the classroom and in the school management, it is reasonable to expect in the future a greater contribution from formal education to the development of informed, engaged and active citizens.

Non-formal education, for its part, can play an important role in fostering the inclusion of marginalized groups and individuals in public deliberation spaces, in equalizing opportunities for participation, and in improving the quality of participation. Through workshops, short courses, popular education programmes and innovative approaches (e.g. legislative theatre), non-formal education could promote the participation of members of marginalized groups who, for a variety of individual and structural reasons, do not tend to participate in public deliberation spaces. Non-formal education can also provide information about concrete opportunities for citizen participation, and for preparing groups to develop the necessary skills for full and meaningful participation.

In other words, if efforts to attract "disengaged" citizens succeed, the next issue for non-formal education would be to equalize opportunities for participation. Indeed, traditionally disengaged groups have less political know-how because they had fewer opportunities to develop the necessary competencies to act in these deliberative spaces than professionals and middle class groups. Factors such as class position, gender, race have significant bearing on the capacity of people to engage successfully in civic learning, because those locations generate different levels of previous educational and political experiences, connections, feelings of confidence and the like. Non-formal educational processes could facilitate information and generate positive attitudes towards participation through the development of feelings of political efficacy. As some interviewees pointed out, being motivated and well informed about the process are key factors for success. In this regard, a variety of courses and workshops could be designed, both prior to and in conjunction with their involvement in the process.

Preparatory courses and workshops can support these efforts by placing a greater emphasis on the knowledge, skills and attitudes necessary for political participation, rather than by the perpetuation of politics as a spectator sport. Potentially, this would give newcomers a better baseline or starting point in regard to civic skills, and the confidence that they can make a difference. In planning these courses, curriculum designers may consider the statements of many interviewees that one of the best learning strategies for being effective participants is to seek out people knowledgeable about the issue being considered, and people affiliated with the municipal government. These "pre-service" efforts can be complemented with the development of civic training centers in local communities, in alliance with social movements and unions. "In-service" courses and workshops could be implemented throughout the process to make members more self-conscious of the informal learning that occurs during participation, thereby enabling participants to organize, systematize and pass on their experience to the next generation of participants. Indeed, as mentioned previously, the absence of pre-service and in-service courses and workshops was perceived by members of the STF as a missed opportunity to improve participation, to make tacit learning more conscious, and to enhance the informal learning acquired experientially.

The previous discussion raises two challenges (one theoretical, the other more practical) for researchers and practitioners of citizenship education. The first is to develop a theory of lifelong and lifewide citizenship learning that examines the civic knowledge and attitudes acquired throughout life (from primary socialization to late adulthood) and in different educational settings (formal, non-formal and informal). The challenge is not only to examine the learning experiences in each setting and age period, but also to examine the continuities and the tensions among them, including the ways in which individuals negotiate those different learning experiences. The second challenge is to nurture more fluid linkages between formal and non-formal citizenship education programmes, on the one hand, and between these programmes and informal learning processes, on the other. This would help to maximize the learning potential of public spaces and to build capacity for the radical democratization of social institutions. Addressing these two challenges together can contribute to the development of the theory and practice of a holistic "pedagogy of democracy."

References

Abers, R., 1998, Learning democratic practice: distributing government resources through popular participation in Porto Alegre, Brazil, in M. Douglass & J. Friedmann (Eds.), *Cities for Citizens*, Wiley, New York.

Abers, R., 2000, *Inventing Local Democracy: Grassroots Politics in Brazil*, Lynne Rienner Publishers, Boulder, CO.

Almond, G. & Verba, S., 1963, *The Civic Culture: Political Attitudes and Democracy in Five Nations*, Princeton University Press, Princeton, NJ.

Arnstein, S., 1969, A ladder of citizen participation, *Journal of the American Institute of Planners*, **35(4)**: 216–224.

Bandura, A., 1977, *Social Learning Theory*, Prentice Hall, Englewood Cliffs, NJ.

Barker, J., 1999, *Street-Level Democracy: Political Settings at the Margins of Global Power*, Between the Lines, Toronto.

Berry, J., Portney, K. & Thomson, K., 1993, *The Rebirth Of Urban Democracy*, The Brookings Institute, Washington, DC.

Bourdieu, P., 1984, *Distinction: A Social Critique of the Judgment of Taste*, Routledge, London.

Bourdieu, P., 2000, *Propos sur le Champ Politique*, Presses Universitaires de Lyon, Lyon.

Carter, L.H. & Elshtain, J.B., 1997, *Task Force on Civic Education Statement of Purpose*, P.S. Political Science and Politics (December), 744.

Church, J., 2001, Citizen participation in health (care) decision-making: what we know and where we might go, in: *The Shift: A Newsletter on Shifting Paradigms in Health and Health Promotion*, 3 (3), University of Alberta, Edmonton, Canada.

City of Toronto, 1997, *Coming Together: Healthy City Toronto 1993–1997*, City of Toronto, Toronto.

City of Toronto, 1998, *We've Got to Stop Meeting Like This*, City of Toronto, Toronto.

City of Toronto, 1999, *Building a City for All Ages*. Final report of the Toronto Seniors' Task force, City of Toronto, Toronto.

Cogan, J. & Derricott, R., 2000, *Citizenship for the 21st Century: An International Perspective on Education*, Kogan Page, London.

Dewey, J., 1927, *The Public and Its Problems*, Swallow Press, Athens, OH.

Eraut, M., 1999a, Non-formal learning in the workplace – the hidden dimension of lifelong learning: a framework for analysis and the problems it poses for the researcher, Plenary paper presented at *the First International Conference on Researching Work and Learning*, Leeds University, Leeds.

Eraut, M., 1999b, Non-formal learning, implicit learning and tacit knowledge, in F. Coffield (Ed.), *The Necessity of Informal Learning*, Policy Press, Bristol.

Fedozzi, L., 1997, Orçamento Participativo: Reflexões sobre a experiência de Porto Alegre, FASE, Porto Alegre.

Frazer, E., 1999, The idea of political education, *Oxford Review of Education*, **25**: 5–22.

Gear, J., McIntosh, A. & Squires, G., 1994, *Informal Learning in the Professions*, University of Hull: School of Education, Hull.

Hahn, C., 1998, *Becoming Political: Comparative Perspectives on Citizenship Education*, State University of New York Press, Albany, NY.

Ichilov, O., 1998, The challenge of citizenship education in a changing world, in O. Ichilov (Ed.), *Citizenship and Citizenship Education in a Changing World*, Woburn Press, Portland, OR.

Layton, J., 1990, City politics in Canada, in M. Whittington. & G. Williams (Eds.), *Canadian Politics in the 1990s*, Nelson Canada, Scarborough, Ontario.

Livingstone, D., 1999, Exploring the icebergs of adult learning: findings of the first Canadian survey of informal learning practices, *Canadian Journal for the Study of Adult Education*, **3**: 49–72.

Morrow, R. & Torres, C.A., 1995, *Social Theory and Education. A Critique of Theories of Social and Cultural Reproduction*, SUNY Press, Albany, NY.

National Advisory Committee on Aging, 1999, *1999 and Beyond: Challenges of an Aging Society*, available on-line at http://www.hcsc.gc.ca/seniors-aines/pubs/beyond1999/intro_e.htm

Niemi, R. & Junn, J., 1998, *Civic Education: What Makes Students Learn*, Yale University Press, New Haven, CT.

Nylen, W.R., 2002, Testing the empowerment thesis: the participatory budget in Belo Horizonte and Betim, Brazil, *Comparative Politics*, **34(2)**: 127–145.

Offe, C. & Ronge, V., 1975, Theses on the theory of the state, *New German Critique*, **6**: 137–147.

Pateman, C., 1970, *Participation and Democratic Theory*, Cambridge University Press, Cambridge.

Polanyi, M., 1966, *The Tacit Dimension*, Doubleday, Garden City, NY.

Pontual, P., 1999, O Processo Educativo no Orcamento Participativo: Aprendizados dos atores da sociedade civil e do estado, Unpublished doctoral dissertation, Pontificia Universidade CatÛlica de Sao Paolo.

Putnam, R.D., 1993, *Making Democracy Work: Civic Traditions in Modern Italy*, Princeton University Press, Princeton, NJ.

Putnam, R.D., 1995, Bowling alone: America's declining social capital, *Journal of Democracy* **6(1)**: 65–78.

Raphael, D., Brown, I. & Wheeler, J. (Eds.), 2000, *A City for All ages: Fact or fiction? Effects of government policy decisions on Toronto seniors' quality of life.* Centre for Health Promotion, University of Toronto. Available:www.utoronto.ca/seniors/Toronto/sept2000Report.htm

Statistics Canada, 1999, *A Portrait of Canada's Seniors*, Statistics Canada, Ottawa.

Schugurensky, D., 2000, *Citizenship learning and democratic engagement: Political capital revisited*, Proceedings of the 41st Annual Adult Education Research Conference, Vancouver: AERC, 417–422.

Schugurensky, D., 2001a, *The enlightenment-engagement dilemma and the development of the active citizen: Lessons from the Citizens' Forum and the Participatory Budget,* Proceedings of the 20th anniversary conference of the Canadian Association for Studies in Adult Education (CASAE), Quebec City.

Schugurensky, D., 2001b, Grassroots democracy: the Participatory Budget of Porto Alegre, *Canadian Dimension*, **35(1)**, pp. 30–32. Jan/Feb.

Schugurensky, D., 2006, "This is our School of Citizenship. Informal Learning in Local Democracy." In Z. Bekerman, N. Burbules and D. Silberman (eds), *Learning in Hidden places: The Informal Education Reader*. New York: Peter Lang.

Torney-Purta, J., Schwille, J. & Amadeo, J., 1999, *Civic Education across Countries: Twenty-four National Case Studies from the IEA Civic Education Project*, Eburon Publishers, Delft.

Torney-Purta, J., Lehmann, R., Oswald, H. & Schulz, W., 2001, *Executive Summary: Citizenship and Education in Twenty-eight Countries: Civic Knowledge and Engagement at age Fourteen*, International Association for the Evaluation of Educational Achievement, Amsterdam.

Tough, A., 1971, *The Adult's Learning Projects: A Fresh Approach to Theory and Practice in Adult Learning*, The Ontario Institute for Studies in Education, Toronto.

Vygotsky, L.S., 1978, *Mind in Society*, Harvard University Press, Cambridge, MA.

Chapter 6
While No One is Watching: Learning in Social Action Among People who are Excluded from the Labour Market

Kathryn Church, Eric Shragge, Jean-Marc Fontan, and Roxana Ng

Introduction

This chapter profiles non-profit community/trade union organizations[1] run by/for marginalized groups. Under the pressures of a turbulent social and economic context, many have evolved a contradictory practice that blends social and economic development. While breaking with earlier traditions of opposition, they have fostered new traditions that operate "while no one is watching" to transform the lives of individuals facing a rough ride in capitalist societies. Informal learning is a significant part of this shift.

The authors of this chapter have been involved for many years in community organizations and/or trade unions. Our argument draws on several years of collaborative research done with three such organizations in Montreal and Toronto, Canada. It documents informal learning arising from practice in three areas: learning to participate; learning to re/connect with others; learning a new definition of self. We view these as core features of what Foley (1999) calls "learning in social action." For us, this phrase references actions ranging from informal conversation to formal collective process. In aligning ourselves with Foley's work, we are contributing to a stream of literature on informal learning that could be characterized as "learning power and action in resisting communities" (Adams, 1997). It encompasses the learning struggles of women, First Nations and other racial/ethnic minorities, youth and the elderly.

As much as possible, we have written this chapter in plain language with words in common use. We did not want the academic use and histories of words to take precedence over their every day meanings. Also, we have organized the presentation of our findings in generic categories. This strategy arose from our discomfort with the ways in which terminology used in previous drafts, term such as "political learning" or "solidarity learning," required us to reference and position ourselves with respect to academic debates (Church et al. 2000). Against the grain of academic practice, we chose not to privilege the categories derived from our work over the case descriptions that give them life. Thus, while broadly locating ourselves, we have resisted establishing our legitimacy in this way. Our primary focus is on the community organizations we have studied, and how their participants live

K. Church et al. (eds.), *Learning through Community: Exploring Participatory Practices*.
© Springer Science+Business Media B.V. 2008

out informal learning. The categories we use are intended merely as a functional framework on which to "hang" our descriptions and observations.

Context

We begin with the political and economic restructuring of the late 1970s. In the decade that followed, community responses were shaped by government's redefinition of its role and by changes in waged work. New community practices emerged around a commitment to pragmatism and concrete forms of problem solving. These changes were in response to rapid and substantial shifts in economic and political life. The working class and other social groups, people who made some gains with welfare state expansion and post-war employment opportunities, were faced with deteriorating social and economic conditions. Further, ideological attacks from the Right challenged social gains made through the welfare state and the legitimacy of the state playing an active social role. Budget cuts on the social side were the order of the day, with those at the bottom bearing the burden of fiscal conservatism.

Economic changes paralleled the redefinition of the role of the state. Unions were put on the defensive as employers sought more "flexible" workplaces to enable greater competition in global markets. This push and accelerating technological innovation brought massive unemployment in the 1980s and much of the 1990s. The new jobs that replaced traditional blue-collar work were neither unionized nor stable. As a consequence, unemployment remained high for most of the period between 1980 and 2000. Further, finding a job did not mean that people were able to escape poverty (Jackson and Robinson, 2000). Those who did not find work found themselves under attack. Rather than targeting poverty, governments launched offensives against the poor themselves, and other marginal populations, not only by removing programmes and benefits but by also assailing the basic entitlements to these programmes (Leduc Browne, 1996, 2000). There seems to be little for those with progressive social vision.

How did the community sector respond to these changes? At first, activists in the community sector opposed the cutbacks in government spending on services and programmes. As the years passed, it became clear that the Right was gaining rather than losing ground. As the new economy emerged from the restructuring, it appeared that a return to post-war employment patterns and the welfare state was unlikely. Community organizations and organizers faced a dismal situation. There did not seem to be the energy to continue the social action struggles of the 1960s and 1970s. Poverty and unemployment coupled with a reduction in social programmes drove large numbers of new clients to community-based organizations and services to seek help. The community sector responded with social solidarity and innovative programmes.

Many community organizations repositioned themselves from an oppositional stance to one of collaboration, from seeking confrontation and challenging the power structure to finding common ground on which to build a new social consensus (Albrow, 1996; Teeple, 1995). Further, both governments and private foundations have embraced this new orientation. These bodies have subsequently supported many of the new initiatives that use this approach. Part of the reason for this is that community organizations have cushioned the blows to the poor and the working class that resulted from the changes we have described. One of the new directions of practice is a blending of economic and social development, a process often expressed as social integration through the labour market. This has been expressed through practices such as community economic development, a mixed form of community intervention that creates businesses that have a social vocation (Shragge and Church, 1998). These new practices embody the tension between the more militant practices of the past and new ways of responding to new realities. The learning involved in this process is the theme of this chapter.

Evolving a Collaborative Method

At the opening session for the Network for New Approaches to Lifelong Learning, it became obvious that the four of us shared a common orientation towards community organizations working with people who are excluded from the marketplace. Using the Network's resources, we joined forces to enrich our individual study of these sites, and to extend them into collaborative work that would enable us to go beyond what any one of us might have generated alone. The decision reflected a common curiosity about how community organizations are responding to their redefined relationship to the state and the consequent redefinition of waged labour in the context of entrepreneurial ideologies that underpin the process of globalization.

By focusing on our commonalities, we do not mean to imply homogeneity of interest or approach. In fact, one of our major challenges has been to work across race/ethnic, gender, language and geographical differences. Further, we have different theoretical orientations, use different methods, have different weightings of theory to practice in our intellectual projects, and different degrees of intensity in terms of our community engagement. Bridging these differences was not easy. What has carried us through as a team was our agreement to begin from the sites themselves, i.e. to be most heavily informed by action/observation and reflection on the ground. We started from tensions, contradictions and transformations within community/union organizations.

Our research focused on three sites. The *Homeworkers' Association* (HWA) is a labour-supported organization that works with immigrant women who are unemployed members and homeworkers in the garment and textile sector. Designed as a place of training for people on social assistance, *Chic Resto Pop* is a community restaurant located in a low-income, working-class community in Montreal. A member organization of the Ontario Council of Alternative Businesses, *A-Way Express* is a courier service that is operated by psychiatric survivors in Toronto.[2]

Each of these sites was subject to the same global trends. Yet, because of historical social and political configurations, each was responding differently to the resulting

changes. Together, they demonstrated a range of organizational strategies for coping with restructuring and marginalization. Rather than "measure" that capacity
using standard indicators, we wanted to portray it in narrative "snapshots." A year
into our work, we noted our interest in "looking at people's experiences, and trying
to understand how the larger context (provincial, municipal, sectoral, social policy,
cultural, etc.) shapes their experiences. In turn, we look at how they respond to and
innovate around constant structural change." (Team Notes, May 1998)

From the start, we wanted to do comparative work that did not compromise what
we had begun with our selected communities. These individual sites remained the
primary focus of analysis. Every 4–6 months, we would meet face-to-face in an
attempt to forge some kind of synthesis, or joint framework. Periodically, we
worried about the need for symmetry in our approach. For example, on the brink of
fieldwork, we discussed developing a common interview guide. But our entry
points were too diverse for this uniformity. In the end, we used different data collection
methods in different sites.

- In Montreal, Eric and Jean-Marc built on previous study and writing about Chic
  Resto Pop by hiring a student researcher to do several weeks of observation at
  the restaurant. This initial work laid the ground for a second student researcher
  to interview key informants about learning at three levels: individual/personal;
  collective, staff and leadership; and organization, community, society.
- A student researcher who spoke Chinese spent several months doing initial
  observation with the Homeworkers Association in Toronto. Upon her departure,
  Roxana took up the task, of observing pattern-making classes, and English as a
  Second Language (ESL) classes over 1 year. She also attended their executive
  meetings. Her interpretations relied on observations and fieldnotes.
- Kathryn did a retrospective reading of research reports and interviews arising
  from six previous years in the field of psychiatric survivor-run businesses in
  Toronto.[3] She drew on individual interviews, focus groups, and large group
  discussions from two major research studies, rereading the results using "informal
  learning" as a fresh conceptual lens.

Using mixed methods to facilitate our comparative analysis made sense because our
relationships to and histories with our sites were different. The symmetry of our
study arises from shared questions about work and social life, about community
organizations and their engagement with formal definitions of work.

Learning Through Social Action in Three Sites

Although definitional issues were actively debated within NALL, the context was
dominated by a concept of informal learning as planned, intentional and rational.
This reflected Alan Tough's influence in the area of self-directed learning.
According to Percy et al., he was oriented towards "rationalistic, time-segmented,
project-based and quantitatively defined series of related concepts such as 'learning

projects' and 'learning episodes'" (1994, pp. 36–37). NALL's national survey (Livingstone, 1999) was built directly on the prior research of Tough (1968) and Penland (1979). Livingstone's post-survey writing emphasizes the importance of "explicit informal learning" as a discrete (rather than diffuse) learning experience. It can be consciously identified as significant by the learner and retrospectively recognized both in the form of knowledge and the process of acquisition. It is distinguished from basic socialization or tacit informal learning where "learning and acting constitute a seamless web in which it is impossible to distinguish informal learning in any discrete way" (1999, p. 51).

Tough's research demonstrated a preference for individually-conducted learning among members of dominant social groups. As a result, "Collectively-conducted learning processes continue to constitute the least well-documented part of adults' informal learning" (Livingstone, 1999, p. 53). Specifically, few researchers have studied popular struggles and social movements for their learning dimensions. "The potential field of study is huge," asserts Griff Foley, "and almost untouched" (1999, p. 140). He references his own work (Foley, 2001a) and that of Michael Welton as the only case studies of learning in social action of which he is aware. Welton is concerned with learning as an intersubjective process. "I have wanted to find a way of thinking about the various domains of human (adult) interaction as a social learning process" he explains. "How can we understand the family and the workplace, public life and social movements as learning sites?" (Welton, 1995, p. 9).

Tough's approach also failed to take seriously the "dormant, unintentional, incidental self-directed learning" (Percy et al., 1994, p. 17) that falls outside of its frame of reference. Over the years, there have been efforts to rectify this (see, e.g. Berger, 1990; Melville, 1987; Peterson, 1987). The one that resonates most closely with our own sense of things is Foley's articulation of learning in social action or learning in the context of struggle against oppression. This kind of learning is not linear. Rather, it is complex and contradictory, inductive and dialectical. It includes recognitions that reproduce the status quo as well as recognitions that critique the status quo. It is often conflictual.

Most significantly for us, Foley claims that learning in social movements "is largely informal and often incidental – it is tacit, embedded in social action and is often not recognized as learning. The learning is therefore often potential, or only half-realized" (1999, p. 3). Learners may retrospectively recognize their own learning but it is not essential that they do so. It is our task as researchers to "expose" and articulate the learning they acquired through struggle. This is not to denigrate or eliminate explicit forms of learning – as many types happen at once. "We learn as we act," Foley insists, "and our learning is both tacit and explicit. This is indeed a complex tapestry difficult to "unpick" (Foley, 2001b, p. 284). The learning that we observed in our sites tends to be highly dynamic, ad hoc rather than planned, and often incidental to the primary purposes of the organization.

The subjects of our research carry particularly high social stigma. Writing in this volume, Diane Meaghan notes that prostitutes are typically constituted in policy around fear and danger, disease and disorder. They are seldom viewed as individuals/

groups possessing a specialized knowledge that could be broadly useful. Instead, in medical/scientific as well as popular discourse, they are seen as a social problem. With various shadings and nuances, the same discourse is applied to the psychiatric survivors, social assistance recipients and immigrant women whose labour we profile. Rarely are they visible as learning subjects.

Our chapter begins to address this problem by taking up three non-profit community organizations run by and/or for marginalized groups as sites of learning. Our attempt is complicated somewhat by the fact that two of the research sites are a hybrid form: both community organizations and workplaces. There is a growing body of research on informal learning in workplace environments from a range of disciplines: education, sociology, cognitive psychology, cultural psychology, ecological psychology and anthropology. This literature is split between those who are skeptical about the workplace as an educative environment, and those who favour it as a rich base for learning experiences (Garrick, 1996; see also Boud and Middleton, 2003).

We are similarly torn. We take to heart Butler's argument that "techno-capitalism" requires entrepreneurial, change-oriented worker-learners who "willingly accept responsibility for the ongoing development of their personal exploitable capacities" (Butler, 2001, p. 65; See also Dehli and Fumia, this volume on issues of govern-mentality). We can see that government enthusiasm for entrepreneurial solutions and related training programmes in the community sector is part of this emerging "meta-governance." As workers ourselves, we experience the contradictory "dismantling (of) the habits of permanent, round the clock, steady and regular work" for more flexible work patterns and non-standard employment.[4]

Sympathetic as we are to Butler's analysis, we do not view the workplaces that we have studied as sites of restriction only. Nor are we automatically warning against the dangers of entrepreneurial initiatives in the community sector. Our response stems from knowledge of the long histories of exclusion that have shaped the groups involved in these projects. In western capitalist societies, paid work is the organizing principle "around which self, family, society and state revolve" (Gint, 1998, quoted in Butler, 2001, p. 64). To be excluded from this sphere is powerfully debilitating in both material and social terms. For those who have lived this reality, coming into a productive social role as workers – even if they themselves have to create it – can be transformative.In the end, we take a dialectical position in the debate over informal workplace learning: restriction and release are simultaneous features of the experience. As Foley argues, people's everyday experience "reproduces ways of thinking and acting which support the often oppressive, status quo, but that this same experience also produces recognitions which enable people to critique and challenge the existing order" (1999, pp. 3–4). From our observations of community/union organizations, informal learning takes place at a number of levels: between individual participants, between organizations, and, significantly, between organizational representatives and their founders. In the following section, we discuss these interactions in terms of three themes that emerged from our project: learning to participate; learning to re/connect; and, learning a new definition of self.

Learning to Participate

Engestrom (1999) argues that standard theories of learning are "closed" in the sense that they are primarily concerned with a subject's absorption of an established body of knowledge. His interests lie in the opposite direction, in a curiosity about those places in which people are transforming their lives and their organizations by creating a course of action without knowing the path. He called for a learning theory that can cope with situations of continuous uncertainty. The examples that most interest him are people adjusting to changes in the labour market. Engstrom's curiosity parallels our own and brings us to the first kind of learning that we observe in the community sector: learning to participate.

Jonathan Barker argues that "political participation requires a space in which people can meet; it requires a time when people can be present together and hear one another" (1999, p. 27). Steering away from larger phenomena such as mass protest, he makes a case for local organizations and small meetings, referring to them as "activity settings" that are the "contextual or situational unit out of which the idea of political space is built …" (1999, p. 30). We find this formulation useful. It helps organize our interest in how community organizations run by and for marginalized groups learn to position themselves within entrepreneurial culture. They are "foci of social energy; they contain and organize social forces that impel action just as surely as individual needs, desires and strategies do" (Barker, 1999, p. 29).

The roles that community organizations might take up in a restructured economy are not immediately obvious. Some, such as business development, have been actively resisted. As Shragge and Church point out, for community organizations, business as private enterprise has always been the enemy:

> Class formation polarizes the interests of those who own and control the means of production; owners versus both employees and the wider consumer society. In addition, one can add an ecological critique on the limits of growth, and a gender analysis of who has power in business. Yet, one of the main functions of [CED] is to promote business development (1998, p. 37).

However, profound contextual changes are forcing community organizations to learn the "entrepreneurial curriculum" – and quickly – if they are to survive. The problem becomes how to build programmes that will fly in the new economy and receive viable support in terms of government policy while simultaneously carrying forward historical concerns for social and economic justice.

For an example, we turn to Chic Resto Pop, a community restaurant located in an old industrial neighbourhood in Montreal's east-end.[5] Its dual purpose is to create jobs for the founding members and others on social assistance, and to provide quality, hot and inexpensive meals for the poor in the community. Now about 15 years old, Resto-Pop serves hundreds of people 3 meals a day, 5 days a week. Most are single men, average age of 45, who live alone, and are receiving welfare or Employment Insurance. The organization has introduced a mobile kitchen to provide meals to local schools, and day camps in the summer. In 1992, it introduced a musical festival, which is now an autonomous organization.

Resto-Pop is a non-profit organization managed by a board of directors and funded by government and its own entrepreneurial activities. There are 19 full-time employees under the supervision of the director. The restaurant takes in roughly 100 trainees each year for periods of 6–15 months. They are accorded the responsibilities and rights of workers. The goals of the training are to rebuild confidence, improve general work habits and learn new job-oriented skills. However, the restaurant is also a place for socialization. Community organizations use its space for information and discussion sessions on issues such as the social origins of poverty and welfare recipients' rights. In marrying these two functions, the Resto displays what it has learned about being an actor in civil society.

The founders of Chic Resto Pop wanted their initiative to respond to fundamental daily needs and problems in the community. In order to get financing, they established close connections with the government. Reflecting on that step, Benoit, a key organizer argued: "I don't think all public authorities are crooked. It's always easy to challenge; but when it comes time to build something, it's not easy." Building in alliance with the state created problems on two sides.

On the one hand, the Resto's relations with government were often conflictual. As the organization made an increasing number of claims, it experienced barriers with respect to programme accessibility or extension conditions. It had to overcome the inflexibility of regulatory norms and structures that are too often inappropriate for responding to concrete needs. Duguay confirms that:

> The Resto established privileged links with the Employment and Solidarity Ministry which allowed activity to continue. The business maintains co-operative relations with the Ministry, marked by a certain degree of restraint. The Chic Resto Pop is making sure to reduce the possibilities of interference from its partners in the orientation and development of the business, always looking to avoid playing the role of subcontractor. The relationship is equally marked by claims. The Resto Pop's autonomy is protected by a constant negotiation with public authorities. (English translation, 1999, p. 33)

While negotiating on that front, the Resto faced the wrath of popular organizations. They criticized its integrative services as collaboration with state politics of disengagement. The organization had bent to the deficiencies of the State, they argued, and become the transmitter of its politics. Said Benoit:

> The Resto was considered to be a pariah by a lot of community groups, like rights protection groups. That even brought about a debate in the newspapers at one time. They accused the Resto of exploiting workers. The community milieu was quick to take offence in response to divergent opinions that we were facing.

Caught in the middle, the Resto looked for ways to maintain equilibrium between a collaborative process (to respond to short-term needs) and a critical one (to defend its ideological positions). Its services helped it gain credibility among the local population. Its increasing number of interventions on behalf of marginalized populations helped it achieve a certain degree of broader social renown. In fact, the Resto actively involved itself in several groups, coalitions, and round tables on poverty, hunger or employment. For example, it organized a 2-day discussion on the causes of Québec unemployment. Nearly 350 clients, neighbourhood residents, and Resto workers, participated in this forum. Out of it a workers' declaration emerged that was then delivered to the Minister of Revenue Security.

Chic Resto Pop could easily have been an organization that limited itself to a narrower focus as a service business. In principle, no one could have foretold the role that it would occupy at the social level. However, the Forum example illustrates the voluntary social engagement emanating from the Resto. This learning trajectory is situated at two levels. On the one hand, the Resto's social activism depends on the degree of involvement manifested by the actors who drive it. These managers are increasingly conscious of the influence and growing social weight accorded them. Without prior training in "social marketing" but rich in experience gradually acquired in the field, they knew how to seize opportunities to occupy an important place in public and political debates. On the other hand, social recognition of the Resto also flows from organizational development that is increasingly independent from the individual will of its promoters. The "public image" conveyed by the organization transcends the individuals who work there.

The same dynamic shapes the work of the psychiatric survivor-run Ontario Council of Alternative Businesses (OCAB), of which A-Way Express is a member. Faced with the government's Ontario Works programme, its leaders used consultation to shape new legislation so that "the disabled" were transferred from workfare to a separate income support plan. After publicly supporting the legislation that made this possible (Ontario Disability Support Programs Act), they came under fire for "selling out" from critics both in and outside of the survivor community. While absorbing those charges, OCAB played a key role in organizing across the divisions of the survivor community to protest the government's move towards outpatient committal or community treatment orders. Thus, like Chic Resto Pop, OCAB lives the contradiction of being funded by government and on record in support of some policy directions, while maintaining a vocal critic and organizing against the government on others (Church, 2000).

In striking this delicate balance OCAB's image, too, is of crucial importance. Its leaders have learned the value of documenting the knowledge that psychiatric survivors generate through their actions, both to "re/member" it for their own members and to pass it along to others (Church, 1991). Position papers and research reports commissioned by the organization have acted not only as a touchstone but also as a wedge into debates on broader social issues. The organization has circulated them strategically to key publics including mental health professionals, bureaucrats, politicians and academics. Its leaders have used them to inform but also to create legitimacy and political support for their efforts. Like economic development itself, the practice of "working a document" was also learned by doing.

Meanwhile, at A-Way Express Couriers, employees relate to each other as co-workers but also as active participants in the running of the business. These workers are drawn not just into jobs but into decision-making roles: on the Board of Directors, the management team board or advisory committees. These are forums in which employees struggle collectively with issues facing the businesses, where they take up positions of responsibility in how things are run. Employees learn a range of skills as a result, from how to run a successful meeting to how to work with other people. For example, one employee talked about gaining a capacity for compromise and consensus building as a result of doing committee work. Being depended upon rather than depending on others is novel and important. For some it leads to more extensive participation as an employee from one business might be asked to sit on the board for another.

Workers come to know not just the business but the broader environment in which the business operates: bureaucracy and government; funding and social policies; the psychiatric survivor movement and its leaders. From our point of view, the movement connection is particularly significant. To give an example, one employee talked about how psychiatric survivors have to work together to build political support in order to keep their businesses alive. This knowledge of a broader collectivity was gained in relationship to key survivor leaders and other survivor groups. It was not a structured teaching/ learning, but occurred in the context of daily life at A-Way, at annual general meetings and yearly conferences. At A-Way and similar sites, leaders of the survivor movement find and develop new members for movement activities: attending rallies, representing survivors on government committees, or sitting on the boards of mental health programmes. For some employees, this led to new forms of political identification, in which the term "survivor" became a positive identifier.

Within the Homeworkers Association, a similar kind of learning is most clearly evident in its executive meetings. Here, the coordinator can and does motivate workers to develop their leadership and organizational skills. The current coordinator does this very well, albeit, not always in a conscious way. An example is her insistence that the executive members (elected from the HWA membership) conduct the meeting according to a set agenda. She urges them to think through how the organization and the activities they undertake can be improved and modified.

One executive member commented during an informal interchange that she liked this style of conducting meetings much better. Before, she felt that executive meetings were another social occasion where they just came together to chat; the past coordinator took their ideas and attempted to develop activities. This did not leave room for the executive to take initiative. Now, she sees clearly what they are discussing, and what decisions are being taken because minutes are written up and sent to the executive members afterwards. The coordinator also asks the members explicitly to take on more responsibilities for developing activities, and for organizing them. Thus, members develop a sense of ownership for the outcomes.

These meetings are also a place where recruitment of members is discussed, and where members' grievances (for instance, when they are treated unjustly in the workplace, or when subcontractors fail to pay them) are raised. Executive members brainstorm the courses of action that can be taken by the Association. These meetings can be very animated, where different and divergent views are expressed and debated. Frequently, sewing machine operators, especially if they are home-based workers, have few options in redressing their working conditions. However, out of the discussion, executive members gain a different and broader understanding of how their work is situated in a larger context, and learn how they may navigate, collectively and individually, their livelihood in the constantly evolving labour market of the garment industry.

Learning to Re/Connect with Others

In his book of case studies, Griff Foley describes how women involved in a struggle over a school in a Philadelphia neighbourhood, "un-learned racism and learned solidarity" (1999, p. 22). These Edison High activists "developed ways of acting and learning built on values of affiliation (and) nurturance" (pp. 22–23). The character of initiatives such as this is captured in the words of an organizer who was attempting to transform a group of South American women from a domestic sewing course into an occupational training course:

> Within the first three months everything we thought the course would be fell apart ... The course became their space. They spoke much more freely about a number of things from the start than we did ... things like sexuality, their intimate relationships ... things we hadn't anticipated discussing in the group (quoted in Foley, 1999, p. 99).

As a result of taking on controversial topics related to women's bodies and health, the group left its church base to form its own organization. These brief examples lead nicely into the second form of informal learning that we have observed in the community sector: learning to re/connect with others.

All of the organizations we are studying are immediately concerned with preparing participants for labour market (re)entry or creating an alternative market. However, only some of the activities that participants engage in are directly related to the curriculum of the programme and the job. Others take place through social interaction in and around formal organizational practices. Thus, our interest in these organizations is not so much in the formal outcomes of business development or job placement as it is in the learning that takes place simply because these settings bring (often isolated) people together.

For an example, we turn to Toronto's garment industry where, between the 1980s and the mid-1990s, there have been significant factory closures and massive worker lay-offs. This restructuring affected female immigrant workers, who are mainly sewing machine operators, differently from male immigrant workers, who are mainly pattern enlargers and cutters. In downsizing garment plants, the latter (numerically much smaller) group is retained while the majority of sewing machine operators are laid off. They are now sewing garments at home on a piece rate basis, thus becoming homeworkers, earning non-union wages, and possibly extending their work day to make the same amount of money (Ng, 1998, 1999). Union strategies in response to garment worker displacement depart from the traditional tactics of organized labour. One of them was to form coalitions with other groups and to organize home-based workers into the Homeworkers Association (HWA).

The biggest challenge in organizing homeworkers was locating them, often by word of mouth, through the underground network of contract work. A multipronged strategy of training courses, social activities, and service provision was found to be effective and continues to this day. As a voluntary, non-union organization, funding the HWA was a challenge; it could not maintain its ongoing services solely on the basis of its low membership dues. It did some outreach to the Spanish and South Asian communities in the early 1990s when the HWA first formed. However, as funding sources dried up, a decision was made to focus on organizing within the Chinese community because they are the largest group of homeworkers. (For details, see Ng, 1999).

The most interesting aspect of HWA's organization is the transition that its parent organization (International Ladies Garment Workers Union) made from the old style business unionism to social unionism to what activists in the early 1990s characterized as community unionism. Community unionism expands on social unionism by advocating that unions become integrally involved within their communities and form coalitions with other groups working on similar issues. As capital consolidates and expands its power base, some unionists recognize that it is important for unions to expand beyond their traditional base and organizing strategies (see Dagg, 1996).

The HWA provides an interesting example of how community organizations, in this case affiliated with a union, respond to the crisis of work and develop entrepreneurial ways of participating in the restructured economy. In order to recruit members and to provide services for its members, the HWA organizes English classes as well as training, up-grading and other courses and workshops (e.g. basic, intermediate and advanced sewing; sewing machine repair) as a key area of its activity. In addition to acquiring additional skills and abilities, classes are places where worker socialization takes place.

It is through interacting with each other in classes, not only around learning the formal curriculum, but also in informal exchanges, that garment workers develop a sense of collective consciousness and identify themselves as workers and as immigrants. For instance, in observing the pattern-making classes, it is clear that this is one place where homeworkers meet each other; this helps to break down the isolation of home-based work and provide an opportunity for women to come together to discover the common conditions of their lives. Apart from learning from the instructor about how to design and produce patterns, class members help each other with drawing and cutting patterns. In these exchanges they also talk to each other about their work and family situations, enabling a process of solidarity and friendship to emerge.

Thus, the classes serve an important social and educational purpose. Socially, workers meet other workers who share similar working conditions and experiences. While this shared sense of self is implicit in the classes, it becomes explicit when they interact with each other during coffee breaks. Over tea and cookies, workers inquire after each other's working conditions, wages, and so on. When there is a perceived injustice, they encourage and support each other to launch a complaint. This is a form of political socialization through solidarity learning.

As a concrete example, we call up a scene that took place during a break in a pattern-making class. Here, one participant mentioned how she and other workers in her factory did not get paid for a long weekend when they were sent home early. Unless they were told ahead of time, according to the law, they should be paid. Attempts to talk to the supervisor and one of the owners had produced no result. At that point, another worker suggested a strategy that eventually worked. Here we see the cementing of worker solidarity that occurs during class breaks. In these moments, workers learn from each other strategies for negotiating their lives as non-English speaking immigrants who may not initially know how to assert their rights as workers.

Thus, whereas during class time workers acquire formal knowledge about certain subject matters (e.g. how to make a pattern or speak workplace English), it is during the workers' social time together that they acquire a collective worker identity and informal knowledge about negotiating lives as immigrants and as working people. This is not the kind of learning that is explicitly cultivated and encouraged by the HWA. It simply evolves out of the interactions among members. Nevertheless, this form of social learning can certainly be made more explicit and intentional by the organization.

We see this pattern repeated in our two other sites. At A-Way Express, employees identify with the business and take pride in it as a collective enterprise. They talk about it in terms of happiness, enjoyment and enthusiasm but most often in terms of "comfort." A-Way is a place in which they feel settled, stable and adjusted – difficult qualities to come by. They can be themselves without having to hide past experiences or current difficulties. Employees stay with the business for a rare solidarity, empathy and an acceptance of difference that they find with each other. "We're all in the same boat," said one, and that creates very strong bonds. At A-Way, amidst the delivery of parcels, some people make lifelong friends.

At Chic Resto Pop the general atmosphere is one of openness and respect for difference. As one worker said: "Here people talk to each other, and if someone has a problem, we try to help and to understand. ... No one leaves you in your little corner, they seek you out. That's how they taught me to open up and to speak more easily." Workers benefit from the sensitivity and support of a variety of individuals, generally growing out of a sense of affinity. In fact, the more experienced workers-in-training act as counsellors, explaining certain tasks to volunteers. Thus, a woman who was initially nervous and withdrawn now asserts that she is ready to supervise others: "I like to put them at ease. I like to show them and help them feel secure."

The workers also often offer different kinds of personal support, such as reading and explaining an administrative form or offering solutions to a personal problem. As one worker explained, "It's for problems at home, a fight or problems with welfare. Or sometimes people who have a hard time understanding or who don't know how to read." Thus, sharing a common socio-economic condition facilitates certain kinds of exchanges between workers and provides for learning opportunities that are not directly related to work. This also means that access to different local resources depends in part on information obtained through friendships and acquaintances. Similar to the classes organized by the Homeworkers Association, the Resto represents a place that encourages the development of personal contacts; it provides for a valuable broadening of social networks.

Over the course of our observation period, several old-timer workers frequented the Resto not just to eat. In fact, we observed that vacationing workers, as well as ex-workers or others returned to work as volunteers. One permanent employee confirmed that this was common practice and that these substitute workers were very much appreciated because they filled in temporarily vacant positions. Such is the case of an experienced volunteer, ex-worker-in-training, who came in to work cutting vegetables. She preferred to keep busy at the Resto rather than be bored at home.

This case is not unique. A variety of different people – young and old, single or parents – offered a helping hand in different sectors for reasons beyond the economic. Of course, like other workers, the volunteers benefit from a free meal after 4 hours of work, but the Resto certainly represents something more than an opportunity for a free meal. For many clients and ex-workers, it is also a place for social exchange, expression and fulfillment that breaks up the daily isolation. Among many ex-workers and clients, a feeling of membership develops distinct from that generally seen amongst the affordable-meal clientele. The higher degree of attachment amongst the volunteers is probably based on a more direct rapport with the regular personnel and the de facto recognition of their participation in a dynamic business. Moreover, in some cases, the work is perceived as community activism and translates as social consciousness. From another point of view, the organization of human resources does not seem very closed and rigid when faced with this manpower. On the contrary, it is characterized by an unplanned inclusiveness and thus it reveals a certain kind of learning made possible through its organizational flexibility.

Learning a New Sense of Self

Analysing new social movements as learning sites, Michael Welton (1993) explicitly addresses the "unlearning" of old identities that accompanies movement participation. Ecology movement activists are attempting to replace anthropocentric with ecocentric conceptions of our relationships to nature. Peace movement activists are attempting to replace violence with pacifism as a way of problem solving. Women's movement activists are attempting to replace degrading with valuing and empowering conceptions of self. And so it is with participants in the community organizations that we studied. They go through both obvious and subtle transformations as a result of being immersed in contact with other participants. This brings us to the third kind of informal learning we have identified: learning a new sense of self.

For an example, we turn to A-Way Express, a psychiatric survivor-run courier company in Toronto.[6] After almost two decades of operation it has acquired 45 couriers, 17 part-time office staff and roughly 1,200 customer accounts – over half in the private sector. Employees move around the city by subway or streetcar/bus on instructions from a central dispatcher. The business operates on revenues generated from its service as well as government grants. Couriers work on commission at a rate that is seventy percent of service charges. A minimum shift is 4 hours; the average number of shifts worked is 3.

After some years of development and struggle, the importance of being survivor-directed and controlled has become firmly entrenched in A-Way's culture and practice. Staff members are decision makers on the board, management team and through other participatory mechanisms. A-Way is overt about its politics. Through promotional material and clearly marked courier bags, the company works to educate the public about the productive capacities of the survivor community. Employee participation in public hearings and government consultations attempts to ensure that psychiatric survivors are broadly heard.

One of the most striking things about A-Way employees is their sense of future. Not only do they have an active work life, most can see their lives going forward in some way. We understand this as part of the revisioning of self that these sites can foster, particularly with respect to various authorities that govern people's lives[7]. Similar to activist learning in a campaign to save the Australian rain forest, psychiatric survivors who work at A-Way develop "a more critical view of authority and expertise, and a recognition of their ability to influence decision-making" (Foley, 1999, p. 4). This is a mark of empowerment. In the next few paragraphs, we trace this process through the life of one person.

Laurie was an employee of A-Way Express for 8 years. She entered the business after a traumatic adolescence: psychiatric hospitals, medication, suicide attempts, temporary employment, and life on the street. A turning point for her was realizing that the institutional "solutions" did not work.

> For years I went to hospital thinking someone has to know how to fix this. But nobody knows. There is no answer and there is no medication that can fix it. There was a sadness to realize that a solution never could be found there. On the other hand it was a relief, a freeing feeling. Taking back that control meant all of a sudden there was something I could do about it.

The first benefit of employment at A-Way was the relief of not having to hide visible and invisible scars. The second was finding a place where she could both recover herself and acquire new skills. In other words, the business functioned for her as an "organizing circumstance." Rather than pre-planning her "project" in the way suggested by Tough's research, Laurie and learners like her "tend to select a course from limited alternatives that occur fortuitously within their environment and which structure their learning project" (Spear, 1988, p. 201). As you will see, Laurie's learning was not linear. Rather, circumstances created during one "learning episode" become the ground for the next step in the process.

Laurie entered A-Way Express as a courier but soon began to take advantage of other openings. In her first couple of years, she moved from courier to answering phones to more management-type roles in the company.

> I filled in for an administrative assistant who was away sick. Basically I was doing the banking and that sort of thing. I added a lot to that job: typing minutes from meetings, for example. At the time we were getting in some computer systems so I started to learn about computers. When the marketing manager left there wasn't anyone to replace him and I wanted to attempt the job. Then when the business manager left, I applied and was moved into that position.

During a particularly difficult crisis in the company, Laurie worked alongside interim directors to get things back on track. She was then hired into the role of executive director. One of her biggest challenges as a manager was to comfortably occupy a position of authority – difficult for someone who had previously been damaged by various institutional authorities.

> It was a very difficult transition. You may have been reactive to authority all those years
> but now you're it. It was very hard for me to learn to make decisions and be firm about
> things. The majority of survivors that I have seen are extremely sensitive people. You have
> to be very aware of where other people are at, and also very sensitive to where they're
> coming from. It's about self-esteem and also shyness.

Using extensive consultation with employee board members, Laurie learned to lead
by anticipating distress. Being an effective survivor leader involved reading
and changing the anxiety level of the setting by attending to the ebb and flow of
laughter, jokes, conversation and silence. It was subtle emotional work.

Early in the executive director role, Laurie learned that she could not run A-Way
Express without understanding and influencing the systems (health, social services
and welfare) with which it interacts. A big part of her job was to connect and
interpret the business to bureaucrats responsible for funding, and mental health
professionals providing other kinds of programmes. At the same time, and in direct
tension with this, Laurie formed relationships with leaders of the psychiatric survivor
movement. They profoundly influenced her development not just as a manager but
as a political activist.

Laurie's workplace biography is similar to the life histories that Finnish
researcher Antikainen (1996) used to arrive at the concept of a "significant life
experience." At the core of this kind of learning are interlocking transformations of
both self-identity and social environment. Three factors make this possible: the
expansion of the person's world view or cultural understanding; the strengthening
of their voice so that they have the courage to participate in dialogue or even break
down the dominant discursive forms; and the broadening of the field of social identities or roles. An exemplar of this process, Laurie moved from expertise forged
through difficult personal experience to knowledge gained from interaction with
systems and social movements. Her identifications range from "crazy" person to
psychiatric survivor leader, from employee to executive director. The range is
difficult to encompass.

> It's hard to walk between worlds. It's almost like living a double life, and I still struggle
> with that a lot. There are things in the survivor context that give me – for lack of a better
> word – qualifications to be a leader. I can tell stories that people will think are funny; they
> will understand what I mean. When I go home at night or when I go out with friends out-
> side of the survivor circle, I find that my situation changes. The personal experiences of
> being a psychiatric survivor that qualify me in my work just don't transfer easily into the
> outside world. In some ways, they still put me on the bottom of the heap.

Because of her 8-year journey through A-Way Express, Laurie understands better
than most people that transformations of skill and identity take a long time. Even
when they appear complete, vestiges of the past remain. Many A-Way employees
identify ongoing "mental health problems" as a feature of their lives. Consequently,
they struggle for self-confidence and retain a sense of personal limitation. They
blame themselves for previous job failures and remain nervous about their abilities.
As one person put it, "I don't feel capable of more than what I'm already doing."
This sense of self limits their employment goals and opportunities both within the
company and in mainstream employment.

Chic Resto Pop trainees also rediscovered attitudes, behaviours and interactional abilities that they believed were lost. They regained confidence and improved self-esteem. After several months' work, most workers felt improvements in communication, patience, perseverance, tolerance and motivation. The work experiences supported the development of new social interaction. Like A-Way, Resto has always given priority to this type of reintegration. It gives the organization trainers who have "been there" – although they are not specialists. Said one key informant: "There's a complicity, a way of speaking, a way of saying things. There's something in the dynamic that's interesting."

Conclusion

The settings we have examined pose troubling political and social questions. Created to respond to difficult social issues and problems, they have used a combination of community organization/development traditions and economic tools. How should we understand these settings and their practices? Do the organizations become social regulators that fit people into low-wage jobs? Do they accept the limits of the new economic order and keep practice as defined within limited parameters? Or can these settings act as a place of opposition and if so, how? It is easy to dismiss them as oriented toward training for the labour market or creating marginal jobs for a population that usually does not work. However, this is only a small part of the picture. In exploring the question of social learning and examining the processes and underlying values of the organizations, a different picture emerges, one that is far more complex.

We view our research sites as examples of what Elaine Butler refers to as "spaces of contestability" (Butler, 2001, p. 68). In this chapter, we have attempted to insert them into a discussion where they do not typically appear, namely, inside "the seductive, official rhetoric about lifelong learning for and at work" (68). At the same time, clearly, "contestatory" (emancipatory) and "regulatory" practices coexist. The regulatory aspects are those practices that push people into the labour market as a primary focus of the work of these organizations. The emancipatory practices contribute to building democratic opportunities, social solidarity between participants, a redefinition of self, and the ability to act to make changes in the world.

The community/union organizations we studied have possibilities for social regulation and social integration. Learning happens on both sides of this dynamic. In other words, you can learn how to be "normal" (accept the status quo), or you can learn how to contest "normal" (challenge the status quo). In fact, both can happen at once. So, for example, the waged labour that these organizations create or facilitate makes a fundamental contribution to people's lives but without necessarily addressing longstanding problems with, for example, job hierarchies, low wages, and poor working conditions. At the same time, the organizations use waged labour as a means to other, non-economic ends.

One way of picturing what is happening here is to see these community organizations as having core and peripheral functions. The core activities of these groups are structured, pragmatic and economically oriented – for example, readying workers for entry into the job market. In other words, their formal mandates are compliant with the socio-economic shifts of the mainstream. The peripheral activities are interactive, social, political and cultural. In other words, through unstructured social interactions – in effect, while no one is watching – important political work appears on the periphery. Even as this analogy helps to illustrate our point, it creates an uncomfortable dualism. In fact, the "core" is shot through with the "periphery." The two are clearly interdependent. It may be that only under the pressures arising from the current context does their separation become more sharply defined.

In our case studies, it is the informal processes in the organization that reveal their politics. If it were only the specific tasks carried out that define the organization, we would see them as far more regulatory. However, informal learning and its related social processes are the practices that move participants in new directions. Thus, informal learning becomes a defining element. It is through processes of informal learning that personal/collective transformation can occur, and participation in political processes is put in place. The danger here lies in the indirect, diffuse nature of this more political practice. Because of founder pressure and professionalization of these organizations, these practices can easily be lost.

Debates about these issues are ongoing but we agree on one basic point: community organizations perform an informal educative function that is generally unrecognized – by their own leadership/membership, as well as state, market and academia. Liberatory, counter-hegemonic possibilities emerge from informal spaces as well as from the formally mandated functions of these organizations. Our research asks community organizations to recognize this and their own importance as learning sites. We want the leaders of these organizations to understand the importance of informal processes, and without over-regularizing, to encourage and make space for them. We want to validate them in this labour so that they will consciously maintain and enhance opportunities for potentially transformative learning in social action.

Endnotes

[1] The Homeworkers Association that we studied functioned more like a community organization than a union. For simplicity sake, from hereon in, we refer to all sites simply as community organizations.

[2] For more detailed descriptions of these three sites, the researchers' relationship to them, and the changing context that is shaping their operation, see our working paper (Church, Fontan, Ng and Shragge, February 2000) on the NALL web site: *www.nall.ca*

[3] Griff Foley points out that "Detailed accounts of particular struggles exist in the literature of labour history, women's history, urban studies, development studies and associated fields. The learning dimension can be 'read into' such studies … and much more needs to be done in this

regard (1999, p. 140). Kathryn's re-reading of her own previous accounts of psychiatric survivor action through economic initiatives is a contribution towards this end.

[4] To produce this work, the research team constantly juggled the impact of changes affecting not only the relatively stable employment conditions of its university members but also the uncertainties, limits and strains of Kathryn's only partially chosen self-employment. Reflecting on the schisms and dysjunctures opening up in both locations has been an ongoing part of our conversations.

[5] A longer, more complete description and analysis of Chic Resto Pop can be found, in French, on NALL's web site: *www.nall.ca*

[6] A more complete analysis of informal learning in psychiatric survivor-run businesses with a particular focus on A-Way Express can be found on NALL's web site: *www.nall.ca*

[7] This is consistent with findings observed at other, similar sites: one such, Turnaround Couriers, founded in 2002 by Richard Derham, provides work for at-risk youth (Toronto Star, 2005).

References

Adams, M., 1997, *Preliminary Bibliography of the Research Network for New Approaches to Lifelong Learning (NALL)*, Centre for the Study of Education and Work, Toronto.

Albrow, M., 1996, *The Global Age*, Stanford University Press, Stratford.

Antikainen, A., 1996, In search of the meaning of education and learning in life histories, revised version of a paper delivered at the *Crossroads in Cultural Studies Conference*, Tampere, 1–4 July 1996. Department of Sociology, University of Joensuu, Box 111, 80101 Joensuu, Finland.

Barker, J., 1999, *Street-Level Democracy: Political Settings at the Margins of Global Power*, Between the Lines, Toronto.

Berger, N., 1990, *A Qualitative Study of the Process of Self-Directed Learning*, Doctoral dissertation, Virginia Commonwealth University, Division of Educational Studies, Richmond, Virginia.

Boud, D. & Middleton, H., 2003, Learning from others at work: communities of practice and informal learning, *Journal of Workplace Learning*, **15(5)**: 194–202.

Butler, E., 2001, The power of discourse: work-related learning in the "learning age," in R.M. Cervero, A.L. Wilson & Associates (Eds.), *Power in Practice: Adult Education and the Struggle for Knowledge and Power in Society*, Jossey-Bass, San Francisco.

Church, K., 1991, *Re/Membering Ourselves: Psychiatric Survivor Leadership Facilitation*, Available from the author at 511-155 Dalhousie Street, Toronto, Ontario M5B 2P7 or email *k3church@ryerson.ca*

Church, K., 2000, Strange bedfellows: seduction of a social movement, in E. Shragge & J.M. Fontan (Eds.), *Social Economy: International Debates and Perspectives*, Black Rose, Montreal.

Church, K., Fontan, J.M., Ng, R. & Shragge, E., February 2000, *Social Learning among People who are Excluded from the Labour Market: Part One: Context and Cast Studies*, Network for New Approaches to Lifelong Learning, Toronto, Canada.

Dagg, A., 1996, Organizing homeworkers into unions: the Homeworkers' Association of Toronto, Canada, in E. Boris & E. Prugl (Eds.), *Homeworkers in Global Perspective: Invisible No More*, Routledge, London.

Duguay, P., 1999, Le chic Resto Pop: entreprise communautairs et d'insertion, *Cahiers du CRISES* No ES9907, University du Quebec, Montreal, Canada.

Engestrom, Y., 1999, Expansive learning at work: toward an activity-theoretical reconceptualization, Paper presented to CLWR *Seventh International Conference on Post-Compulsory Education and Training*.

Foley, G., 1999, *Learning in Social Action: A Contribution to Understanding Informal Education*, Zed Books, London.

Foley, G., 2001a, *Strategic Learning: Understanding and Facilitating Organizational Change*, Centre for Popular Education, New South Wales, Australia.

Foley, G., 2001b, Emancipatory organizational learning: context and method, in *Conference Proceedings from the Second International Conference on Researching Work and Learning*. Faculty of Continuing Education, University of Calgary, Calgary, pp. 278–284.

Garrick, J., 1996, Informal learning: some underlying philosophies, *Canadian Journal for the Study of Adult Education*, **10**(1): 21–46.

Gint, K., 1998, *The Sociology of Work*, 2nd edn., Policy Press, London.

Jackson, A. & Robinson, D., 2000, *Falling Behind: The State of Working Canada*, Canadian Centre for Policy Alternatives, Ottawa.

Leduc Browne, P., 1996, *Love in a Cold World: The Voluntary Sector in an Age of Cuts*, Canadian Centre for Policy Alternatives, Ottawa.

Leduc Browne, P., 2000, The neo-liberal uses of the social economy: non-profit organizations and workfare in Ontario, in E. Shragge & J.M. Fontan (Eds.), *The Social Economy: International Perspectives and Debates*, Black Rose, Montreal.

Livingstone, D., 1999, Exploring the icebergs of adult learning: findings of the first Canadian survey of informal learning practices, *Canadian Journal for the Study of Adult Education*, **3**: 49–72.

Melville, N., 1987, Bubble and streak: an independent learning project, *Adult Education*, **59**(4): 317–323.

Ng, R., 1998, Work restructuring and re-colonizing third world women: an example from the garment industry in Toronto, *Canadian Women Studies*, **18**(1): 21–25.

Ng, R., 1999, *Homeworking: home office or home sweatshop? Report on current conditions of homeworkers in Toronto's garment industry*. Network for New Approaches to Lifelong Learning, Toronto, Canada.

Penland, P., 1979, Self-initiated learning, *Adult Education Quarterly*, **29**(3): 170–179.

Percy, K., Burton, C. & Withnall, A., 1994, *Self-Directed Learning among Adults: The Challenge for Continuing Educators*, Association for Lifelong Learning, Lancaster.

Peterson, R.E., 1987, Present sources of education and learning, in R.E. Peterson & Associates (Eds.), *Lifelong Learning in America*, Jossey-Bass, San Francisco.

Shragge, E. & Church, K., 1998, None of your business? Community economic development and the mixed economy of welfare, *Canadian Review of Social Policy*, **41**: 33–44.

Spear, G., 1988, Beyond the organizing circumstance: a search for methodology for the study of self-directed learning, in H.B. Long & Associates (Eds.), *Self-Directed Learning: Application and Theory*, University of Georgia Adult Education Department, Athens, Georgia.

Teeple, G., 1995, *Globalization and the Decline of Social Reform*, Garamond, Toronto.

Toronto Star, Ideals on Wheels, *Toronto Star*: 22 March 2005, pp. A8–9.

Tough, A., 1968, *Why Adults Learn: A Study of the Major Reasons for Beginning and Continuing a Learning Project*, Ontario Institute for Studies in Education, Toronto, Canada.

Welton, M., 1993, Social revolutionary learning: the new social movements as learning sites, *Adult Education Quarterly*, **43**(3): 152–164.

Welton, M., 1995, *In Defense of the Lifeworld: Critical Perspectives on Adult Learning*, State University of New York Press, New York.

Chapter 7
Knowledge Collisions: Perspectives from Community Economic Development Practitioners Working with Women

Mary Stratton and Edward T. Jackson

Introduction

The concept of an interrelated world economy, generally termed "globalization," has become an inevitable component of academic, media, government and everyday discussion. For developed countries such as Canada, this process of globalization supposedly moves our economy from a resource-manufacturing base towards one primarily concerned with knowledge production suitable to the new "information age." In this new context, albeit with different interests and intents, academia, business, government, and lately, civil society, have increasingly focused on how and what people learn. "Entrepreneurship" and "microenterprise" have become catch words of this new economy. However, the ideology behind them often poses problems for those involved in community economic development (CED) and adult education, who insist on a component of social transformation as well as economic advancement. In the words of one CED practitioner:

> We want people to go out and be able to succeed in the mainstream economy, but we don't want to buy into a system that puts the economy ahead of the people that participate. ...
> We're here to give a shot to those who don't usually get one.

Focusing on issues of learning, knowledge and practice, we explore some of the tensions, problems and possibilities that CED practitioners confront as a necessary part of their job. We are concerned with two closely related arguments: First, the tensions that arise among individuals and groups that hold different learning perspectives lead to collisions that create barriers and boundaries which are detrimental to gaining and applying new learning and thus, inevitably, to successful CED practice. Second, out of this discord of knowing emerges a new synthesis of knowledge that enables CED workers to challenge resistant boundaries and intercedes to mediate constructive solutions that allow both social and economic development.

In 1998–1999, the Centre for the Study of Training, Investment and Economic Restructuring (CSTIER) at Carleton University conducted a study that encouraged front-line community economic development workers across Canada to explore the ways they gained information needed to work with women participants in community

K. Church et al. (eds.), *Learning through Community: Exploring Participatory Practices*.
© Springer Science + Business Media B.V. 2008

economic development (CED) initiatives. Although it is a university-based research centre, CSTIER's primary goals were more pragmatic than academic. Research funding offered an opportunity to initiate much needed Canadian research related to CED practice and awareness of gender issues and to disseminate the findings among the Canadian CED community. Thus, even at the outset of the project, differences in knowledge orientations were an essential dynamic of the research relationship. The clashes that inevitably occur between academic ideals and theory, and the pragmatic necessities of frontline CED practice, constitute an active part of the development of our discussion. This discussion has evolved as a result of the interactions among the CSTIER research team, the CED practitioners who took part in the study, and members of the Network for New Approaches to Lifelong Learning.

Background and Methodology

CSTIER's core purpose is to provide a bridge between academia and front-line community economic development practice. In 1997, the centre launched the Community Economic Development and Technical Assistance Program (CEDTAP), a US$3 million initiative that, over the next 3 years, matched nearly 100 community-based organizations with technical support and advice provided by a pool of more than 30 experienced groups of CED professionals (Jackson, 2001). In 1998, aware of the lack of Canadian resources on CED practice with women, CEDTAP was in the process of establishing the Gender and Learning Group, an electronic list dedicated to exchanges of information of use to CED practitioners. The present NALL-CSTIER project, *Women and Community Economic Development: Changing Knowledge, Changing Practice,*[1] was complementary to this and other centre projects focusing on CED and gender. The three-member research team (who all combined academic associations with community development experience) generated a set of research questions that reflected the team's academic interest in learning processes together with a concern to gather information of practical application and usefulness to CED practitioners.[2] The main focus of the study was on how practitioners, engaged in CED that includes or is specific to women, gain new information relevant to their work and incorporate that new learning into their daily practice. Interview questions focused on sources of information, learning opportunities and processes, the relative usefulness of different kinds of knowledge, and methods and opportunities for applying new knowledge. The questions of "if" and "how" gender issues affected learning and practice were central to the inquiry. Identifying problems experienced by practitioners, along with their suggestions for improvements, was also an important element.

As both NALL and CSTIER were committed to applying research methods which include the participation of those who are the subject of the study, the methodology was designed to be as collaborative as possible. A draft inter-view schedule was presented to a focus group of Toronto-based CED workers. From the outset, the boundaries of knowledge and learning in relation to CED and the proposed study were questioned. The CSTIER research team did not directly employ the terms "formal," "non-formal" and "informal" learning in developing the research instrument. We did ask about formal education, generally recognized to refer to credentialized, course-based learning obtained in an accredited, government-recognized institution. The boundaries between non-formal and informal learning, however, seemed problematic, and blurred from a CED practice perspective. NALL considered non-formal learning to be that which does not qualify as "formal' but which is organized by an instructor/facilitator. It includes a vast array of possibilities, such as all interest courses, Sunday School, amateur sports, workshops and conferences. As CED practitioners are often those responsible for organizing community-based "non-formal" events, we anticipated that they might not readily conceptualize this form of learning as distinctly separate from other learning activities. Consequently, we took a very broad and open approach to asking about learning. Our introduction to interviewees stated only that we wished to "find out how practitioners involved with women and CED gain new information relevant to their work, and how they incorporate that new learning into practice" (interview schedule[3]).[4]

In the study's pilot phase, when the draft research instrument was given to a focus group, the members generated many more critical points and questions concerning how learning is considered, how it occurs, and whose knowledge counts. The following extracts from the focus group transcript illustrate the interactive process by which these questions were generated and addressed:

E: [The project], is it learning about how gender influences CED, or how the learning that happens in CED is gendered?

E wonders if she made sense.

R [the researcher] doesn't quite know what to say. The others are impressed with the question! R says she thinks it is hard to really separate the two things. She suggests the goal was to find out how CED practitioners learn, but agrees that all the issues the group has raised are involved in this, which makes it very complex and difficult to get at. She suggests this project is exploratory, just a beginning.

C: From one hour to the next...there are different experiences, moving from one place to the next ... [*murmurs of agreement from several participants concerning these changes in working context*] ... it's hard trying to explain [what it is like to do that] and how I fit into those different roles. If I have to think of it as a gender-based identity – it would take years [to explain] [*laughter, Pause*]

A; ... it's not what you'd call a routine job ... [*laughter*]

E: The understatement for the afternoon!

C: Just look at the way we've come to these questions. They're kind of linear [*laughs*] even though open-ended and we've done what we do – well, you know what, we get the essence of what you want to know, but let's talk about it in a language that's familiar to us and in a format that's familiar

[Someone] One that's bouncing all over the place?

C: – Well, and it's story telling.

The input from the focus group strongly influenced the thinking and expectations of the CSTIER research team and, ultimately, the research instrument.

The final interview schedule, designed to collect closed-end quantitative and in-depth qualitative information, was applied in a preliminary study with 15 key informants who were employed by CED organizations across Canada. Telephone interviews (approximately 1 hour in length) were conducted with practitioners from a variety of different geographical, economic and social contexts who are concerned with promoting CED activities that include women as participants and beneficiaries. The qualitative components of the interview transcripts were ana-lysed by developing a thematic grid to identify common concerns and viewpoints. A summary of the study results was developed and distributed to the research participants, other members of the CED community, and the NALL network members. Results from the study were also presented and discussed in a roundta-ble session at the 1999 conference of the Canadian Research Institute for the Advancement of Women (CRIAW). The summary of that session subsequently became part of the overall data set.

One of the major issues emerging from the study data was the existence of knowledge clashes. Collisions concerning what counted as legitimate knowledge and how this was learned were pivotal discussion points that challenged neat aca-demic divisions between formal, non-formal and informal learning. Imbedded in the participants' responses were tensions that went far beyond the initial focus on gender. Clashes between theory and practice at many different levels and locations emerged, and tensions deriving from the interaction of gender and social classes were pronounced. This chapter developed as a result of these insights from the research participants, and takes their anecdotal explanations as the primary platform for further exploring the collisions, barriers and possibilities to which they collectively point.

The Resistant Boundaries of Discordant Knowledge

Theory and Practice: The Academic Versus Front-Line Divide

It is increasingly well recognized and documented that the structural conditions of the academy and those of actual practice are markedly different and have different cultural rules as well as practical necessities. Both front-line teachers and commu-nity development workers view academics as generally out of touch with the pres-sures and necessities of everyday practice (Hansen et al, 2001; Heaney, 1993; Lewis, 1999). Heaney (1993) goes as far as to argue that conducting research and developing knowledge that is truly participatory is counter to the very existence of universities, which are founded on the premise of a knowledge elite. Ultimately, the university institution must attempt to co-opt and reown knowledge created in this way. There are, nevertheless, many scholars with a genuine philosophical commitment to the use of participatory research approaches and partnerships to challenge dominant knowledge assumptions and effect social change (CSTIER and NALL being examples of this). Church (2000) refers to the members of such community–academic partnerships as "bridge people" (p. 4).

Heaney's concerns cannot, however, be lightly dismissed. First, although there are a few attempts in the United States and Canada to develop university programmes specific to CED practice, there are significant structural barriers to initiating programmes that truly include community-based knowledge (Lewis, 1999; Lovett, 1997). University courses inevitably tend to emphasize the theoretical, whereas effective practitioners need to acquire a combination of community development, business and political management skills. It would seem clear that those with actual practice experience should be involved in the design and delivery of CED courses, but few have the Ph.D. credential demanded by the university (Lewis, 1999). Most formal educators, however, lack the skills required to design and/or deliver community education (Lovett, 1997). The CSTIER research participants heavily underlined this gulf between academic teaching and what CED workers need to learn and how they want to learn it:

> The least useful [knowledge] is from academic conferences and publications, because the written "publish-or-perish" syndrome often requires a language that is impenetrable. At academic conferences, presenters are often out of touch with the real people that they are supposed to be talking about.

> [It's about] the way the women want [the learning]. [About] finding out how they learn and then giving the information to them in that way. It's letting them tell me how they learn and responding to that. I call it sharing information – not teaching. ... Noting the difference in the way women learn compared to men, and paying attention to hands-on application is very important. Using useful resources and applying them in our practice. But this is not how you get taught at a technical school, where the guys are.

> I feel my big stumbling block, having just come from graduate school, is not lack of ideas, but the ability to implement them. Can I learn from others about resources that would allow me to implement ideas?

As these remarks suggest, the divide between the academy and CED practice perspectives also pertains to written material on CED practice. There is little time and money available for CED workers to write about their own practice and few avenues to have such material published and widely circulated. The majority of literature concerning CED that is readily identifiable and attainable is published by academic sources in a style most suited to readers with university level education. This is far from ideal. As one participant explained, "I'm biased against academic literature. I need something to work with that's my way of learning. I prefer case studies – just theory [alone] is difficult to apply."

Although style and language are noted as a barrier to the usefulness of academic literature,[5] most emphasized is the collision between ungrounded academic theory and the learning content CED practitioners believe they require. Academic publications have traditionally followed a formula of thesis generation prompted by analysis of previously published literature on the matter. Even when the topic to be researched is issue-based, the generation of research questions and methods is usually derived from existing published work rather than in consultation with the people about to be "researched." We are convinced that a traditional academic approach to the issues discussed in this paper would have failed to generate the discussion that has become its focus. Most of the published literature cited within this discussion was only located *after* the participants had identified the problem of knowledge clashes and after an extensive cross-disciplinary search. A preliminary literature search focusing on women, CED and practice, conducted prior to discussions with CED workers, was found to be of limited utility and mainly demonstrated that specific attention to gender issues in CED practice in Canada was minimal. Such sources as were available did not really address the question of how CED practitioners gained and applied new learning relevant to their work.[6] The point here is twofold: Traditional academic approaches to research and publication can actually create barriers to incorporating insights relevant to applied practice. If identifying relevant material can be challenging for academics, front-line practitioners have even less time to negotiate the boundaries of different disciplines, theoretical orientations and competing sets of often impenetrable jargon.[7]

The multifaceted divide between academic knowledge and front-line practice creates a persistent problem for many CED practitioners. Knowledge generated and endorsed by academics is generally accepted as "legitimate" whereas other forms of knowledge that are not recognized and endorsed in formal learning institutions are not. Without legitimization of their knowledge perspective, many CED workers face constant barriers to further professional training and to applying their knowledge in everyday practice. Asked what would help in the latter regard, one study participant was very clear about the matter:

> [What is needed is] for others to recognize that professional development and training of CED practitioners is essential (as academic training is for academics, etc.). We need an integrated knowledge program. Leaders in the field understand that and the importance of having opportunities and networks to [allow] discussion and exchange of ideas. ... Funders must recognize ... [that] training for practitioners about the complex world is needed ... that it is ongoing, continuous learning – not a matter of educational credentials. And academic learning may interfere with community-based learning and put me out of touch. For example, an MBA is perceived as valuable but community-based learning is not.

Theory and Practice: The Economic Versus Social Development Clash

Academic theory about the social side of community development is only one component of information tapped by CED practitioners. Another vital aspect is business-related (technical) knowledge, which might be gained from academic institutions, but more often via the business and economic sector. As one study participant explained, however, "What knowledge means to the practitioner is practical tools to do our job," and traditional business is no better at providing this than the academy. Another participant outlined the problem and the CED workers' creative, multitask approach to resolving it:

> There is nothing out there in traditional business development programs to address these [gender-related] things. ... Women are more about creating   links and services – but these are not appreciated. There are two streams within the project team. The business trainer draws from traditional sources and her challenge is to ... [be] really creative to adapt to the scale of business we work with (more informal, lower than the traditional small businesses edge). She has to adapt it so as to take into account women's ways of learning (group and participatory oriented). She gets a lot from within herself and the women she works with. CED initiatives are easier ... because they take many of the issues into account ... [but] they still focus on economic indicators – the money they make – whereas we focus on a sense of autonomy, confidence, and getting out of isolation. We feel we are out in the forefront with the other women's CED groups, having to invent ourselves.

The preceding quote outlines the multifaceted nature of CED practice and the frequent tensions imbedded therein. The mission of CED is to bridge the divide between the business model approach to economic development and the social justice view, which holds that the social development of a community is paramount and in tension with market interests. Thus, by its nature, CED is rife with diverse, sometimes opposing views that give rise to the contradictions and tensions that are part of the everyday life of CED workers. While this may lead to the development of integrated learning, it is not surprising that it also at times generates discordant knowledge.

A further tension arises between economic and social interests because CED organizations (CEDOs) in Canada rely heavily on state funding. While many programmes funded in this way have achieved CED goals, there are also undeniably powerful interests within government at all levels that prefer more traditional economic development. These tend to work to marginalize CED policies and programmes (Jackson, 2001, p. 6). Thus, the structural context of CED practice is a contradictory one, and the response has been a permanent debate about how to best respond and interact within such conditions.[8]

CED workers often have no real option other than to live with, constantly think about, and attempt to understand the dilemmas provoked by structural tensions. In the CSTIER study, most participants reported that they attempt to find solutions that further CED ideals as they understand them. Publications and other public opportunities for debate generally require the presenter to take a clear position, and for this reason it is possible that these media tend to overemphasize the divisiveness of the debate.[9] Nevertheless, opposing perspectives are also sometimes present in front-line practice (Lennie, 1999; Lewis, 1999; Rubin, 1997). For example, a strong critique of the microenterprise model of CED emerged at the 1999 CRIAW round-table, where most participants were engaged in social advocacy rather than economic development. They argued that people (especially women) needed food and shelter before they could even begin to think about being trained to start a small business. They also questioned the economic potential of microenterprises succeeding against large, dominant corporations.[10] As Rubin (1997) notes, though, if such clashes of perspective lead social activists and theorists to actually oppose some development projects, it can be extremely detrimental to overall community development. Using the example of affordable housing development, he argues that social justice ideals and concerns about the economic bottom line must, and can, be reconciled without demobilizing social advocacy.

Although they recognize the dangers inherent in attempting to negotiate the competing interests of government and corporate partnerships, many CED practitioners concur with Rubin that possibilities for successful outcomes can be found (Chambers, 1997; Church et al., 2000; Jackson, 2001; Torjman, 1999). A CSTIER-study participant described the complexity and constraints practitioners face:

> [We need] more sources of knowledge ... [something]that mixes traditional business knowledge with CED philosophies. Something to bridge and interpret the traditional into CED. ... A fundamental philosophical dilemma for CED (and it's more complex for women) – are we just interpreting the mainstream or do we realize that this doesn't apply, and go back and develop new approaches, which [then] become very marginalized? [We need] learning where you question the system that is giving you learning knowledge; [where] you have to learn on your own and with those you interact with everyday, who are sharing their problems with you.

These observations also point to the danger of co-optation of egalitarian philosophies and methods at the economic level of CED initiatives as well as at the academic (noted earlier). As Lennie (1999) illustrates, "empowerment ideology" is a key concept in development theory, but in practice supposed "participatory" methods of community consultation can become diluted, even corrupted by incorporation into models which remain essentially patriarchal and hierarchical. There is a danger that development workers (and academic theorists) who consider themselves committed to egalitarian processes may overlook the deep structure of such power dynamics (Lennie, 1999; Rao, Stuart and Kelleher, 1999). A failure to fully recognize such dynamics may leave a practitioner convinced that an open consultation has been provided, when in fact what has occurred has been "mainly a one-way process of obtaining information from the community" that has left the community members frustrated and cynical (Lennie, 1999, p. 104).

No matter how aware the CED worker is of co-optation dangers, s/he faces a daunting task. Alternatives to public funding are equally fraught with problems. Regardless of how financing is obtained, there is considerable agreement that embracing microenterprise approaches, and/or business models of evaluation can lead to "reproducing and reinforcing neoliberal globalization" (Jackson, 2001, p. 4). Fontan and Shragge (2000) warn that the government will support microenterprise projects only "as long as the objectives remain social integration and not social change, the costs are low, and it does not become a point of confrontation" (p. 6). A CSTIER study participant complained, "we're strangled these days. You can't say the words "advocacy" or "lobby" now or we won't get any funding from the government or foundations." However, Church et al. (2000) argue that, despite the difficulties of developing funding proposals to meet government requirements, "in Ontario, community organizations have learned to replace the forbidden term 'advocacy' with still acceptable references to 'public education'"(p. 5). In general, CED practice "is steeped in the challenge of integrating social goals with economic goals" (Lewis, 1999, p. 181), and achieving this without abandoning core values is something the CSTIER research participants reported struggling with:

> Sometimes it is attractive to an organization to go where there is money. We've done it and found ourselves contracted out with no control of the elements of it, which [may] compromise our program. The organization has learned from this to be selective.

> I think government has put [partnerships] in there as a bottom line thing…but from a CED view, I think it's a good learning tool. … [We've] learned new skills by sharing the specific skills we already had.

> Some projects we don't do because there is no money for child care. We hope we can always get the money (somehow), so we don't have to *not* do it. We don't apply for funding that won't cover child care. … This is our general principle for all programs, [that there be] support … either directly or through our liaisons.

These statements from practitioners reflect high awareness of the tensions and contradictions that arise from a clash between economic and social development interests. Yet, they remain willing to engage with the resulting discord in order to find effective ways to deliver the kind of CED they know their communities need.

The Power Dynamics of Community: "It's Not Just about Gender"[11]

Chambers (1997) points to simplistic, dichotomous thinking (such as male/female, wealth/poverty, social/economic, academic/community and powerful/powerless) as a great impediment to successful development projects. He argues that the power dynamics of communities are far more complex. There is no simple homogeneous grouping of "types" of people. Within every social group, Chambers argues, there are "uppers' and "lowers," that is, some people have relatively more or less power than other members. The capital (or lack of it) attached to being an upper or lower in any given social situation is cumulative – having power in one setting tends to allow opportunities in other areas, and vice versa. The reality of deep poverty becomes multifaceted deprivation, although even among the most deprived groups there will be, in relative terms, some uppers. These complex power dynamics, which are always present and constantly reconstructing themselves, must be recognized and continually challenged by CED practitioners. Of course, this is not easy. Using Chambers' framework in relation to the community members they seek to assist, all CED workers are inevitably uppers. Moreover, as power tends to blind and distance the holder to the realities of others, it becomes not only a communication barrier but also essentially a learning disability.

Chambers offers an effective way of looking at the intersections of gender with social class, ethnicity, geography, physical ability, sexual orientation and other social status markers. CED practice with women requires an awareness that we all hold gendered world views that affect the content and experience of knowledge, learning opportunities, and everyday life, but considering gender alone is not enough (ID21, 2000a; Lennie, 1999; Naples, 1997). Academic literature and front-line practitioners have long identified a set of barriers specific to the successful CED participation of women. Lennie (1999) argues that these barriers stem from male-defined approaches to planning and consultation that contrive, in a variety of ways, to disallow space for women's concerns. This combination of barriers serves to silence women and reduce their visibility (possibly making them completely invisible) in the development process (pp. 98–99). Comments from the practitioners in the CSTIER study highlight some of the ways this can occur:

> Women's issues differ from those of men, for example providing day care, transportation, work situations, clothing. So many government initiatives do not consider these kinds of things.

> [Women] learn in a classroom setting that the way they conceive a problem is not right ... Formal settings present knowledge in a way I can't understand ... things are removed from the way I normally learn and understand.

> When men are involved in funding decisions we sometimes feel that we have a harder sell. If the man has no feminist conscience and thinks women should be at home with the kids (and we have encountered that), then it is a very hard sell.

In addition to recognizing structural barriers to CED participation for women, female CED workers are sometimes aware of how their own work interactions are constructed in a gendered fashion, although their experience of this may differ:

> I struggle with being female and doing the work I do. I suspect it's the same thing for other people, but I don't know if it is. ... The chief [here] is male, which strikes a particular dynamic, and learning how to [manage] that is a huge part of what I do.

> I have worked in a segregated environment (all male dominated, or predominately women). I was asked once how I would handle working in a predominantly female environment, given the conflicts that were bound to arise. Why would they ask that? Assume conflicts are greater among women? It's not like that.

> There is too much of our role as a team of four women, of our experiences as women and mothers, to ignore in any of the work that we do (if we were four men it would look completely different). ... When I do go out and see CED organizations that don't have a focus on women and try to apply a male-defined business model, something is missing. [The male model] only works for women who have education and resources to deal with that, who could do it anyway because they have the culture and language (the talk, the dress, the aspirations, the approach). For me this is *not* CED.

This final quote illustrates the complexity of gender interacting with other social statuses, as well as reference to the economic/social development divide noted earlier.

The friction related to social class issues was often highlighted by study participants. As one practitioner put it, "it's not just women for me – it's low income women – the mixture of class as well as gender."

The tone of the comments from CED workers seems to suggest that class divisions are deeper and harder to overcome than barriers that relate solely to being a woman. Furthermore (in keeping with Chambers, 1997), they permeate every dimension of the CED process (funding, practice and programme participation), and reveal mixed perspectives among the practitioners themselves:

> A funder walked in [to the centre] in a mink coat [and was] afraid to get it dirty. She's funding women on welfare! That sucks. It's totally inappropriate. There are class and economic conflicts between people investing in the program and the participants.

> The women's centre … would be a good partner [but] … accepts the micro-economy uncritically. We are serving a different group … so, the question is whether they would see us as a partner. The class issue is within everything. In this case within the gender issue.

> There is real sympathy for low-income women, and single parents in particular. The problem is [that there is also] a recognition that it is so much harder for those women to succeed in business, and of the limits of the support we can offer. We end up thinking, "can this woman pull this off? I don't think so."

> In my case I'm dealing with a group of women, so the gender thing is built in. … And I've struggled with a lot of these issues in my own life – the violence, the abuse, the whole thing, the homelessness, the poverty … but the class thing – as a middle-class person I couldn't tell my family that I was on the street … I don't have to pretend [with the women in the program] that I haven't had those experiences.

> Some of the [participant] group … can get frustrated with some of it [problems the other women have]. [They] … have a high level of [formal] education, though they are now low-income. They don't have the understanding of [some of] the issues.

These comments indicate that the CED practitioners themselves hold (or have held) different class locations. Generally-speaking, front-line workers are more likely to be aware of the programme participants' knowledge perspectives than are the organizational board members or funding representatives. But, even when practitioners do their utmost to convey programme users' views to controlling organizations, that experience is still inevitably mediated. Cawley (1996) suggests that the more CED workers speak the language of the community, the greater will be their marginalization by those who hold powerful positions and conservative views that are legitimated by professional credentials. Such complexity of power relations and knowledge perspectives raises many questions about how community needs and solutions are defined. Who is involved and who excluded (Naples, 1997)? Saleebey (1998) argues that the dominant knowledge position tends to be problem focused and pushes practitioners in that direction also. The result is negative labelling of the community as dysfunctional. In contrast, a recognition and tapping of a distressed community's resources and strengths are necessary to successful development. Comments from a group of women raising children on social benefits underscore this point. One woman took aim at school breakfast programmes (usually run by middle-class women), asking why the mothers were not given the food so that they could directly feed their children. She wondered about the language of government advertising that claims "children can't learn if they are hungry." Would it be all right if they could do so? As long as children eat, is it OK for their mothers to starve? Another woman pointed out that it was the chicken she needed, not lessons on how to cook it (Landsberg, 1997). These women had been excluded from designing the programmes they really needed – and the reason was not their gender, but their social class.

Class and gender also interact with other social factors adding to the complexity of the community power relations facing CED workers. In terms of the present study, although the focus group noted race and ethnicity as important factors, the rest of the research participants had little to say on the matter. While two thirds reported their projects as considering ethnicity issues quite or very well, half also reported that there was very little representation from diverse groups of women. Some noted that this was an area they were working on, while others claimed there were organizations/programmes elsewhere specifically aimed at minority women, and thus it was not really their mandate. Barriers and tensions relating to ethnic diversity were an issue almost never volunteered by the participants. This may suggest an area where some Canadian practitioners lack the necessary knowledge to analyse and address issues.

Geography, particularly the difference between rural and urban situations, is another factor that has considerable impact on how the complexities and dynamics of gender, class and race play out in everyday life. Obviously geographic factors influence what work is available and thus what training and development is appropriate. Lovett (1997), however, suggests that although rural issues are understood in theory, there is a tendency in practice to bypass this knowledge. Decisions are often made, and programmes initiated and implemented, at a regional (or even provincial) level which are not actually appropriate to the needs of individual rural communities. The rurally located practitioners in the CSTIER study were engaged in local programming, and thus did not raise this particular issue. They did raise the problem of distance, though, which has a variety of effects on their practice. Lack of opportunity to attend CED conferences or training events was noted. Although the growth of electronic communications had alleviated this problem somewhat, it did not make up for a lack of face-to-face interaction with other practitioners. Furthermore, telecommunication systems in some remote areas are still unreliable. In one case, a practitioner reported having to fight to retain her Internet and fax connections when her organization's board members thought these were an unnecessary cost. As will be discussed below, informal learning opportunities are important to all CED workers, but to rural-based practitioners they are often all that is available.

The picture of community that emerges, therefore, is one in which complex knowledge perspectives and power dynamics create a shifting terrain which both the CED worker and programme participant must constantly negotiate. These shifts constitute the everyday reality of CED practice – knowledge clashes will arise, and as we will argue, can be a positive influence for constructive change. But when the boundaries of present knowledge, especially the privileged knowledge of uppers, is resistant to new learning and responsive change, "knots" of discord result which severely hamper successful CED practice.

Knots of Discord: Not Recognized, Not Funded, Not Sustainable

Lewis (1999) comments that there seems to be "a stubborn reluctance and/or inability to learn from what is working in community economic development ... [and] part of the problem appears to be the extreme reluctance of politicians and bureaucrats to adopt the longer-term investment perspective required" (p. 212). This kind of climate results in part from the failure to confront and unravel the resistant knots of discordant knowledge we have previously discussed. As the following quote illustrates, such a climate can generate frustration and anger among CED workers as well as marginalized community members:

> Why doesn't the government fund CED initiatives? I don't understand that! Given the fact that it is proven [successful] in countries all over the world, women's CED initiatives can be, and are, successful in financial terms and in building a safe community, why is the government reluctant to give long-term funding to get these projects off the ground? [I would like to see a] recognition of realities. It takes three years to get a small business established, but it is only supported for 12 months. This guarantees failure – why? In order to guarantee there will always be a scapegoat for the government to blame.

Recent literature concurs. Naples (1997) complains that although long-term, equitable, and choice-driven strategies have been identified, women's economic needs continue to be ignored because this alternative perspective is viewed as more risky than a conventional economic approach. Indeed, the importance attached to training poor women is apparently currently decreasing, despite a growing body of international research demonstrating such training is a key component of successful development. Some agencies and programs have abandoned training entirely in favour of microcredit schemes (ID21, 2000b). Church et al (2000) argue that this entrepreneurial culture exerts pressure on the way community organizations define themselves and, in turn, leads to unstable and insufficient funding. Lovett (1997) contends that this type of funding climate leads community groups to compromise goals and standards in order to secure finances.

Obtaining suitable and sufficient funding was a major concern for all of the participants in the present study. Their programmes generally relied on a mosaic of funding, to which the various levels of government were the primary contributors, followed by businesses and foundations. Practitioners frequently noted the gulf between available funding and what they knew to be needed in order to effect sustainable community development. Statements made by the participants are the best way to illustrate these problems and how they relate to learning/knowledge and practice:

> Lack of time and funds can be a vicious circle preventing the application of new learning from taking the priority it should. It's less tangible and easy to dismiss in the face of more pressing deadlines and priorities.

> We want to build a show home in the city featuring accessible options. ... But everyone says "why build in the inner city where it's run down?" But that's where many of our women live. [Other people] say it's not worth as much if we build it in the inner city, but we want it in an area that is home to the women.

> If people are not eligible (are not on Social Assistance, EI, whatever) the regulations can be very frustrating for them. There are those that don't fit these categories, that are

interested [in our programs]. ... It should be for all who want/need it, so people don't have
to fit the system – it should be the other way around.

So many things just come down to funding. ... Everyone expects you to do things for nothing, but you just can't. A business pays a CEO really well, but if you look at what CED
CEOs are paid it is ridiculous. ... Government is one of the biggest culprits. It gives money
to organizations with only a small amount [allowed] for salaries. [Government] will fund
job subsidies or overhead ... [but staff] are undervalued and underpaid.

If I had a cushy government or business job, I could get city hall to listen to me and pay
attention. But I'm talking about an ideal world, because they ... don't allow that my knowledge is legitimate – they shut you right down.

Some Board members (about half) have yet to meet even one of our borrowers. When it
comes down to operations, the expectations of what is in a business plan and the payment
schedules are not in keeping with the abilities of our clients.

Clients are not well represented on the Board ... program participants originally had more
of a voice but now the organization has defined itself more as a CED provider to constitu-
encies of client groups living in long term poverty.

For the CSTIER study respondents, all forms of professional development for the
CED practitioners – including formal education courses, conferences or informal
networking opportunities – fell into the category of things funding agencies did not
view as important. Nearly 70% of the practitioners interviewed had personally
contributed to the cost of their own learning opportunities, and 30% had covered
all costs themselves. Twelve percent had also personally borne the costs of integrating new learning into practice.

In summary, resistant knots of discordant knowledge encourage a socio-
economic climate that is contrary to that identified as necessary to effective and
sustainable CED. As one practitioner commented, "I have the impression that university ... business life, and everyday [CED] client's life, are very different worlds."
The factors that contribute to a divide between the differing knowledges of theory
and practice intertwine with the complex power dynamics present in any community to prevent constructive change. As long as those in control of what is currently
regarded as legitimate knowledge refuse to open their minds and institutional doors
to those who have learned something different, the experience and insights of most
community members and workers will not be recognized. Until they *are* recognized, CED programmes will not be sufficiently and appropriately funded. And, if
they are not properly funded, they will ultimately not be sustainable.

Consensus amid Discord: Possibilities from Collisions

Our litany of difficult problems paints a rather pessimistic picture of the conditions
of doing CED. To contemplate, as we have suggested, "confronting and challenging" them all, may seem daunting to the point of being immobilizing. Nonetheless,
many CED workers *do* confront these issues everyday. Furthermore, what we will
now argue is that, out of the discord of knowing different things, there often

emerges a consensus among practitioners concerning both the problems and the possible solutions. As already indicated, CED practitioners of necessity need to obtain and apply different kinds of knowledge to their work. The participants in the CSTIER study described how they achieve this, and what they revealed was a process of integrating knowledge that relies heavily on informal learning components. The result, we contend, is a particular, synthesized knowledge set that blurs socially constructed boundaries across discrete categories of learning. This synthesized knowledge also generates an ability to intercede among opposing groups and opinions in order to identify and mediate new possibilities for sustainable community development. To outline this dynamic in more detail, we first explore the role informal learning plays, and then illustrate the process of knowledge integration that practitioners described.

Challenging Boundaries: The Social Process of Informal Learning

Livingstone and Sawchuk (2000) have argued that subordinated groups widely employ creative and primarily informal, learning strategies as a means of producing an alternative body of knowledge which is more relevant than dominant forms to their lived cultural experience. Such learning is an expansive social phenomenon that is inherently oppositional because it is counter to the dominant knowledge perspective. Lovett (1997) suggests community education that occurs *with* the community is most effective and is generally informal in approach. Further, Lewis (1999) argues that CED practitioner knowledge is derived from "learning from the trenches" (p. 191), in that, "they know because they have contributed their blood, sweat and tears. ... They know the hope that has been created in the lives of disadvantaged people, neighbourhoods and communities" (p. 193). The participants in the CSTIER study strongly endorsed this concept of learning by doing, as can be seen in the following quotes. They also described the social process of such learning, placing a heavy emphasis on shared experience and personal reflection. This process was viewed as having a vital role in determining both programme content and practice approaches:

> Learning by doing is the only way at this point that we learn, going ... [in] and doing stuff, finding out what people want or need. ... In the [program] learning amongst the community members always happened there because someone else was doing something and someone else said, 'hey, that's cool, how do you do that?' ... or they would find something in a book and say, 'how do we do that ... we can figure that out' ... it was a matter of a collective learning and doing.

> My learning I think of as being forced by development – personal and professional development. ... learning is an on-going process through practice that never ceases to amaze me.

> The knowledge and experience I gained personally [by] being a sole-support mother, with a handicapped child, on social assistance. This was, and is, most helpful in my dealings with low-income women because I understand what *they* are experiencing. It

is the sapping of energy [because of poverty] which prevents/immobilizes women from participation.

However, respondents did not value all kinds of informal learning equally. The foregoing comments underline the importance of social interactions, of listening and relating to the experience of programme participants, and then translating the resulting information into programme practice that meets those self-identified needs. In contrast to this highly valued form of informal learning, practitioners also tended to rely heavily on informal learning from text-based sources (including the Internet) because these were among the only opportunities open to them. While such sources had value, they were seldom viewed as ideal, as one participant argued:

> [Most of my learning is] self-directed, via the Internet, from the office and from home, [plus an] occasional conference ... [and a] community college certificate program. ... No, these are not the best places. There is a lot of importance in networking with other practitioners, and there has been very little of this in the province to date. Learning with peers and colleagues would be the best conditions.

Learning from text-based information, whether gained formally or informally, generally had to be analysed and adapted before it was of any real use to local CED practice. Opportunities to interact with other practitioners and programme participants were found to make this task much easier, helping to prevent practice errors. Learning via social interactions was therefore crucial. In stark contrast to the presumed process of formal classroom-based learning, it was also multidirectional and transferable. As one practitioner explained:

> [I learn] on the job. For example, while driving the truck, personal interactions with the workers take place. I get personal information about how [the women] want to learn. We put emphasis on this – the participants telling us how they want to learn. ... I've made it a point not to forget the struggle of learning for me ... and I'm more patient with the women and encourage them to be more patient with themselves to expect to need more than one attempt. Mistakes are OK, we learn from them. ... One thing we do is attempt to relate learning to skills we already have – skills transference – for example, if you can thread a needle you can fit a drill bit. We encourage [the women] to get over the idea they have "done nothing, just raising children." This is a job with tremendous skills. They need to recognize the accumulation of life skills they have and how these relate to [other] jobs. For example egg whites to paint mixing, and so on. ... Then, when that woman turns around and teaches another woman about those skills and fears, I get all choked up. They're doing it all – I'm instigating and organizing – they're making it happen.

Blurring the Confines of Learning: "It has to be Integrated"[12]

Despite their critique of formal education (especially of university academics), and the heavy emphasis placed on the importance of personal experience and social exchanges, CSTIER study practitioners did not dismiss a valuable contributing role for formal learning. Rather, they argued that formal education provides only some components of the overall knowledge needed to conduct successful CED practice. As they explained, the nature of the work demands the integration of various kinds of knowledge, otherwise "there's not much point:"

> The most useful by far is integrated knowledge; not just theory and applied, but the political and financial realities, the interactions, communications, and the technical. For example, I had technical knowledge on how to write a heck of a business plan to get financing from a bank. But I need to make that relevant to my political, social, financial context.

> We have to deal first with individuals and ways of learning ... then, the political and technical issues and knowledge are involved – neither can be ignored. ... There are lots of resources for the technical, and information for the political, but if you can't listen to the personal stuff, then you can't integrate the other knowledge. ... In the end, integrated learning is what counts, but the above [description] is the process.

> It's impossible to separate [types of learning]. ... Each member has different skills in the technical area (so some of the team might say they draw more on one area), but as a team [our knowledge] is very integrated. That's what makes the program women-based, women-centred. It's an unquestionable principle – it must be based on integrated knowledge. ... For me the integrated learning is right in the inception of the process. Analyzing [the clients'] own lives is the beginning point, starting from their experiences to evaluate what they can do and how they can do it.

The CED practitioners in the CSTIER study describe a process in which the various kinds of learning are combined and the boundaries between them become blurred. Even if various aspects of information were gained from different sources, at different times, these are not viewed as useful knowledge until they are integrated. Furthermore, the necessary kind of knowledge requires that the practitioners shuttle back and forth between formal, non-formal, and informal learning activities.[13] Respondents indicated that, for the CED worker, doing and learning are inseparable activities, and integration is part of the "doing" involved in creating useful knowledge.

Other researchers looking at the role of informal learning in community settings have also noted at least some aspects of this boundary challenge. Church et al. (2000) observe that marginalized groups tend to see types of learning as part of an "overlapping and simultaneous process" (p. 35). Lovett (1997) identifies informal learning as an essential component of converting knowledge imparted via formal education into material useful to community education. Clover and Hall (2000) also argue that community knowledge challenges the utility of continuing to think of learning as something that can be divided into discrete types. Overall, the community-knowledge message is that, without the component of informal learning, there is merely information. To apply this, or to pass it on effectively, we must personally act upon it and integrate it with what we already "know." Such insight is entirely compatible with cognitive science. So why do formal learning organizations continue to so marginalize informal, community-based knowledge? The reasons, which we have discussed earlier, have little to do with learning and much to do with relations of power and control inside formal institutions.

Knowing How to Intercede: Mediating Possibilities

Community development work necessitates confronting power dynamics at every level, and gaining the knowledge required to do their job often compels CED practitioners to blur the knowledge and learning boundaries academic institutions construct and uphold. Having created the new, integrated knowledge they need, these community workers then apply it to challenging the resistant boundaries created by different and discordant knowledge, which is held by others involved in the development process. Interceding and mediating among individuals and groups holding contrary knowledge perspectives is at the heart of successful community development. The non-constructive, oppositional views of both "uppers" and "lowers" must be confronted in the process, and CED workers need to create a bridge between them. That bridge may be shaky and imperfect, but without it there is no pathway toward change. Practitioners generally understand this, and within recent practitioner-generated literature (originating from a variety of disciplines), a consensus seems to be emerging about the kinds of knowledge base and practice approaches required for successful CED (Gutierrez and Lord, 1998).

An important segment of the literature does not dismiss or minimize the difficulties practitioners face, but acknowledges that practitioners must confront these challenges in an attempt to find ways to move forward. There is agreement that such work requires a special kind of knowledge (Chambers, 1997; Rubin, 1997). Rubin describes it as allowing the worker to survive in the niche between the business deal and the social action (1997, p. 82). He argues that, no matter how hard it is to achieve, CED requires the recognition of a "double bottom line" – one that addresses both fiscal and social realities. Arriving at such a recognition requires the mediation skills to convince those controlling the fiscal end that, in a distressed community, "profound personal problems" *are* the economic conditions (p. 62). Those concerned with the social issues must understand that even though the tensions may be irreconcilable (it is "trading with the enemy" in some respects), successful development means negotiating anyway. Using housing development as an example, he suggests that practitioners should first get the money for the physical development (without it, how will the area improve?). Next, they should argue that the social interventions (child care, adult education, teen programs, etc.) are necessary to protect the physical investment.

We have noted earlier the problem of co-optation. There is some agreement in the literature that avoiding co-optation requires constant vigilance and an ability to be self-critical and embrace error as part of the continuous learning experience (Chambers, 1997; Lennie, 1999; Rubin, 1997). The authors emphasize the importance of using: truly participatory approaches to ensure the involvement of a wide range of community members; support structures (community assets) already in place; and extended networking through the use of the language of the community rather than that of the dominant structures. Chambers (1997) underscores the necessity of step-by-step work that builds out and up from the grass roots, small and slow perhaps, but with a commitment to continuity, training, encouragement and using the many points of leverage within organizations at all levels (pp. 230–232). Comments from the CSTIER study participants are aligned with this view, and offer illustrations concerning the process in practice:

> In the beginning [applying new knowledge to practice] was always a problem, but that's why I see CED as an educational process. I go around and get people excited about it and convince them to get involved and support it. It's a question of having enough time. It has never happened that a new idea was implemented 1 month later. It can be quite a bit longer, but we've never said that we won't do it. We take it one step at a time.

> In the past the organization has been insensitive to the needs, issues and changes [for women]. Now it is gaining more sensitivity to participants. ... For example we have teamed the abled participants with the disabled. We are identifying transportation difficulties of seniors and trying to address them. It has been a learning process for the organization. ... We are trying to boost the local economy. ... To create a climate for investment in the community in [terms of] business *and* social programs. ... Change is occurring now – but very slowly and carefully. I [use] extreme sensitivity ... [t]here are so many changes to be made, naturally everyone resists.

> One way we respond is, if there is an ongoing program established by a funding body, we will not go in meeting their agenda. We will go in redesigning their program rather than ours. For example [we might say] "you talk of individual counselling; we do group counselling. We believe in it because (whatever reasons). Can we get funding?" If they refuse us we won't do it their way. Generally, we get a chance – not always at first crack, but we're like the puppy – they take us home and see how we do. ... We're always on a trial basis – but really hard to get rid of!

> With something new there is always resistance ... so you have to ... look for people who are willing to work on it, and not worry too much about the opposition. We need to respect the diversity, yet work with those who do support that [particular] vision. ... [T]here are always people who are movers and shakers, and I'm a strong believer in finding them and working with them. I could say all the other things too: that it moves slowly, and that things are entrenched. But, my philosophy is to look for an open door and not to get stuck at a closed one.

While these practitioners convey a pragmatic view of practice that recognizes the very real difficulties to be faced, their approach is also inspiringly positive. The challenge of conveying the value and importance of CED initiatives is perceived as an exciting educational process. Instead of seeing an overwhelming array of unrelenting barriers, the study participants identify an agenda-setting task full of possibilities. Their ultimate goal is to create more inclusive, egalitarian communities that are both socially healthy and economically viable. These CED workers are determined to achieve this goal by utilizing their simultaneous roles as knowers, teachers and learners to create innovative practice and effective approaches to negotiation.

Conclusion: Imperfect but Forward

Participants in our CED study showed innovation, determination and a positive orientation, but they continue to face a difficult political climate and a constant battle to "prove" that their knowledge is valid, important and effective. Without support, in the face of short-term success stories proving unsustainable, too many CED workers are likely to burn out and become immobilized by hopelessness. The current situation is full of tensions and contradictions. Co-optation is a continual threat. Oppositional power dynamics are a constant. And the very best of CED practices are still imperfect. Community development work is messy, still too often exclusive of many citizens (especially those viewed as "uneducated' and thus not possessing the "correct" knowledge perspective). However, non-action is not an option. Real action is needed, and quickly. So where do we go from here?

Referring critically to the postmodern academic position as unhelpful and unacceptable to those engaged in front-line development practice, Chambers (1997) asserts that even if we have to work "on the edge of chaos," we can, and must, bring into view and make intelligible dominant trends that justify and obscure social injustice and inequality (p. 222). He argues that a recognition and celebration of multiple realities can lead the way to rich and sustainable communities. Understanding that there is no single, final truth, no ultimately correct belief or behaviour does not in itself have to be immobilizing. We may stumble forward imperfectly, but we *can* move forward. Chambers and others (such as Fontan and Shragge, 2000; Rao et al., 1999; Rubin, 1997) suggest that there are many points of leverage to be identified and used within any organization. Challenging tensions and contradictions can be a powerful way of opening the door to constructive change, but this must be recognized as a permanent task.

Chambers and the CSTIER study participants have taken the position that, in order to move towards long-term structural change, ways must be found to moderate and engage dominant and oppressive structures and processes in the short term. Drawing on the accounts of experienced Canadian CED practitioners, we have suggested that knowledge collisions contain important possibilities for action. CED activists have no real choice but to utilize such opportunities in order to relate to, and mediate among, distressed communities, the corporate world, and the various levels and agents of the state. The possibility for progressive social change exists because, ultimately, all of these groups must take a position that balances social peace *and* a viable economy. Within the tensions that arise from such a necessity, the interests of the social and economic must converge. Literature on CED is beginning to provide detailed examples of how this might be achieved, and Canadian CED practitioners have built a wealth of practice-knowledge to be recognized, tapped and shared.

Formal education institutions (particularly universities and colleges) that seek to provide professional education to CED practitioners must find new and creative ways to encourage, value, validate, systematize, blend, and disseminate the integrated knowledge that is generated by CED practitioners. Educational delivery systems – whether they are face-to-face or online, individual or group-based – must also understand and promote this kind of integrated learning. Opportunities for CED education that are so organized are likely to be effective and, thus, create a continuous demand for such services in the CED sector, and possibly, also within other social sectors.

The School of Community and Public Affairs at Concordia University has broken ground with a new programme offering a graduate diploma in community and economic development. Programme co-founder Lance Evoy, and the coordinator of programme development, Michael Chervin, have discussed how this initiative is confronting the resistant boundaries we have outlined in this chapter.[14] Their comments indicate that principles of effective CED practice have been applied to the process of establishing this graduate diploma.

Chervin and Evoy emphasize a number of important points that fall into two basic areas: challenging the traditional university structures, and innovative programme content. Challenging traditional practices within the university, along with the structural need for co-optation of new knowledge, meant first recognizing and acknowledging these as problematic and then "going against the grain of that need." To do this successfully, it was essential to create a network of people within the university who shared the same basic values and vision (albeit from different perspectives), and who could credibly speak from within the institution about the importance and value to the university of a CED programme. In a context where tension is inevitable and reversals an ongoing risk, this, however, is a task that is never finished. Chervin recommends "continuous engagement with the contradiction of both going against the grain of conventional university 'needs' and of strengthening, in very practical ways, the university's more transformative or emancipatory functions."

Innovative programme approaches require the same unremitting engagement with challenge and change. Chervin and Evoy argue that the tension between theory and practice is an important aspect of the relation between the two that must be creatively engaged, grounded and fully integrated by soliciting and responding to "what and how critically reflective practitioners yearn to learn." The Concordia programme explicitly guides its instructors to take up these ongoing challenges. Administrators use focused advertising of part-time positions, along with team-teaching, to allow practice-based instructors to be part of the programme. Input is consistently sought from students and shared among faculty and other students. Assignments emphasize the integration of knowledge about theory, policy, practice and personal experience. Such approaches clearly echo the preferred two-way, integrated learning approach advocated by participants in the CSTIER study. Evoy remarked on how struck he was by the degree of sophisticated integration reflected in the discussions among the CED programme students, while also observing that it could sometimes be a major issue for academics to understand the integration process.

The Concordia programme provides an excellent model of a way forward for relevant academic approaches to CED learning. However, at present, there are few Canadian formal education programmes designed specifically for CED practitioners. There is, nonetheless, much more that the academic world can do to generally recognize and support the value of different kinds of knowledge. The NALL network's collaborative, community partner structure, and its focus on informal learning activities, provides an example of the possibilities in that regard. Like CED practice, the experience has been imperfect, uneven, and contested, but has definitely also broken ground by challenging the boundaries of traditional formal learning organizations and academic alliances and practices across different levels of "uppers" and "lowers." Those who have been involved will not in future think about knowledge and learning in the same terms, and will have ongoing opportunities to spread what has been learned.

The importance of creating strong networks and identifying alliances that can achieve change (even if these structures are sometimes tense and difficult to manage) is a point of general agreement among development practitioners everywhere. CED workers are aware that there is discord in knowing differently. We believe that they need to use this knowledge and experience to create discord in mainstream thinking by disrupting it with strong arguments for new learning and different approaches. In Canada, we suggest, practitioners have room to make more effective use of the multiple knowledges they recognize and apply to their personal practice approaches. Although governments and business place much emphasis on a knowledge-intensive economy, to date CED has tended to focus on low technology initiatives and training – which in itself is a reflection of the internalized fallacy that those lacking formal education credentials also lack intellectual (learning) ability. There is an opportunity, therefore, to bridge that divide. CED *is* knowledge intensive, for both practitioners and programme participants. CED workers need to take that recognition and their negotiating skills and apply them to new knowledge production by producing methods that lead programme participants to better jobs and more learning opportunities. They have to "sell" CED as a knowledge-intensive, important and vital part of the new global information-based economy. If lifelong learning is held to be a necessity of the new economy, it must follow that it is also an essential part of CED work – for practitioner and participant alike. A convincing case can be made that both government and business should invest in CED training and development, and make a commitment to stable and longer-term funding.

It is interesting to note that the high-technology sector has itself gone the furthest of all sectors in breaking down barriers between formal and informal learning – both before and after the "tech-bubble" burst. Practical ability was, and remains, more important to the industry in the development and application of front-line technology than paper credentials. Technology companies operate facilities that allow their workers to share knowledge and integrate their social networks with their professional lives – they push the sharing of knowledge and teaching through intentional networking. There is almost always money and time for technology workers to learn. Why should the same opportunity not be made available for CED workers and the participants in CED projects? Development workers concerned with contesting social inequality worry about dominant groups co-opting, mainstreaming, and rendering ineffective, their methods of practice. However, we contend that CED workers can co-opt some mainstream ideas and practices to successfully advance community development projects.[15]

We do not want to in any way minimize the strategic and tactical risks inherent in partnerships with dominant power groups. But, CED cannot proceed without forming them. CED work is imperfect, but imperfect local action is better than no local action at all. CED will never be perfected because it is necessitated in the first place by an imperfect world. Still, CED could be much improved if practitioners at all points on the CED spectrum were to benefit from training that was ongoing, and organized around the integrated knowledge model that practitioners themselves identify and prefer. Engaged scholars, CED practitioners and all community members concerned with social justice must continue to struggle forward, imperfectly, recognizing both the barriers and possibilities contained within multiple and discordant knowledge perspectives.

Endnotes

[1] *Women and Community Economic Development: Changing Knowledge, Changing Practice* (Stratton and Levine, 2000) is a summary of the results of the study available from CSTIER (in French and English) and on the Internet at *http://www.carleton.ca/cstier*. It is also available from NALL as Working Paper 12-2000. A copy of the interview schedule containing a full description of the results is also available from CSTIER upon request. In 2004, CSTIER changed its name to the Carleton Centre for Community Innovation to better reflect its new strategic focus.

[2] Barbara Levine, who was with CSTIER as an Associate Director in 1998–1999, was the original Principal Investigator for the Women and CED project. She identified the research concern and wrote the initial proposal to NALL.

[3] Only one question late in the interview actually suggested categories of knowledge/learning and these were "technical," political," "personal" and "integrated." These categories were suggested by Barbara Levine, based on her own experience of CED practice and the language and areas of knowledge familiar to practitioners.

[4] We recognize that there are further conceptual issues imbedded here. NALL has generally used the terms "knowledge" and "learning" interchangeably (as well as learning/training/education). We have added to this the term "information." Data from our project seems to suggest these terms are not synonymous, but take on different roles in a learning/ knowledge creation process. Sorting out such tangled conceptualizations has been given very little previous attention and is beyond the scope of the present discussion. NALL's attempts to date have served more to muddy than clarify the matter.

[5] It should be noted that all but one of the research participants had some post-secondary education and over 70% had at least one university degree. Their criticisms of academia are grounded in experience of these formal institutions and do not derive from an inability to interact successfully with formal learning structures.

[6] To be completely fair, some of the cited literature was only published after the date of the initial literature search, and electronic search engines have improved greatly in the interceding 20 months, Nevertheless, it was the focus on knowledge clashes in community development (rather than gender, CED and learning) that proved to be most productive.

[7] This matter of competing disciplines, theories and jargon needs to be emphasized. A detailed discussion is outside the scope of this paper, but it is worth noting that the cited literature spans six to eight different disciplines (depending on how one divides them up), located internationally. It offers an even larger number of theoretical approaches to analysing the problems and employs different terminology to describe the same basic issue. There are, for example, myriad (and often poorly defined) terms relating to participatory research approaches and/or community consultation methods, and Lovett (1997) notes various interpretations of "community education." NALL members have noted this diversity among their work (Church, 2000). As academics, we have found the exposure to it challenging and often rewarding, but it nevertheless underlines a barrier that exists *within* academia as well as *between* it and the broader community.

[8] The authors found it particularly challenging to present the discussion of these differing perspectives and ongoing tensions in a balanced and nuanced way that neither exaggerated, nor minimized, their divisiveness.

[9] There are many examples among academic publications. While some authors emphasize CED as a strategy for social change and underline the dangers of cooptation by state and corporate partners, others argue a need for social advocates to increase entrepreneurial approaches and broaden capacity building skills. Still others argue it is possible to negotiate the pitfalls without sacrificing social development goals. For some examples see: Fontan and Shragge, 2000, Jackson, 2001, Murray and Ferguson, 1998; Rubin, 1997; Shragge, 1997; Torjman, 1999.

[10] There are also probably misunderstandings regarding what is actually meant by some terms. For example, participants in Oberdof (Ed.) (1999) contended that microenterprise and microfinance are not the same thing. There is little agreement, however, concerning the exact role of microfinance in CED. Discussants argued that it depends on context and available alternatives.

[11] During the pilot study phase of the CSTIER research, early in the focus group discussion, one of the participants declared, "it's not just about gender." This statement is definitive of the complexity of relations that emerged in the subsequent research.

[12] When asked what kinds of knowledge they found most useful to CED practice, participants in the present study repeatedly argued that various kinds of knowledge had to be integrated.

[13] This boundary crossing is increased because CED practitioners are often responsible for designing and implementing non-formal community learning and training experiences. To do this, they combine various elements of their own learning, and learn informally through the experience of providing the non-formal activity. For them a non-formal opportunity might be a conference workshop where practitioners exchanged such experiences. But they might learn equally well from an informal opportunity to do the same. It is not, therefore, surprising that these academic conceptual distinctions tend to be viewed as meaningless by many people involved in community-based learning.

[14] This section is based on personal communications with Michael Chervin on 26 February 2001 and Lance Evoy on 1 March 2001. We are indebted to them for their insightful in-depth comments, which are worthy of considerably more attention than is possible within this paper.

[15] We are not oblivious to the competition and profit motives that "inspire" the technology sector to provide such worker supports. What we are arguing is that just as the governments, etc. often co-opt the language of participatory community partnership to forward dominant goals, so might CED practice take the language and methods of dominant groups to forward its own.

References

Cawley, R., 1996, The incomplete revolution: the development of community work in Quebec CLSCs, *Community Development Journal*, **31**(1): 54–65.

Chambers, R., 1997, *Whose Reality Counts*? Intermediate Technology, London.

Church, K., 2000, *The Communal "We?": A conversation piece on the richness of being a network*. Network for New Approaches to Lifelong Learning (NALL), Toronto, Canada.

Church, K., Fontan, J., Ng, R. & Shragge, E., 2000, *Social Learning among people who are excluded from the Labour Market: part one, context and case studies*, a working paper: NALL, Toronto, Canada.

Clover, D. & Hall, B., 2000, In Search of Social Movement Learning: the growing jobs for living project, presented at *Contested Terrain: The boundaries and practical impact of informal learning: The 4th Annual NALL Conference*, October, Toronto, Canada.

Fontan, J. & Shragge, E., 2000, Tendencies and visions in the social economy, in E. Shragge & J. Fontan (Eds.), *Social Economy: International Debates and Perspectives*, Black Rose, Montreal.

Gutierrez, L. & Lord, C., 1998, Toward a social constructionist method of community practice, in C. Franklin & P. Nurius (Eds.), *Constructivism in Practice: Methods and Challenges*, Families International, Milwaukee.

Hansen, H., Ramstead, J., Richer, S., Smith, S., & Stratton, M., 2001, Unpacking participatory research in education, *Interchange*, **32(3)**: 295–322.

Heaney, T., 1993, If you can't beat 'em, join 'em; the professionalization of participatory research, in P. Park, M. Brydon-Miller, B. Hall & T. Jackson (Eds.), *Voices of Change: Participatory Research in the United States and Canada*, Bergin & Garvey, Westport, CT.

ID21 Development Research, 2000a, *Sustainable Perspectives? A Gender Analysis of Environmental Change*. [Research reporting service] http://www.id21.org/static/5acj1.html

ID21 Development Research, 2000b, *Training for Empowerment: The Impact of Training on Women's Microenterprise Development*. [Research reporting service] http://nt1.ids.ac.uk/cgi-bin/dbtcgi

Jackson, E.T., 2001, Accompaniment philanthropy: Canada's Community Economic Development Assistance Program, in D. Bruce & G. Lister (Eds.), *Rising Tide: Community Development Tools, Models and Processes*, Rural and Small Town Program, Mount Allison University, Sackville, NB.

Landsberg, M., 1997, Gritty, witty view of poverty from the front lines, reproduced in *NAPO News 62* (February, 1998), The National Anti-Poverty Organization, Toronto http://www.napo-onap.ca/nn62.htm

Lennie, J., 1999, Deconstructing gendered power relations in participatory planning: towards an empowering feminist framework of participation and action, *Women's Studies International Forum*, **22(1)**: 97–112.

Lewis, M., 1999, Community economic development, in K. Battle & S. Torjman (Eds.), *Employment Policy Options*, Caledon Institute of Social Policy, Ottawa.

Livingstone, D.W., 2003, Exploring the icebergs of adult learning: findings of the first Canadian survey of informal learning practices, *The Canadian Journal for the Study of Adult Education*, **13(2)**: 49–72.

Livingstone, D. & Sawchuk, P., 2000, Beyond cultural capital theory: hidden dimensions of working class learning. Draft paper circulated to NALL, March 2000.

Lovett, T., 1997, Community education and community development: the Northern Ireland experience, *Studies in the Education of Adults*, **29(1)**: 39–50.

Murray, J. & Ferguson, M., 1998, *Exploring Priorities: Women's Economic Development in Canada*, Eko Nomos, Toronto, Canada.

Naples, N., 1997, Contested needs: shifting the standpoint on rural economic development, *Feminist Economics*, **3(2)**: 63–98.

Oberdof, C. (Ed.), 1999, *Microfinance: Conversations with the Experts*, Micro-enterprise Policy Institute, Bolivia.

Rao, A., Stuart, R. & Kelleher, D., 1999, *Gender at Work: Organizational Change for Equality*, Kumarian, West Hartford, CT.

Rubin, H., 1997, Being a conscience and a carpenter: interpretations of the community-based development model, in M. Weil (Ed.), *Community Practice: Models in Action*, Hartworth, Binghampton, NY.

Saleebey, D., 1998, Constructing community: the emergent uses of social constructionism in economically distressed communities, in C. Franklin & P. Nurius (Eds.), *Constructivism in Practice: Methods and Challenges*, Families International, Milwaukee.

Shragge, E. (Ed.), 1997, Community economic development: conflicts and visions, *Community Economic Development: In Search of Empowerment*, Black Rose Books, Montreal, Canada.

Torjman, S., 1999, *Are Outcomes the Best Outcome*? Caledon Institute of Social Policy, Ottawa.

Chapter 8
Teacher's Informal Learning, Identity and Contemporary Education Reform

Kari Dehli and Doreen Fumia

Introduction

The second half of the 1990s was a period of a great deal of turmoil and change in Ontario's schools, as a neoconservative government, first elected in 1995, pushed ahead with its version of reform in the name of standards, accountability and efficiency. In this small study, conducted in 2000, we examine how teachers were being positioned and how they understood themselves in the complex milieu of intense education reform.[1] One of the central questions that we asked is how notions of effectiveness, improvement and accountability shape images of the good teacher in reform discourses, and how these notions are woven into teacher talk as they "account for themselves" in interviews (MacLure, 1993).

Twelve teachers were interviewed. Some were participants in the original research. Some were selected because they had worked as teacher representatives on school advisory councils, others because they teach grade 3 or 6, whose students were targeted for yearly provincial testing. The teachers were asked to comment on contemporary school reform, particularly those aspects having to do with curriculum, assessment and reporting. However, because the interviews were open-ended, several teachers took the conversation to topics that we did not elicit. For example, they talked about stress, burnout and health-related problems that they experienced.

Working Knowledge, Informal Learning and Making "New" Teacher Identities

Notions of informal learning provide ways to describe connections teachers make between the more general discourses and practices of reform and the ways and conditions in which they articulate what they do and their "sense of self" in relation to them (Avis, 1999; Coldron and Smith, 1999). On the one hand, this kind of learning is situated and embodied (Church et al., 2000) in the everyday working knowledge of teachers. On the other hand, it is embedded in the more general discourses and conditions of reform. We consider first some of the teacher

K. Church et al. (eds.), *Learning through Community: Exploring Participatory Practices*.
© Springer Science+Business Media B.V. 2008

identities that are assumed, preferred and legitimized in contemporary education reform discourses and practices, and then explore where and how teachers encounter these identities, and how they learn to "take them up" (Walkerdine, 1990) or "work them through" (Farrell, 2000). How are different bodies differently situated in relation to new teacher identities? What kinds of embodied learning might be involved in the take up or refusal of identities, what rewards, risks and costs might be attached to "the labour of identity" (Adkins and Lury, 1999)? At the end of the chapter we speculate about how such learning, risks and costs are gendered and racialized.

We frame our interpretive questions around identity because the workplace is one of the central sites where identities are formed and learned (du Gay, 1996; Miller and Rose, 1995). This might be especially so for teachers, whose work has historically been described as "more than a job," and whose workplace is at the same time thoroughly known and recognizable to anyone who has attended a school, yet mysteriously opaque to anyone who is not an educator (Britzman, 1991). Moreover, a great deal of research on educational change and improvement is preoccupied with teachers' identities, seeking variously to "develop" individual teachers' inclinations towards, and capacities for, change; to "empower" teachers to find and express their "voice" and capacities as "change agents," or to engage teachers in research and reflection on their practice (Fullan and Hargreaves, 1992; Sikes, 1992). Such ideas proliferate in pre-service teacher education, and they are also appropriated into some of the rhetoric of official, government-sponsored policies and discourses of reform. In a 1998 paper, for example, the Deputy Minister of Education for Ontario advised teachers to "be the change you wish to see" (Lacey, 1998). At the same time, the Ontario government's interventions in schooling have served to seriously compromise the environment wherein such ideals might be realized, creating conditions where "being the change you wish to see" has become nearly impossible for many teachers (Gidney, 1999; Ontario Secondary School Teachers' Federation, 2000). Nevertheless, notions of the efficient, forward-looking and self-reflexive teacher who collaborates with colleagues and seeks ways to involve parents are very much "at work" in educators' talk and reasoning. This is so even as schools are subjected to budgets cuts, restructuring of governance and standardization of curricula, testing and reporting. How do teachers make sense of this? How do we?

The notion of governmentality (Foucault, 1991; Rose and Miller, 1992; O'Malley et al., 1997) is helpful for thinking about the multiple ways in which power is exercised in schools and rationalized in contemporary education reform discourses – whether generated by and circulated among researchers or asserted through official policies and political debates. According to Gordon (1991) governmental forms of power characteristic of neoliberalism work by (more or less) indirectly shaping general conditions and capacities for conduct, particularly individuals' exercise of freedom, self-reflection and self-improvement. In this account, freedom is not an essential capacity of human subjectivity standing in opposition to power. Rather, freedom is viewed "as an array of competencies that are ascribed to different agents and can only be realized in relation to specific conditions of possibility" (Barnett, 1999, p. 383). Freedom and agency are simultaneously the "condition of possibility" of power and its "effects" (Foucault, 1990; Rose, 1996b; Hall, 1996).

Hunter and Meredyth (2000), Popkewitz (1998, 2000) and Popkewitz and Lindblad (2000) have made use of governmentality to rethink the discursive and spatial organization and effects of contemporary education policy and research. Popkewitz, in particular, has explored relations between reform, research, teachers' "reasoning" and practices of inclusion and exclusion. In this chapter, governmentality enables us to think about "education reform" as one of several contemporary fields where discourses and practices of "improvement," "effectiveness" and "accountability" shape general and everyday conditions of teachers' work and teachers' thinking. It opens up questions about how, in addition to its enactment in legislation and its capacity to control teachers, "reform" also operates through teachers' self-reflexive practices and "labour of identity" (Adkins and Lury, 1999). However their "dispositions" may be shaped, teachers' actions and ideas cannot be fully predicted or controlled. There is always something in excess of, or not quite like, the "rules of reason" that education reform provides (Popkewitz, 1998). Indeed, by exploring the "spaces" where teachers encounter and "take up" new identities, we may be able to see where education reforms reach (one of) their limits. At the same time, these encounters may be ones where indirect and governmental forms of power meet up with more direct modes of containment and discipline, and more overtly ideological and political rhetoric.

How did teachers in this study make sense of different and contradictory discursive resources to explain their work, their students and themselves? In order to address this question in detail we relied on research into teacher biography and identity, in particular the work of Deborah Britzman. In analysing interviews with student teachers who were developing teacher identities, Britzman draws on the antagonistic push and pull of discourses to create new meanings (1991, p. 111). Teachers, Britzman argues, "take up" identity through both compliance and resistance to a normative, stereotypical notion of "the teacher." She suggests that a "normative voice ... defines what a teacher is and does in relation to the kind of authority and power teachers are expected to display" (p. 115). A "resisting voice" on the other hand, "speaks to one's deep convictions, investments and desire" (p. 115). Within the destabilizing terrain of contemporary reform, the teachers we interviewed express a range of feelings as they negotiate "new" identities, drawing on contradictory discourses of power and freedom, deep convictions, disavowal and alignment. Some of the conceptual implications of Britzman's insights go beyond the scope of this chapter. However, the attention she brings to questions of psychic investment and desire suggests that relations between "rationalities of government" (Foucault, 1991) and the formation and actions of subjects cannot be adequately explained through theories of power that focus solely on notions of control and resistance. Nor can they presume the transparency of language and the rationality of subjects.

As many researchers and advocates of school improvement would agree, reform programmes are most effective when teachers "freely" adopted them rather than viewing them as external and political impositions (Sikes, 1992; Carter, 1998; Kruse and Louis, 1999). The recognition that education reform will work to the extent that teachers take them up as their own has generated a wide range of initiatives that seek to make individual teachers responsible for students' achievement and to shape teachers' dispositions towards ongoing improvement. During the late 1990s the provincial government in Ontario introduced requirements for teachers to enrol in prescribed courses and to submit to regular, mandatory testing to maintain their certification. In addition to this overtly directive approach, more benign notions such as lifelong learning, the culture of improvement and the learning organization were added to the more established vocabulary and practices of pre-service and in-service teacher education and professional development. Many reform efforts in Ontario in this period were aimed at teachers' learning and knowledge and, indeed, Canadian teachers do engage in large numbers of learning activities, formal and informal, to maintain or enhance their knowledge and skills (see Chapter 9 by Bascia, this volume; Smaller et al., 2000).

Our concern in this small study was not so much with organized learning activities in which teachers participate as with more embedded and embodied forms of learning. Within a more general discursive environment where change and reform were asserted almost as slogans and where teachers' knowledge and skills were called into question, we were interested in learning that entails negotiating new identities. One interesting feature of (some of) the teacher identities that are generated in contemporary education reform discourses, including research discourse about reform, is their appeal to and emphasis on, individual teachers' freedom, flexibility and accountability. Related to this is the emphasis on individual schools' capacity to develop collaborative relations within and beyond the school to promote students' achievement. Such freedom – particularly from the purported bureaucratic constraints of school boards and collective agreements – continues to be touted as a central feature of reform efforts. However, while teachers in this study told us that the new curriculum promised some freedom to design suitable teaching and learning strategies, they also voiced a number of complaints: Targets of achievement or "outcomes" were set externally and they assumed very specific notions about what counts as learning, and students' (and teachers') performance was more insistently measured than ever before. Moreover, report cards and tests were standardized in ways that are highly prescriptive, and the work of preparing for these new accountability practices takes up an inordinate amount of teachers' and students' time. Some teachers we talked to were frustrated that over the 5 years preceding the study they had to abandon more innovative, equity and activity-oriented approaches in favour of traditional teacher-centred pedagogies in order to "cover" all the concepts and skills on which students would be evaluated.

The devolution of responsibility and risk to local schools and individual teachers also brought with it other modes of accountability, particularly ones that purport to open up the schools to different forms of "involvement" and "partnership," and to make the work of teachers and the learning of students more transparent, especially to parents. In turn, during the 1990s, parents in Ontario (and elsewhere) were increasingly positioned as consumers of children's education (Deem et al., 1996;

Crozier, 2000; Robertson, 1999; Whitty et al., 1998). In the name of reducing bureaucratic control, in the late nineties the Ontario government introduced regimes of regulation that were every bit as prescriptive as earlier ones, and this in turn was depicted as evidence of commitment to raising standards of quality and excellence. For teachers, the balance between freedom and accountability would seem to be heavily weighed to the latter. They were "free" to pursue appropriate strategies to ensure that students in the classroom, no matter their circumstance or the resources of the school and community, meet the targets established by centrally determined curricula, tests and reporting tools.

Discourses of Reform: School Improvement as Common Sense

Late twentieth century education reform policies were pursued through a range of heterogeneous practices that sought to raise and measure standards, and provide greater accountability to the "consumers" of education. Promoted by political conservatives and social democrats alike, contemporary reforms in Canada and other English-speaking "western" countries mandated a panoply of initiatives that put in place modes of governance and management that accord with "market" principles and practices (Deem, 1990; Ball, 1994; Dehli,1996, 1998; and Chapter 9 by Bascia, this volume). Canadian provincial governments appealed to the challenges and threats of an emerging "knowledge economy" and the potentials and risks of global competitiveness to focus attention on what critics described as falling standards and waste in schools. And while there are ideological differences in how governments identified problems and justified reforms, most urged teachers and students to raise standards, and schools and school boards to reduce bureaucracy, increase efficiency and "do more with less." While raising the achievement of students and improving the efficiency and accountability of schools were touted as desirable goals, governments cut budgets, "restructured" modes of governance, and introduced new modes of reporting and accounting. Alongside the theme of raising standards and "retooling" schools for global competitiveness, education reforms in Ontario (and elsewhere) also invoked a pernicious nostalgia for a well-ordered past when women knew their place (in the heterosexual family), when young people were deferential and well behaved (submitting willingly to teachers' authority at school), and when "we" knew who we were as a nation (white, European and integral to the British Empire). This mixing of the modern and forward looking with nostalgic appeals to tradition, generates normative and exclusive visions of the social and the individual, of who belongs and who is excluded from the community and the nation (Epstein and Johnson, 1998; Gillborn, 1999).

The political rhetoric used by governments to justify interventions in education made effective use of "progressive" market discourse, on the one hand, and authoritative assertions of "traditional" notions of discipline and order, on the other. Subjected to a "discourse of derision" (Deem, 1990; Kenway et al., 1993), teachers were variously accused of being self-interested, unaccountable and lazy, or lacking the skills and qualifications required in the "new global economy." It was as though control of education must be taken away from educators, "the producers," and transferred to its "consumers," and particularly parents and employers (Deem, 1990). Significantly, teachers were referenced as members of powerful collectives, the teacher unions, or rigid bureaucracies, the school boards.

The Ontario government's "Common Sense" ideology was especially virulent in the way that teachers and the unions representing them were targeted and demonized (Urquhart, 2000). Between 1995 and 2001, the government introduced several bills in parliament to fundamentally reorganize – through simultaneous centralization and decentralization – the education system. At the same time, when teachers were solicited to participate in improvement or reform efforts, the appeal was made to them as individuals, who are professional, hard-working and caring. A number of regulatory bodies with an "arms length" relationship to the government and to teacher unions and school boards were established to administer and monitor progress on the road to improvement and higher standards.

Teacher unions and education activists resisted many of this government's initiatives. Indeed, Ontario teacher unions were among the best organized and most articulate critics of Tory initiatives, culminating in a 2-week protest strike in October–November 1997 which closed virtually all publicly funded elementary and secondary schools in the province. But while the unions had some success in explaining their objections and mobilizing large scale resistance to budget cuts and centralization of power in education – areas where overt forms of power are very much in evidence and lines between "us" and "them" can be clearly drawn – the broader agenda of reform and improvement was a more difficult and diffuse target (Lewington, 1998). Even critics of government-mandated reforms (including some of the teacher federations, and teachers we interviewed) agreed that schools needed to change. The curriculum did require "modernization" and consistency, and students' achievement should be raised and closely monitored (a search of teacher federation newsletters and web sites would support this claim). Thus, calls for greater transparency of teachers' work and accountability of students' learning received substantial support, not least among the diverse constituency of parents whose interests were frequently invoked to justify education policy initiatives. There was much less agreement among these groups, however, about what a good curriculum would or should include, what kinds of teaching strategies were desirable and effective, or what was meant by transparency and what kinds of practices would provide accountability.[2]

The introduction of a province-wide curriculum, testing and reporting on students' achievement in terms of outcomes was justified in terms of accountability, both to parents and to "taxpayers" (a category that predictably appeared in government discourse whenever budget cuts and efficiency measures are introduced). The new curriculum, along with standardized tests and report cards, seemed to represent a substantial shift in both orientation and practice of teachers, a shift that was justified in order to create a "culture of improvement." For students, externally set norms of achievement lifted out particular aspects of learning (those that can be measured and accounted for through techniques of testing and reporting) which then came to stand in for everything worth doing and knowing in school.

Regimes of reporting and testing, no matter how objective and comprehensive they are designed to be, construe particular kinds of students as normative and good, while many students are positioned as beyond the norm (Burgess and Carter, 1992). The Ontario curriculum's strong emphasis on display of particular kinds of reasoning and problem-solving strategies naturalized notions of "the good and reasonable person" associated with the white, heterosexual middle class.[3] Definitions of what is normal, true and good were asserted in terms that appear to be outside political debate and beyond teachers' capacity for critical reason, as students' performance was to be mapped onto predesigned categories of assessment levels or outcomes. For teachers, these aspects of reform would seem to have profound implications for their view of learning and of children, as well as for their own work and professional identity and autonomy.

While parents were promised greater choice and involvement, and teachers were enticed with greater freedom and responsibility for designing their own teaching strategies, new daily and time-consuming monitoring and reporting practices ensured that learning and teaching were accounted for, and that outcomes were noted and explained. Self-observation and self-reflection are integral to the linked practices of freedom and monitoring, requiring teachers to engage in daily record keeping of students' activities and achievement, and to interrogate their own performance. These forms of accountability rely on and are successful to the extent that they engage individual workers – or teachers – in practices of self-regulation or self-government (du Gay, 1996; Popkewitz, 1998). That is not to say, however, that all teachers were, or continue to be, willing or able accomplices in these processes.

In schools, such regimes of observation and self-regulation can have profound effects, both on the learning and assessment of children and on the work and identities of teachers (Slee and Weiner, 1998). The push for greater accountability, focused on outcomes and more intrusive and regular auditing, testing and reporting procedures, reduces teachers' autonomy and professionalism (Sikes, 1992; Hextall and Mahony, 1998). Further, such techniques privilege certain kinds and terms of knowledge and learning and recognize certain groups of students as competent. Many forms of teaching and learning are thereby rendered invisible or irrelevant, while many students are marginalized or excluded from participation in "normal" activities and spaces of learning (Walkerdine, 1990; Carter and Burgess, 1993; Slee and Weiner, 1998). Such notions inform teachers' reasoning, for example, when they describe the limits of their capacity and responsibility, limits which have become more sharply drawn as schools have lost many of the resources dedicated to support "marginal" students. At the same time, the Ontario curriculum's testing and reporting procedures entailed increased pressure on teachers' time, leaving little time to work with students whose experience and learning differ from the norm (Ontario Secondary School Teachers' Federation, 2000).

Learning Reform: Becoming Change Agents?

When we first started discussing teachers' interview transcripts we were uncertain about what might "count" as informal learning in their talk. It seemed obvious, at one level, that as schools were changing, the people who work in them, including teachers, would learn to do their work in new ways and would be introduced to new ways of knowing and explaining teaching and learning to themselves and to others. At another level, it seemed that what and how teachers were learning involved something more than acquisition of skills and knowledge. It also involved changing their thinking about, and dispositions towards, teaching. Such fundamental relearning is referenced in research and policy in terms of the need to promote teacher development and to encourage a "cultural change" in schools. A discussion document issued by Ontario's Education Improvement Commission in 1997, entitled *The Road Ahead*, typifies such a vision of teachers and schools:

> In our classrooms there will be greater flexibility and interaction among colleagues. Staff will work increasingly as teams. The isolated teacher will become much less common, replaced by a staff team approach that provides for flexibility of grouping and timing based on the needs of students and the nature of the subject being learned. The focus at the school level will move from what is to be covered to how our higher standards of achievement can be achieved. (Education Improvement Commission, 1997: part 2)

This official text – and its title – conjures up a forward-looking teacher, engaged in progressive improvement efforts. This is a teacher who shares important features with those of the "entrepreneurial" subject of the market. It does not immediately follow, however, that teachers recognize themselves in these terms or that they want to become this teacher. In other words, the presence of a discourse, and the subject positions it provides, neither guarantees its effectiveness nor its "take-up" (Walkerdine, 1990). Indeed, a great deal of effort is required to induce teachers to alter their commitments towards the work they do and their identification with teaching. Moreover, there was and is dispute among researchers, policy makers, administrators and teachers about the best means and conditions to facilitate such a shift, thus opening up the very identity of teachers to scrutiny, regulation and struggle (see Hargreaves, 1994; Hargreaves and Goodson, 1996; Fullan and Hargreaves, 1992; Gitlin and Margonis, 1995).

The teachers who talked with us experienced extensive revisions of governing structures, curriculum and assessment practices, and increased pressures to improve the achievement of pupils. Each year since the mid-1990s, there were deep cuts to education budgets and attacks on teachers' collective agreements. And, while teacher unions and school boards were subjected to a great deal of criticism, teachers as individuals were repeatedly told that they are professionals, and invoked as the key agents, along with parents, of education reform. Thus, a number of quite contradictory discourses and conditions surrounded teachers at this time.

Alongside images of the dynamic, forward-looking and flexible professional "on the road ahead," another image of the teacher emerged in government-initiated school reforms and circulated in much of the media coverage of education in the 1990s. This teacher was one who is stuck in the past, has become complacent, and is incapable of adopting new knowledge and refuses to get on with the business of change. What did teachers make of these conflicting images, and how did they see themselves in relation to them?

The teachers in our study had much to say about the politics of school reform. They had strong views about how schools and teachers have been represented in media and government discourses. Their feelings of having been unjustly attacked; their anger and sense of distrust were palpable. One teacher expressed his frustration in these terms:

> But that's not fair so … all these things … and then all of a sudden you get attacked by everybody. You're not doing a good job. And all these things are telling you are not doing a good job. … And to me it's sad, because teaching is a great thing. (Teacher interview #3, August 1999)

Another teacher angrily dismissed attacks on teachers as lies:

> [The government is] lying, they're casting aspersions on teachers, it's slanderous, it's libellous and it makes me angry. I feel powerless to do anything about it. It makes me often wish I were doing anything other than teaching. (Teacher interview #6, July 1999)

One government initiative to which teachers kept returning was Bill 160, a massive piece of legislation introduced in September 1997. It had the effect of centralizing control of curriculum and financial decisions in the Ministry of Education. In opposition to this Bill, Ontario's teacher unions joined together to organize an unprecedented walkout by all of the province's teachers (except those in private schools) in the fall of that year. Lasting for 2 weeks, the scale of and support for this action was massive – both among teachers and among parents (see Hargreaves, 1998). Yet the way the teacher unions' leadership ended the walkout and the lack of any apparent impact on the government's education agenda, left teachers in this study feeling angry, cynical or demoralized.

Teachers talked of this event with mixed feelings. They were proud to be part of an important political event. They were nostalgic for a sense of identification with teachers as a large and powerful group, a feeling that they had subsequently lost. There was also regret and disappointment not least because the outcome of this protest was unsuccessful – Bill 160 was passed into law. One teacher said that

> I would say that the biggest change has been a sense of demoralization among teachers in general. … Bill 160 had thrown everything into a sense of not knowing – where we're at, where we can go, what it is possible to hope for. (Teacher interview #6, July 1999)

On top of the sense of disillusion that not even such a massive mobilization could influence the government, this teacher's comment alludes to another theme in the interviews. One effect of the late nineties wave of reform was uncertainty and fear; teachers did not know who to trust, what was expected of them or what would happen next. It was as though teachers saw themselves as the main victims of reform. Teachers expressed this in different ways often with reference to deteriorating conditions and sinking morale among their colleagues.

> The morale too, in general, the school environment … it's below zero. Teachers are not that happy. The program is not that good. There are not enough books. We don't have science books. They said they were gonna give us money for equipment … I look at the report card … pathetic. They want me to teach music, drama, I mean come on. Too much is too much. … I can't teach music … I don't know anything about music. O.K. I can talk to another teacher who knows about music, I teach their kids computer, they teach mine music, that's fine. (Teacher interview #3, August 1999)

The 1997 protest represented a strong show of collective organization and union power. Yet, several teachers talked about the unions in conflicting ways. While they identified strongly with teachers as a group and supported the protest, they positioned the union at a distance and "out of touch" with the frustrations and stress of teachers' daily work. And beyond the identification with strong collective power derived through the protest, the preferred self-image in several teachers' talk was as members of a profession who deserved respect and trust because of their knowledge and status. In some ways, it seemed as if "official" efforts to address teachers as individuals and to isolate them from unions were effective. However, if we recall our earlier discussion of how discourses provide a range of often contradictory identities and of how people's engagement with or "take up" of identities are complex and ambivalent, we would suggest that teachers made sense of themselves, their belonging and identification, in ways that do not neatly cohere around clear notions of "professional" or "union" categories.

To demonstrate the unfairness of attacks on teachers, some teachers used discourses of professionalism to assert another, more positive, self-image. They compared their treatment to that of other professionals: doctors were preferred as a group that would not be subjected to such criticism and scrutiny. Teachers felt insulted by government and media descriptions but they also talked about how the climate of distrust surrounding schools and teachers had created conditions where parents were more outspoken and demanding.

> And I find it insulting and offensive for somebody to take that attitude. And I know that they would never go into their doctor's office and say "well I think you should do this when you see your patients". They would never do that. That would be rude and offensive, but they do that to teachers. (Teacher interview #5, July 1999)

Contrasting teaching as a profession and teaching as unionized work has a long and contentious history. The claim of professionalism has operated to regulate teachers at least as much as it has protected them from "intrusion" into their domain and expertise by various "outsiders" (Robertson and Smaller, 1996). Moreover, discourses of professionalism also operate to separate teachers from the communities in which they teach, identifying "the teacher" in middle-class and white terms of reason and respectability. To the extent that such notions continue to shape teachers' sense of self, it is not surprising that parents' suggestions about what and how to teach would be viewed with suspicion. At a time when governments, regulatory bodies and researchers appeal to individual teachers' professionalism to win their consent for initiatives and programmes, those very same agencies imposed ever more detailed control of teachers' work, while reducing the resources available to them. As one teacher said, "I'm quite displeased with education and it's because now it's, 'this is the programme, this is what we have to do, sit down and we must get through it' " (Teacher interview #5, July 1999). A second strategy the teachers used to claim a professional identity was to compare the view of present day teachers with an earlier and more respectful position they (presumably) enjoyed in the past. One teacher with 20 years' experience said:

> When I started teaching, I was amazed that they paid me to do what I was doing. I want to keep that. I don't have as many days as that anymore, but I still have them, and I would very much like to finish this teaching career and say, they paid me to do this. ... And this is my work and I love it, but there's a life beyond this. (Teacher interview #9, April 2000)

Other teachers expressed a sense of having to negotiate conflicting and increasing expectations that they themselves, or earlier generations of teachers, were not subjected to in the past. One teacher, who was relatively new to teaching, explained her feeling of vulnerability when people "bombarded" her with questions when they "discovered" that she was a teacher:

> And yet I'm very proud of what I do. But all of a sudden, people out there are ... attacking the profession, and I no longer felt ... you know, as proud about what I was doing. And I felt like I had to defend everything. And that ... I think the ... a lot of people out there really don't know what we do in the classroom. And I think for the first time, I started to realize that. (Teacher interview #8, August 1999)

Another teacher who was teaching in a school in the central part of the city went on at some length about the tensions between deteriorating conditions in the school and the "sudden" changes in the perception and expectations of teachers:

> Because all of a sudden, the government is saying we don't have money for anything. ... This job is becoming very stressful because everybody is so demanding. The principal comes to you and they want special things or projects to please their bosses and to please the parents. And the parents, the SAC [School Advisory Council] want something. And then the teachers want you to do something because they want to put the students first. And they can't do so much because you are called in every direction everyday ... here your life and work goes home with you. (Teacher interview #3, August 1999)

Here we see one of the themes of Total Quality Management – putting the "consumer" first – although perhaps not in a way that this discourse might have envisioned. Rather than providing a clear map for achieving quality, a great deal of confusion and stress result as this teacher (and other teachers in the study) attempted to sort out conflicting expectations and new lines of accountability.

These interviews explicitly sought out teachers' reactions to what we might call the politics of reform "out there." Some seemed to relish the opportunity to vent their frustrations on this topic with us. At the same time, some suggested that teachers had few opportunities and little time or inclination to discuss school reform with their colleagues. Their focus was on their work in the classroom:

> [W]e're so involved, too, with the teaching and the kids, there isn't really a lot of time to sit and talk about this, sometimes morning recess or before school, and then we really have to teach. You have to program and you have all the work that's involved. Now we're involved in a physical move. I would say that we tend to deal with the job, and think about these things just periodically. It's not on our mind all the time, no. Especially when things are running more or less smoothly. (Teacher interview #11, June 2000)

The teacher quoted above was interviewed at the end of the study, 3 years after the protests against Bill 160, when many concrete effects of reform had been worked into the curriculum and organization of schools. While this interview might suggest that teachers' critique of government-imposed reforms was becoming more muted, the transcript segment is also organized around a familiar set of oppositions between "the kids" and "politics," between "teaching" and "sitting around" talking about "these things." Not surprisingly, several teachers described their daily work in terms of "getting on with it." To do this, it was necessary to avoid complaining and to isolate oneself from others who complain, including teacher unions and many colleagues. One teacher, who was disillusioned with both "the government" and "the federation," referred in negative terms to the staff room as a site of "complaints."

> I'm not going to complain. I avoid going into the staff room because the talk is usually negative there ... I think a lot of teachers go in and just let their steam off and then they go back to putting on their happy face again ... but that's just not my scene. (Teacher interview #2, July 1998)

Isolation from colleagues becomes a strategy for managing daily work. Some aspects of discourses of derision can also be seen here, insofar as teachers' concerns and criticisms are dismissed as "negative" and "not my scene." At the same time, however, there is some recognition that teachers – even this teacher – did have cause for "letting off steam" and that many teachers wear a mask, a "happy face," in the classroom. Teachers worked very hard to negotiate a space for themselves in these kinds of contrasting accounts, in different contexts, and with different effects.

Learning to Account for Yourself

The teachers in this study described in vivid detail how they sought to manage and adjust to a new curriculum, testing and report cards, and increased expectations from parents to be involved and informed. As we have said earlier, these descriptions were produced against a backdrop of unfair criticism, demoralization, and diminishing resources. Training or professional development were sporadic and uneven from school to school: principals in the two schools located in middle-class areas were more proactive in this respect. Parent groups in these schools were more successful in raising funds that could be used to provide teachers with "extras," such as computers and printers in each classroom for their use. Thus, teachers were provided with different conditions for carrying out routine aspects of their work. While we cannot generalize from these impressions, they do suggest that a structure which "devolves" many decisions, particularly those concerned with resource allocations, to each school has the potential to increase social and educational inequalities (Gewirtz et al., 1995).

In these different contexts, teachers actively worked "old" approaches to teaching into expectations that the new curriculum subjected them to. One aspect of their work, which we asked them to comment on in some detail, was the introduction of a new outcomes-based curriculum and a standardized report card. Some of the teachers agonized over how to balance caring and nurturing ways to be with students and the new curriculum's emphasis on performance and outcomes. While ostensibly providing teachers with freedom and responsibility to devise their own methods for meeting the curriculum's expectations, teachers' descriptions of how they felt they had to change their approach to teaching were remarkably consistent. They had less time for project and group work, very little time to repeat and reinforce lessons, almost no "social time" with children, and their teaching styles were becoming more teacher – and curriculum – centred.

Some of the teachers were reluctant to abandon the old in favour of the new. Rather, as Carter and Burgess (1993) found in their research with English teachers adopting the National Curriculum in the late 1980s, they sought to integrate different ways of teaching and evaluating. For some, this was a process of trial and error. One teacher described the process of teaching with the new math curriculum for the first time:

> We were just, well me and another grade 6 teacher, we were just scrambling trying to figure out how to implement this program with no resources and the grade 6 was a totally different way of thinking, it's.. more applied, the skills, into a question. (Teacher interview #5, July 1999)

Other teachers also described collaborative relationships with colleagues, particularly those teaching the same grade levels, as they pieced together materials and programmes. Working backwards from the outlines in the different curriculum "strands" and the expectations detailed as concepts to be "mastered" or "competencies" or "skills" to perform, teachers incorporated familiar approaches with new, invented or found, materials. In many ways, the new curriculum appeared open and flexible, inviting innovation and adaptation:

> Well I think at least the curriculum … leaves you open for taking … The curriculum is not so, is not as structured as the grade 3 testing. So the curriculum, you know, as a teacher, you can pick out different aspects that you want to teach, and you can … like I would have no problem modifying it so that my kids understand what concept I'm teaching to what they, you know, what their sort of background is or level and trying to relate that into it, into the curriculum as well and doing (those) parallels.

> So at least the curriculums are a little bit more flexible. I mean it looks like it's not, but there's a lot you can actually do with it. (Teacher interview #7, November 1999)

While the new curriculum provided teachers with some freedom to develop their own pedagogy and programme that would enable students in their classes to perform as well as possible, teachers also talked about having fewer choices, less time and insufficient resources. Thus, the same teacher who approved of the flexibility in the new curriculum went on to characterize the report cards as rigid and formulaic:

> But they give you this formula, you know, and you feel as though … you have to abide by it, or you're not truly reflect … or the child isn't being truly, the marks don't truly reflect the child, and yet it's hard, because all these faces in front of you are so different.

Some explained that whereas they believed in project and activity-oriented teaching approaches, along with a child-centred pedagogy especially popular amongst teachers of younger children, the new curriculum had forced them to abandon these strategies. Moreover, several lamented that the demanding expectations of new curriculum afforded them little time for repetition or to provide weaker students with extra support. In fact, it seemed that a curriculum that appears to offer teachers more flexibility is generating more commonality in teaching, with more teacher-centred pedagogy and curriculum-driven organization of teachers' and students' time. The same teacher who earlier described how she was able to design her own approach later described her frustration with lack of time, particularly for "those little things:"

> [F]or the last year, that's been my hardest, that's been my biggest challenge, is finding time for all those little things. And I think that's what's sad. I mean, we're caught up in making sure that we get everything done in this curriculum, we're caught up (in) making sure that I get this grade 3 testing under way. You know, (everybody's) caught up in all these things and you tend, especially to those students who do lack the confidence or lack … just, you know, a good feeling about themselves … I've had children in this classroom who, you know, it tears my heart out to see what's going on. (Teacher interview #7, November 1999)

Working in urban schools where children's lives and schooling experiences are structured through poverty and racism, teachers encounter many children who do not easily fit the normative student identity around whom the new curriculum and its tests and report cards have been shaped. The mostly nineties wave of reform in Ontario not only ignored these students, but constructed them as outside the norm of expectations, different and marginal even before they enter school (Goldstein, 1998; see also Popkewitz, 2000). At the same time, schools lost many of the supports designed for students with disabilities or special needs, those whose first language is not English or French, and boards had to cut budgets for teaching assistants. Moreover, in the name of distributing resources more "equally" across the province, urban schools have been stripped of resources to fund precisely those programmes that sought to support these students and render their education more equitable. Several teachers in the study were quite explicit about how the curriculum, and the time available to get through it, defined clear limits of their capacity to support struggling students. It was also clear that race, ethnicity and class organized teachers' descriptions and explanations of who these students were. The teachers who talked with us therefore worried a great deal about the cumulative effects of reforms on students who were being further marginalized, and felt that they were less able to assist them now than in the past. However, while teachers lamented the loss of resources, some also mobilized discourses of inadequate families, poor parenting or unsupportive communities to explain that schools and teachers could "only do so much" to assist a child.

When they described the more social and pastoral aspects of education it was, as the teacher above suggests, as though they were conspiring with students to "steal" time away from the curriculum to enjoy a good story or reflect on a sad event. These crucial dimensions of teaching and learning relationships simply do not "count" and cannot be counted in how students' achievement is measured in relation to the new, skills-based curriculum. At the same time, this "social" and "caring" dimension of teachers' work and working identity, historically associated with the figure of the woman teacher, must be subordinated to the image of the efficient and organized teacher who can cover the curriculum and whose students can meet expectations. The notion that "too much" was expected of teachers in the way of "social" support and learning circulated quite widely in government reports and media, making it reasonable to identify the "real" work of teaching – and the core of teachers' identity – in terms of the explicit curriculum and its expectations.

Reporting and Accounting

As we have suggested, not all of the teachers adopted self-descriptions provided in contemporary reform discourses. Even those who tried to do so seemed to have difficulty producing a coherent account of themselves and their work in these terms. The provincial report cards, whose use became mandatory during the first year of this study, provide an illustration of these ambivalences. The report cards were a source of huge frustration and pressure, and completing them involved a great deal of teachers' time. Indeed, during report card time it was impossible to schedule teacher interviews, as every available minute was spent on this task. For some teachers, particularly those who wanted to maintain what they described as a "more personal" approach while also doing well within the terms of the new curriculum, filling in the report cards involved a great deal of time and effort:

> I find just writing the report cards very exhausting. I … You know, they say you don't have to fill up the box, but I do. Sometimes I need to go to a smaller font just to get across what I want to say and I think … the feedback I've received from the parents so far, and this is throughout my writing of report cards, has been very positive. They feel that when they pick up the report card, they get a clear perspective of where the child is at and how that child is doing, and I think that truly comes out of the anecdotals, though. (Teacher interview #8, August 1999)

While completing the report cards is an exhausting exercise, positive responses from parents provide teachers with some reward. At the same time, however, seeking recognition from parents was not always a positive experience. Among the middle class, the anecdotal descriptions that teachers included on the cards were appreciated but they were not sufficient. To this teacher's dismay, some parents also wanted to know how their children compared with other students in her class:

> And that's what I get, I get … parents will come to me and say, well given where this, the grades on this report card, how does my child compete with the rest of the students in the class? Is the child doing … where everyone else is, or are there students in the classroom that are really A+ students, and given that my child isn't doing as well, or … that's what, they come with that question a lot, I find. (Teacher interview #8, August 1999)

Comparing, differentiating and ranking are integral to systems of many forms of assessment and reporting, particularly those that produce grades. Regardless of how they might view their merit (or otherwise), teachers, students and parents become complicit in such ranking practices, particularly in contexts where the "perform-ance" of students and of schools are vested with high stakes and publicized results and comparisons. Nevertheless, teachers' views of the curriculum and report cards were not wholly negative. Some teachers invoked the interests of parents, as well as teachers, to suggest that they represented an improvement:

> For me, for report cards, I think they're trying to make it universal, for right across the province, which in a way is good for, as a parent or as a teacher when you move from one school to another (that) it is exactly the same, so you're not learning a new report system. And parents can also look at it and understand most of it. (Teacher interview #5, July 1999)

But even this teacher, who was quite positive about the report cards and confident about his ability to use them, found their format too prescriptive:

> Only problem with the report card, it becomes very prescriptive, in that we have certain language that is already given us, so it's no longer ... personalized for towards the student. I find them easy to do. It doesn't take me very long to do a set of report cards, as compared to other people. (Teacher interview #5, July 1999)

This teacher attributed his competence with report cards to his computer literacy. A further segment from his transcript suggests that the ability to "cut and paste" with aid of the computer became a key skill for teachers, replacing (at least for this teacher) the "personalized" evaluation and description of each student required in the old report card:

> I'm quite computer-literate so I know how to use it, I know how to cut and paste, and because it's so prescriptive, it's ... if you were an A student, these are the comments that you get. And then you just cut and paste for all A students. And if you were a B student, there are key terms, all the time, most of the time, some of the time, and so that little word just changes for an A, B, C, D student. So, I think depending on the teacher and how they organize themselves for the report card, you could actually do it in a day. It could be that simple. Because you have your grades ... and if it's an A student then that student just gets all these comments. And you just cut and paste.

> So for me, I find them much easier than the old ones to do, because before it had to be very personalized and you'd have to go into all the different skills that the child could or couldn't do ... and also look at social behaviours and interactions. Now, it's very specific outcomes, and ... so I could easily do it in a weekend, and not complain. Where other teachers are probably griping about it. (Teacher interview #5, July 1999)

While this account may seem rather brazen, it also captures something about the move to a curriculum based on skills and "outcomes" and to modes of assessment and reporting that rely on computer technology. While our study was quite small, gendered patterns nevertheless emerged in teachers' talk about the report cards. This was partly related to computer skills, where two of the men we interviewed described how they functioned as unofficial computer "experts" in their schools. For other teachers, having access to and learning to use a computer and the report card software presented a substantial challenge, particularly during the first year. A woman teacher describes her frustrations:

> I: Mm. I want to jump back to report cards. How did you learn how to do report cards? How did you get yourself computer-literate ... or?

T: I don't even know if I am really quite yet. I mean, I've got the discs now and I'm going to call my sister up [laughs] and say, OK, I press this button and I do this and, because, you know, we just got a new computer at home, but … I had a horrible experience at this time last year, because I had to work here at school because my computer at home wouldn't take the information because we were … in the process of getting a new computer. And they would, all of a sudden like, you'd be working on them and it'd be like 5, 6:00 at night, we have to shut down the computers because there's a glitch. Or, something's happened … and so you had.. to go home. And that's so defeating. (Teacher interview #7, November 1999)

We do not want to imply that women teachers are not skilled computer users. Some women described themselves as quite computer literate. One woman in particular was very proactive in seeking out professional development in this area. However, the men teachers made it clear that their proficiency was well recognized in the school, while women seemed less inclined (or perhaps less able) to display their computer skills as an asset to be rewarded. Thus, gender may be at work in how women and men teachers' skills are differentially recognized (see Acker, 1997; Hubbard and Datnow, 2000).

Making a Self by Distancing from the Other

Earlier we suggested that teachers invoked several strategies to compare the stresses of the present with an often nostalgic vision of the past, and to contrast the criticism and control of teachers with the high regard and autonomy presumably enjoyed by other professionals. We turn now to how the teachers made use of strategies of recognition, identification and disidentification, or alignment and disavowal (Britzman, 1991) to construct desirable self-images. In linguistic terms, we can see how teachers were actively "working through" (Farrell, 2000) several discourses, in order to shape new identities that can work for them in changing education environment. These identities, however, are neither as entrepreneurial as some accounts of new workplace identities more generally would suggest (du Gay, 1996; Miller and Rose, 1995; Rose, 1996a) nor are they as closely aligned with reform as school "improvers" and government officials might wish.

Let us consider how one teacher used contrasting descriptions to locate herself as hard-working, efficient and good. She, too, associated the staff room, the space where she might interact with her colleagues, as a place to avoid, except when she was required to attend the Friday morning staff meeting:

I spend my recesses here [the classroom] and I spend my lunch hour in my room. I'm here every morning. I don't go to the staff room except Friday morning I go. I go out once a week for lunch, maybe. The rest of the time I'm in this classroom from 8 in the morning till usually 4:15–4:30. (Teacher interview #9, May 2000)

In this self-description of the teacher at work in the classroom all day, through the lunch hour, she both conveys her commitment to her work and sets up a contrast between herself and her colleagues. Thus, she continues:

> [P]eople cannot whine, you cannot whine if you don't have enough time because you're
> taking an extra half hour for sleep. I take my time out of sleeping time in order to have time
> to get everything done so. ... I think you have to watch and plan. And some people, if you
> were one of those that have to go home and have a nap after school, well then maybe
> you should stay in at lunch and do your work if you're not going to get it done at night.
> (Teacher interview #9, May 2000)

The good teacher, then, watches, plans and manages her time, even sacrificing her sleep to get her work done. In contrast, teachers who complain about not being able to get their work done can be rejected – along with the substance of their claims. They are, in her account, the cause of their own problems by being unable, or unwilling, to make efficient use of their time. A bit later in the conversation, she returns to this rather unfavourable description of her colleagues:

> [At] this school – people get here very late. Like they don't arrive too early here, on the
> most part. There are some of us here before 8 in the morning, Many people come in at 8:30
> and we start here at 8:45. I don't know how they organize their lives. (Teacher interview
> #9, May 2000)

Time – its extent, use, allocation, regulation and management – takes on a significant weight in how she describes herself. She emphasizes her efficient use of time, along with her continuous presence in the classroom, as concrete and practical evidence of her identity as a hard-working professional. The effort that goes into the management of time and organization of space is a visible marker of what Adkins and Lury (1999) call "the labour of identity." At the same time, we are aware that in the context of an interview with university-based education researchers, teachers might be inclined to portray themselves in flattering ways. It may be a situation where an individual would draw attention to her good qualities through an exaggerated contrast between her efficient self and the lacks she identifies in her complaining and not-quite dedicated or energetic colleagues. The interview may be a site where identity is not only laboured, but belaboured.

Nevertheless, this teacher's strategy of aligning herself with a rigorous work ethic and her description of disavowal of pleasure or leisure is not unique. Indeed, teachers, and particularly women teachers, have been actively encouraged to view themselves in this way, with representations of the woman teacher as self-sacrificing and dedicated, shaping discourses of education since the inception of formal schooling (see Prentice and Theobald, 1991; Steedman, 1985; Britzman, 1991; Dehli, 1994).

This teacher also provided some insight into the extraordinary effort that goes into producing or "performing" the identity of the professional woman teacher. Here, she is not wholly unsympathetic to the plight of those whose labour goes unrewarded or who, in her words, have been "forced to swallow" a "very bitter pill":

> I've seen many people who have not been able to maintain that perspective, and
> this has become a very bitter pill that they've been forced to swallow. ... And I
> don't want that, because I think you infect everyone that you deal with. It affects
> the children and it can infect them. And I don't want that. (Teacher interview #9,
> April 2000)

Medical metaphors were used by teachers in other contexts as well. One teacher considered the staff-room a place of risk from contagion, where a complaining or negative attitude might "rub off" on him. Other teachers, in different schools, indicated that they also avoided the staff room for similar reasons. Such statements may seem to lack empathy, but they may also suggest some insight into colleagues who suffer physical illness and psychological strain. Perhaps there is fear that they, too, might succumb to the pressures unless they maintain their focus and efficiency, avoiding contact with those so afflicted. References to the school and the staff-room as spaces of danger and to colleagues as "contagious" may also speak to anxieties and disavowal of those who are seen as different and deficient in reform discourses. Such statements also make visible a view of the self that demands independence, self-sufficiency and individual freedom and responsibility. In one sense, the "choice" to isolate oneself from the social and collegial contexts of the school echoes with the rhetoric of neoliberalism and its elaboration of the autonomous, risk-taking and flexible entrepreneurial subject (du Gay, 1996). In another sense, however, it works against notions of collegiality and teamwork that are also central to education reform. Moreover, the notion that a teacher has the capacity to "rise above" her colleagues, unencumbered by a body that might feel stress or failure and disassociated from the social conditions of her workplace, suggests an investment in an impossible fiction (Walkerdine, 1990).

These interviews provide a glimpse into the possibly substantial health effects involved in "making yourself up" as the autonomous and change-oriented teacher privileged in recent education reforms. Indeed, the depth of insecurity, anxiety and stress that were generated for some teachers surprised us.[4] And while schools and teachers as a group may appear to outsiders as collegial and mutually supportive, the teachers who talked with us about struggling with their work felt that they had individually "failed." For some, it was as though their adjustment – or inability to adjust – to new conditions was literally learned through the body as stress, ill health and failure.

For one teacher, the reforms seemed to generate a diffuse sense of anxiety and insecurity about his ability to perform. In the interview he returned several times, in different ways, to his insecurity about whether and how he could become – and be viewed as – a "good" or "good enough" teacher.

> [The reforms] are a bit cumbersome. … I'm going to have to see how good I am at it. To tell you the truth, I feel as though there are more demands now on me to teach better and still evaluate all those strands. I think I'll have to be more skilled so I'll have to see whether I'm good at it or not. (Teacher interview #2, July 1998)

This teacher told us that he was actively looking for a way out of teaching. Another teacher attributed negative effects on her health to increased stress in the job:

> I've been sick … and I'm a healthy person. I play hockey, I play football, I walk the dog every day. I don't drink coffee, all those things, I don't smoke. I should be a healthy person. But I'm not. … I'm always tired. (Teacher interview #7, November 1999)

A third teacher also complained about the growing pressures of work and worried about the effects on her health:

> I thought, I'm going to take [the summer] off [...] and yet when the summer hit, the first
> two weeks my body just crashed. And ... so I realized that from September to June I put
> my life on hold. Because you know, it's work, work, work, this has to get done. [...] My
> social calendar revolves around what I need to do in terms of schoolwork. (Teacher inter-
> view # 8, August 1999)

While she did dwell on her health and her doubts about her capacity to "cope," thus
framing what she was feeling as her individual problem, this teacher (along with
others) also felt that she would have benefited from workshops, thus indicating that
her predicament might be shared with other teachers. Several teachers complained
about the availability and quality of workshops related to the new report:

> I find that we have had very little training at this point. Now whether there will be training
> in the future, I don't know. [...] [S]o I find just the writing of the report cards is exhausting.
> (Teacher interview # 8, August 1999)

In relation to the new curriculum, another teacher also commented on the lack of
training and resources:

> The curriculum ... there were just so many different topics that we just couldn't even
> address in the one year. I'm sure you heard about the math program. [laughs] Some of the
> math program alone caused enough irate parents and myself, because there was just no
> training, it was just given to us and said, do it, and then we received one day and six hours,
> now you're fully into it, and then, I think six months later there was a workshop after
> school, to learn more about it, so. (Teacher interview #5, July 1999)

Conclusion

The changes brought about through education reforms in the 1990s accord in many
ways with forward-looking and modern "devolved" and neoliberal forms of
governance, in so far as they targeted the general conduct of individuals, seeking to
create conditions where people were provided with a range of opportunities to
practice "freedom," become "agents of change" and make choices. At the same
time, the devolution of choice and freedom also entailed having to take local and
individual responsibility for the choices that are made and the risks that are taken
(du Gay, 1996; Robertson, 1999; Rose, 1996a). Our reading of transcripts of these
teacher interviews suggest that reform and restructuring of schools introduced new
modes of regulation of teachers and their work. Informal learning, along with
injunctions for schools to become "learning organizations" and for teachers to
become "lifelong learners," continue to operate through the details of reform,
enlisting teachers to become subjects in their own governance. In particular, the
skills-based curriculum and the ways in which students' learning must be accounted
for, brought about an important set of shifts in teachers' daily work. Yet, reform
remains elusive and teachers engage in many forms of subversion and resistance.

The effectiveness of reform cannot simply be explained with reference to
increased external control or loss of autonomy, although introduction of centralized
legislative power, budget cuts and restructuring of governance were (and are), of

course, tremendously important and keenly felt by teachers. Similarly, the range of teachers' responses to reform cannot be fully appreciated through frameworks that focus on compliance or resistance, or that take teachers' political or professional mobilizations through their unions as the only evidence of their positions. We do not pretend that our study provides a complete picture, and doubt if such a vision is either possible or desirable. However, by attending to "governmental" forms of power and by interpreting teachers' interviews, we suggest that recent reforms have required that teachers themselves become engaged as "agents of change," but that they do so in complicated and unpredictable ways.

In different ways, these teachers expressed strong disagreement with the provincial government and distrust of their initiatives. Nevertheless, as they described their work, their teaching methods and their assessment practices, it became clear that they could not avoid reform altogether. Reform shaped their work and their identities, even when they strongly disagreed with its goals and methods. Moreover, several teachers described social relations in schools in ways that suggest that democratic and open discussion is very rare (Sarason, 1996), they are contrived (Hargreaves, 1991), or they are dismissed as a futile exercise in complaint. At the same time, some teachers were clearly struggling, individually and in isolation, to "cope" with an increased workload, an ever more tightly regulated schedule, and with contradictory approaches to curriculum and teaching. While it is important to attend to "public" or official politics of reform, many of the apparently non-political features of the curriculum, testing and reporting procedures could have an equally important impact on schools and children, and these features, we argue, also involve new ways for teachers to account for, and identify, themselves.

In many ways, the skills-based curriculum and the increased emphasis on testing and reporting, all administered at a distance from the provincial government by a non-elected agency of experts, provides an ideal example of neoliberal government. While there has been a change in political government in Ontario since we conducted this study, the features of neoliberal government that we have discussed here continue to organize teaching and learning. Teachers make choices and take responsibility for them in their everyday work; in this sense reform is a mode of government that works through the regulation of teachers as "free" subjects, a freedom which these teachers both cherished and lamented. This is how it is worked out in schools. While options are made available for teachers, it also entails individual risk and responsibility for failure.

In these contexts, then, teachers must work through competing discourses and expectations, a process that also involves (among other dimensions) attempts to negotiate, live or "perform" particular, and in some ways conflicting, identities. Moreover, this emphasis on the individual teacher whose performance has become more transparent and closely monitored appears to have led some teachers to isolate themselves from their colleagues, the teachers' unions and from some of the students they teach, particularly those whose performance does not meet "normal" expectations. While some of the teachers we interviewed relished their new freedoms, they were also frustrated by the lack of resources to realize them and with the ways they were made individually responsible for students' or their own "failures." In some ways, the pressures between growing expectations and limited resources, along with the emphasis on individual responsibility and risk, might contribute to some teachers needing to demonstrate their efficiency and success by distancing themselves from their colleagues, while relinquishing responsibility for precisely those students who need them most. These are two areas where markers of difference such as race, class, age and gender, of teachers and students, may come into play in powerful ways (Popkewitz, 1998; Schick, 2000).

Based on this small study (as well as the larger project of which it is a part) we would speculate that the extent and ways in which teachers are able to gain recognition as "change agents" are intertwined with how schools produce and reproduce social relations of power and teachers' different positionings in these relations. We would imagine that how teachers are positioned in gender and racial orders, for example, has consequences for how their efforts to shape new identities are interpreted, whether they are rewarded, ignored, pitied or viewed with suspicion and fear. Furthermore, it also seems that the location of schools, and teachers' common-sense knowledge of schools' populations, have considerable impact on what kinds of reforms, and the expectations they entail, teachers consider appropriate or relevant. While this study considered teachers in relative isolation from such contexts and concerns, future research would need to explore the effects of education reform on teachers' identities, on students and on the social landscapes within and beyond schools.

Endnotes

[1] Doreen Fumia conducted this small study as a follow-up to a larger project (funded by SSHRC with Kari Dehli as PI) that focused on parental involvement in Toronto schools. In addition to Doreen, Anne Bradbury, Grace Puja, Leeno Karamanchery and Karyn Sandlos also worked as research assistants on that project.

[2] Again, see newsletters and web sites of teacher organizatons, as well as groups such as People for Education, Metro Parents Network and the Ontario Parents Council.

[3] For the US, see Popkewitz (1998); for England, see Slee et al., (1998); Epstein and Johnson (1998).

[4] See Blackmore (2000) and Acker (1997, 1999) for feminist research that confirm such impressions.

References

Acker, S., 1997, Primary school teacher's work: the response to educational reform, in G. Helsby & G. McCulloch (Eds.), *Teachers and the National Curriculum*, Cassell, London.

Acker, S., 1999, *The Realities of Teachers' Work: Never a Dull Moment*, Cassell, London/ New York.

Adkins, L. & Lury, C., 1999, The labour of identity: performing identities, performing economies, *Economy and Society*, **28(4)**: 598–614.

Avis, J., 1999, Shifting identity: new conditions and the transformation of practice – teaching within post-compulsory education, *Journal of Vocational Education and Training*, **51(2)**: 245–264.

Ball, S.J., 1994, *Education Reform: A Critical and Post-Structuralist Approach*, Open University Press, Buckingham.

Barnett, C., 1999, Culture, government and spatiality: reassessing the "Foucault effect" in cultural-policy studies, *International Journal of Cultural Studies*, **2(3)**: 369–397.

Blackmore, J., 2000, *Troubling Women: Feminism, Leadership and Educational Change*, Open University Press, Buckingham.

Britzman, D., 1991, *Practice Makes Practice: A Critical Study of Learning to Teach*, State University of New York Press, New York.

Burgess, H. & Carter, B., 1992, "Bringing out the best in people": teacher training and the "real" teacher, *British Journal of Sociology of Education*, **13(3)**: 349–359.

Carter, B. & Burgess, H., 1993, Testing, regulation and control: shifting education narratives, *Curriculum Studies*, **1(2)**: 233–244.

Carter, K., 1998, School effectiveness and school improvement: meanings and traditions, in R. Halsall (Ed.), *Teacher Research and School Improvement: Opening Doors from the Inside*, Open University Press, Buckingham.

Church, K., Fontan, J.M., Ng, R. & Shragge, E., 2000, *Social Learning Among People Excluded from the Labour Market, Part One: Context and Case Studies*, Network for New Approaches to Lifelong Learning (NALL), Toronto, Canada.

Coldron, J. & Smith, R., 1999, Active location in teachers' construction of their professional identities, *Journal of Curriculum Studies*, **31(6)**: 711–726.

Crozier, G., 2000, *Parents and Schools: Partners or Protagonists?* Trentham Books, Stoke on Trent.

Deem, R., 1990, The reform of school governing bodies: the power of the consumer over the producer? In M. Flude and M. Hammer (Eds.), *The 1988 Education Reform Act: Its Origins and Implications*, Falmer Press, London.

Deem, R., Brehony, K.J. & Heath, S., 1996, *Active Citizenship and the Governing of Schools*, Open University Press, Buckingham.

Dehli, K., 1994, "They Rule by Sympathy": women and moral regulation in 19th century kindergarten pedagogy, *The Journal of Canadian Sociology*, **19(2)**: 195–216.

Dehli, K., 1996, Travelling tales: education reform and parental 'choice' in postmodern times, *Journal of Education Policy*, **11(1)**: 75–88.

Dehli, K., 1998, Shopping for schools: the future of education in Ontario? *Orbit*, **29(1)**: 29–33.

du Gay, P., 1996, *Consumption and Identity at Work*, Sage, London.

Education Improvement Commission, 1997, The Road Ahead: A Report on Learning Time, Class Size and Staffing, Education Improvement Commission, Toronto, Canada.

Epstein, D. & Johnson, R., 1998, *Schooling Sexualities*, Open University Press, Buckingham.

Farrell, L., 2000, Ways of doing, ways of being: language, education and "working" identities, *Language and Education*, **14(1)**: 18–36.

Foucault, M., 1990, *Power/Knowledge: Selected Interviews and other Writings 1972–1977*, Colin Gordon (Ed.), Pantheon, New York.

Foucault, M., 1991, Governmentality, in G. Burchell, C. Gordon & P. Miller (Eds.), *The Foucault Effect: Studies in Governmentality*, University of Chicago Press, Chicago.

Fullan, M. & Hargreaves, A. (Eds.), 1992, *Teacher Development and Educational Change*, in *Teacher Development and Educational Change*, Falmer Press, London.

Gewirtz, S., Ball, S. & Bowe, R., 1995, *Markets, Choice and Equity in Education*, Open University Press, Buckingham.

Gidney, R.D., 1999, *From Hope to Harris: the Reshaping of Ontario Schools*, University of Toronto Press, Toronto.

Gillborn, D., 1999, Race, nation and education: new labour and the new racism, in J. Demaine (Ed.), *Education Policy and Contemporary Politics*, Macmillan, London.

Gitlin, A. & Margonis, F., 1995, The political aspect of reform: teacher resistance as good sense, *American Journal of Education*, **103**: 377–405.

Goldstein, T., 1998, Working Toward Equity, *Orbit*, **29(1)**: 14–16.

Gordon, C., 1991, Governmental rationality: an introduction, in G. Burchell, C. Gordon & P. Miller (Eds.), *The Foucault Effect: Studies in Governmentality*, University of Chicago Press, Chicago.

Hall, S., 1996, Introduction: who needs "identity"? In S. Hall & P. du Gay (Eds.), *Questions of Cultural Identity*, Sage, London.

Hargreaves, A., 1994, *Changing Teachers, Changing Times: Teachers' Work and Culture in the Post-Modern Age*, Cassell, London.

Hargreaves, A., 1991, Contrived collegiality: the micropolitics of teacher collaboration, in J. Blasé (Ed.), *The Politics of Life in Schools: Power, Conflict, and Cooperation*, Sage, London.

Hargreaves, A. & Goodson, I., 1996, Teachers' professional lives: aspirations and actualities, in I. Goodson & A. Hargreaves (Eds.), *Teachers' Professional Lives*, Falmer Press, London.

Hargreaves, A. (guest editor) 1998. "From Reform to Renewal: Beyond bill 160." *Orbit*, **29(1)**.

Hextall, I. & Mahony, P., 1998, Effective teachers for effective schools, in R. Slee, G. Weiner & S. Tomlinson (Eds.), *School Effectiveness for Whom? Challenges to the School Effectiveness and School Improvement Movements*, Falmer Press, London.

Hubbard, L. & Datnow, A., 2000, A gendered look at educational reform, *Gender and Education*, **12(1)**: 115–129.

Hunter, I. & Meredyth, D., 2000, Competent citizens and limited truths, in T. Seddon & L. Angus (Eds.), *Beyond Nostalgia: Reshaping Australian Education (Australian Education Review No. 44)*, The Australian Council for Educational Research, Camberwell, Victoria.

Kenway, J., Bigum, C. & Fitzclarence, L., 1993, Marketing education in a postmodern age, *Journal of Education Policy*, **8(2)**: 105–122.

Kruse, S.D. & Louis, K.S., 1999, Professional communities and learning communities: what school leaders need to know. *Orbit (Special Issue on School Leadership in Transition)*, **30(1)**: 9–11.

Lacey, V., 1998, Be the change you wish to see, *Orbit*, **29(2)**: 8–9.

Lewington, J., 1998, Unions find flaws in standardized report cards, *The Globe and Mail*, March 17, p. A8.

MacLure, M., 1993, Arguing for yourself: identity as an organising principle in teachers' jobs and lives, *British Educational Research Journal*, **19(4)**: 311–322.

Miller, P. & Rose, N., 1995, Production, identity, and democracy, *Theory and Society*, **24**: 427–467.

O'Malley, P., Weir, L. & Shearing, C., 1997, Governmentality, criticism, politics, *Economy and Society*, **26(4)**: 501–517.

Ontario Ministry of Education and Training, September 22 1997, *The Education Quality and Improvement Act* (Bill 160), The Ministry of Education and Training, Toronto, Canada.

Ontario Royal Commission on Learning, 1994, *For the Love of Learning. Report of the Royal Commission on Learning*, The Commission, Toronto, Canada.

Ontario Secondary School Teachers' Federation, March 2000, *Impact 2000: Report of the Impact of Government Reforms on Education*, OSSTF, Toronto, Canada.

Popkewitz, T.S., 1998, *Struggle for the Soul: The Politics of Schooling and the Construction of the Teacher*, Teachers College Press, New York.

Popkewitz, T.S., 2000, Reform and the social administration of the child: globalization of knowledge and power, in N. Burbulus & A. Torres (Eds.), *Globalization and Education*, Routledge, New York.

Popkewitz, T.S. & Lindblad, S., 2000, Educational governance and social inclusion and exclusion: some conceptual difficulties and problematics in policy and research, *Discourse*, **21(1)**: 5–44.

Prentice, A. & Theobald, M. (Eds.), 1991, *Women Who Taught: Perspectives on the History of Women and Teaching*, University of Toronto Press, Toronto.

Robertson, S., 1999, "Risky business": market provision, community governance and the individualization of "risk" in New Zealand education, *International Studies in Sociology of Education*, **9(2)**: 171–191.

Robertson, S., and Smaller H., (Eds,) 1996. "Teacher Activism in the 1990's. Toronto, Lorimer.

Rose, N., 1996a, *Inventing Ourselves: Psychology, Power, and Personhood*, Cambridge University Press, Cambridge.

Rose, N., 1996b, The death of the social? Re-figuring the territory of government, *Economy and Society*, **25**: 327–356.

Rose, N. & Miller, P., 1992, Political power beyond the state: problematics of government, *British Journal of Sociology*, **43**: 173–205.

Sarason, S., 1996, *Revisiting "The Culture of the School and the Problem of Change."* Teachers College Press, New York.

Schick, C., 2000, White women accessing dominance, *Discourse*, **21(3)**: 299–309.

Sikes, P.J., 1992, Imposed change and the experienced teacher, in M. Fullan & A. Hargreaves (Eds.), *Teacher Development and Educational Change*, Falmer Press, London.

Slee, R. & Weiner, G., 1998, Introduction: school effectiveness for whom? In R. Slee, G. Weiner & S. Tomlinson (Eds.), *School Effectiveness for Whom? Challenges to the School Effectiveness and School Improvement Movements*, Falmer Press, London.

Smaller, H., Clark, R., Hart, D., Livingstone, D. & Noormohammed, Z., 2000, Teacher learning, informal and formal: Results of a Canadian Teachers' Federation survey, OISE/UT, *NALL Working Paper*, Number 14, Toronto. Available on-line at: www.oise.utoronto.ca/depts/sese/csew/nall/res/index

Steedman, C., 1985, "The mother made conscious": the historical development of a primary school pedagogy, *History Workshop*, **20**: 149–163.

Urquhart, I., 2000, Why teachers? And why now? *Toronto Star*, May 13.

Walkerdine, V., 1990, *Schoolgirl Fictions*, Verso, London.

Whitty, G., Power, S. & Halpin, D., 1998, *Devolution and Choice in Education: The School, the State and the Market*, Open University Press, Buckingham.

Chapter 9
Learning Through Struggle: How the Alberta Teachers' Association Maintains an Even Keel

Nina Bascia

Introduction

Teachers' organizations (associations, federations and unions) have been part of the fabric of public educational life in Canada for many decades. While local ad hoc groups sprang up at various times in response to their members' particular occupational needs, their presence was formalized by the major provincial Education Acts passed during the 1930s, 1940s and 1950s (Young and Levin, 1998) which established their right to legal representation of teachers. While their purview varies from province to province, most have been able to claim the compulsory membership of all public educators (and sometimes school administrators); to play some part in shaping provincial educational policy and negotiating the conditions of educators' work locally; and to have a role in educators' career development by providing formal and informal opportunities for leadership and professional development.

At the same time, teachers' organizations often have not fit easily into the educational landscape. Their engagement in educational decision making is, to a large degree, determined by provincial governments which possess formal constitutional authority over educational policy; their involvement in local and provincial decision making can be legislatively redefined at any time. In many provinces, their purview is restricted to an advisory role with respect to substantive policy issues; the concerns in which they could claim some involvement have been salary, benefits and working conditions, but their ability to negotiate even in these areas can be and are restricted to a shrinking range of issues both by available monies and by provincial legislation (Bascia, 1994, 1998a). Teachers and administrators are largely ignorant about their potential value; only a small minority engages in teachers' organization activities and their work is largely invisible to others (Bascia, 1997). In many places, the news media and public hold images of teachers' organizations as militant, unprofessional, simplistic and selfish in their priorities (Bascia, 1998b).

The tensions surrounding teachers' organizations are particularly significant now. Recent changes in educational policy across Canada have sharply reduced their ability to represent educators as well as having a serious impact on educators'

K. Church et al. (eds.), *Learning through Community: Exploring Participatory Practices*.
© Springer Science+Business Media B.V. 2008

working conditions, opportunities for system leadership and access to educational decision making, more broadly. Teachers' organizations face massive challenges both in terms of their own viability and with respect to the magnitude of stress their members are facing. They have lost support both from the public at large and from their own membership. In some provinces, recent legislation has reduced their claim on teachers from compulsory to voluntary, and in others school administrators have lost their right to legal representation. Fighting to improve conditions for educators who have little official power within the educational system has always been one of teachers' organizations' major purposes, but for many organizations this is a time of particular difficulty.

This chapter considers how one Canadian teachers' organization, the Alberta Teachers' Association, has managed to maintain and even enhance its viability and vitality under particularly challenging political conditions, and perhaps even as a result of these challenging conditions. When teachers as a body or their organizations have been challenged, many teachers' associations become defensive and unable to develop effective countering strategies, but the ATA has been able to "struggle against oppression. ... make sense of what [was] happening" and "work out ways of doing something about it" (Foley, 1999, pp. 2–3). In the process, it has become a more vital organization both internally and in relation to its membership, has created a series of opportunities for educators to mobilize and take some control of their practice, and has redirected the public discourse about education to include at least some consideration of the relationship between educational quality and teachers' working conditions.

In discussing the particular learning strategies employed by the ATA, this chapter draws upon over 10 years of research on North American teachers' organizations (Bascia, 1990, 1994a, b, 1997, 1998a–d, 2000; Bascia et al., 1987; Lieberman and Bascia, 1990), as well as referencing studies on the impact of recent policy directions on teachers' work worldwide (Ball, 1990; Bascia and Hargreaves, 2000; Blackmore, 1999; Earl et al., 1998; Harrison and Kachur, 1999; Robertson and Smaller, 1996; Portelli and Solomon, 2001; Whitty et al., 1998) in order to contextualize the Alberta case. It draws from published analyses of Alberta educational politics (Harrison, 1999; Kachur, 1999) and on the ATA's recent work (Flower and Booi, 1999; Soucek and Pannu, 1996). Its major data source is original research conducted within the ATA during the 1998–1999 school years. This research was initially conceptualized as an analysis of teachers' organizations as sites for teachers' professional learning. Interviews with a dozen organizational staff members in a range of different positions focused on how the ATA carried out its professional development mandate, the role and location of professional development in the larger organization and, especially, how professional development priorities were identified. The interviews revealed an organization deeply engaged with and attempting to influence a complex and volatile environment and even more significant, an organization that conceptualized teacher learning and political action as fundamentally linked, rather than as distinct organizational activities. Because of the way ATA staff articulated and enacted this linkage, the original research focus on teacher learning in rather conventional terms was broadened to allow for a more complex notion of learning that considered aspects of individual but also organizational, sectoral, and social learning.

Much of the published research on teachers' organizations views them as explicitly or implicitly caught up in models, paradigms, and structures that are outdated, simplistic and counterproductive. They are seen by many observers as too single-mindedly intent upon the "game" of adversarial relations (Carlson, 1992) or partisan politics (Lieberman, 1997), operating on a "labour" rather than "professional" paradigm (Mitchell and Kerchner, 1983), and shortsighted rather than visionary (Lawton et al., 1999; Little, 1993; McDonnell and Pascal, 1988). In "choosing" to operate according to such values, they are seen as having made the "wrong choice." The ATA case is useful because it describes the dynamic process of the organization's active engagement in this contested political terrain.

The sections that follow describe recent trends in Alberta educational policy making and practice; identify both the typical and uncommon features of the ATA as a teachers' organization; and describe the organizational strategies that encourage an ongoing process of active learning at multiple levels.

Alberta

Language is perhaps the fundamental medium for the social construction of meaning. The struggle for power, the assertion of dominance, and the maintenance of power structures often occur through the use of language. Powerful norms and structures that organize social life have resulted from rhetorical devices: "God is on our side," "It's the most efficient way," and other compelling phrases have been powerful ideas that have established and perpetuated powerful social institutions. The Christian Church, nation states, mass education, and bureaucratic organizations, to name some obvious examples, have changed society profoundly around the globe (Thomas et al., 1987). The stories told about the emergence of these institutions infer that they were established swiftly and transformed everything in their paths in relatively predictable and uniform ways. We are left with a sense of the inevitability and uniformity of social transformation because many of the most widely promoted histories are those written from the perspective of dominant groups, and because historical and comparative methodologies tend to emphasize a long and distant view. Available records further shape our understanding of the past: we often must rely on the analysis of remaining documents (account books, priests' records, written laws) rather than personal reports, on counting (how many?) rather than qualifying (what was it like?), and thus can only compare static states (before and after) rather than be able to chart the process of change. These factors encourage a view of participants of history as helpless victims unwittingly overwhelmed by mass events.

In our own lifetimes, personally experienced events take on a heightened resonance when others seem to be experiencing them and responding in similar ways. Mass education and mass media make it increasingly likely that we learn of events occurring beyond our own local communities. "Globalization" is both a contemporary social phenomenon we experience and a rhetorical concept that organizes our sense of what is currently happening to us on a mass level. Here, rhetoric is an important part of the package; and here, true to form, we struggle to understand whether social events are beyond or within our control. In the past several years, changes brought about by expanding, interlocking political, economic and technological infrastructures worldwide have been driven in part by the rhetorical rightness of local attempts to maintain economic competitiveness in a newly global economy. Invoking the rhetoric of globalization, many governments have cut public spending and jobs, reduced economic regulation and privatized government services, impacting educational systems profoundly (Harrison, 1999). The ideas promoted by such governments emphasize the adoption of "idealized" private sector models in the public sector. In education, as in other public sector institutions, "globalization" promotes the emergence of quasi-markets.

"Political narratives" are important political strategies in their own right. David Corson (1995) suggests that such narratives "take on a power of their own ... structural relations of domination become represented as "legitimate" through the stories that are told to justify the exercise of power by agents who hold it" (1995, p. 5). The employment of particular discourses can result in broader changes than merely policy setting and enforcement. In recent decades, political leaders have increased their use of the "bully pulpit," persuading others of the logic and inevitability of certain ideas in order to shift educational practice ahead of and beyond the limits of the actual introduction of specific legislation by (Jung and Kirst, 1986).[1] Thus, has the Progressive Conservative administration of Ralph Klein in Alberta, like many other contemporary western governments, adopted a rhetoric of "global competitiveness." Jerrold Kachur writes:

> The [Alberta] government promoted "doing more with less" as if it were a natural need. ... With a crisis management plan in hand, the spin-doctors complained — contrary to fact — that the education system was falling apart. Alberta students, they said, were not exiting the system prepared for the new world order and the system was too costly, with teachers paid too much for doing a lousy job. Alberta's schools needed market-discipline. The business model would offer up a good spanking to those who wouldn't sit up straight and listen to the music (1999, p. 62).

Many current educational theorists characterize the changes brought about by claims of globalization as "unprecedented" in their magnitude, intensity, and invasiveness. Jill Blackmore ascribes recent changes in Australian educational practices to a "frenzy of policy-borrowing of educational solutions across western nation states to what appear to be common social and economic problems" (1999, p. 9). Andy Hargreaves suggests that the boundaries around public schooling that gave it at least an appearance of autonomy have been weakened by the "willful intrusions" of commercial and market forces, and that schooling is more politicized and therefore more transparent than in the past. And as a result, rather than conceptualizing teaching and learning as "nested" within a bureaucratic structure with clear organizational boundaries, it is more useful to view them as the product of relationships between what is inside and what is outside of schools (Hargreaves and Fullan, 1998), to look at the forces that shape education as "flows rather than states, focusing on networks and the layered connections that know them together rather than simpler linear histories of circumscribed events or settings" (Nespor, 1997, p. xiv, cited in Bascia and Hargreaves, 2000, p. 16).

Globalization takes specific forms and has particular effects, but education has been caught up in international relations for over a century (e.g. colonization and imperialism). What is unique about the globalization phenomenon may simply be that it is the current manifestation of such relations, and that we are therefore able to catch glimpses of the struggle for domination which it represents. Alberta is a useful case to study because it has been caught up in the discourse of globalization in ways that parallel in a particularly exaggerated way what has recently occurred in other Canadian provinces (Earl et al., 1998) and, indeed, other parts of the world (Whitty et al., 1998). An export economy, in recent decades driven by fluctuations in petroleum prices, has fostered Alberta's sensitivity to global market trends (Harrison, 1999). Flower and Booi (1999, p. 125) suggest that educational expenditures began to decline in real dollars in the early 1980s after the "oil bust" (see also Soucek and Pannu, 1996), even when every other Canadian province saw increases, often significant, in funding for education. The episodic opportunities for educational innovation and growth possible in other provinces (e.g. Manitoba, British Columbia and Ontario) have not occurred in Alberta since the late 1980s; instead, Alberta educators experienced a combination of "rising expectations and shrinking resources:" shifting social conditions and greater expectations of schools in general and teachers in particular to be "social workers, psychologists and nurses," integrating students with "special needs" into most classrooms, and providing individualized instruction and complex assessment (Flower and Booi, 1999, p. 124).

The Progressive Conservative government headed by Ralph Klein argued that the province's economy required a reduction not only in government spending, but also in government itself (Harrison, 1999). Health, social services and education budgets all shrank in the early 1990s. Many public employees lost their jobs; teachers saw their salaries reduced by 5%. Alberta Education, the province's ministry of education, was reduced in size and restructured. Like other provinces, where changes in Education Acts tightened the province's hold on educational administrators, Alberta Education tinkered with governance issues, taking unto itself, for example, the appointment of school district superintendents. The intensified corporate agenda and the accompanying new rhetoric transformed educators' roles and relationships. What Alberta educators characterized as a "business style of management" encouraged principals to "become managers instead of educators" and switched both the rhetorical and lived emphasis from learning to "accountability and outcomes." According to government statements, the devolution of some decisions to the local level was accomplished to ensure that money reached classrooms more efficiently but, like in other jurisdictions where site-based decision making and budget restrictions have occurred simultaneously (see Bascia, 1996), practitioners reported that "power hasn't shifted down, but problems have."

Educators experienced reduced opportunities for interaction, communication and feedback to provincial policy making. Alberta Education suspended a long-standing tradition of participating in teachers' subject councils. There were several attempts in the provincial legislature to diminish the authority of the ATA by abolishing administrators' rights to representation, though none of these efforts was successful. The province considered dissolving school districts entirely, as New Brunswick had, to reduce infrastructure costs. Like Nova Scotia, British Columbia and Ontario in recent years, however, Alberta ended up merely reducing the number of districts through amalgamation, a shift which resulted in reduced support for teaching. District consultants who had provided professional development and support for teachers lost their positions; regional professional development consortia were set up for a 3-year period and then disbanded; teachers saw their professional development funds reduced to US$2 per student and then lost them entirely. Monies for education were reduced and reallocated; Alberta educators reported that "We spend more money on testing than on curriculum development" (Earl et al., 1998, p. 11). "We've gotten very good at assessing for special needs but we have no money to serve them" (p. 19). Alberta educators reported having to "find money in alternative ways" including teachers' own pocketbooks, donations from parents, private sector involvement through activities such as advertising on school buses and computer screen savers, and "user fees for students, even for regular classes like science" (p. 12). The reduction of funding was accompanied by reduced time for learning and preparing for new mandated practices: "You're on your own for implementation. There is no teacher preparation for the changes" (p. 15).

The rhetoric of globalization and the logic of reduced public spending; the expansion of achievement tests, the "manipulation of results," "negative media reports"; the introduction of charter schools – these governmental actions were met by and matched with eroding public support for the educational system. "Privatization is the goal. Parents are making choices other than pubic education" (Earl et al., 1998, p. 11). Educators reported that "the government is constantly bashing education and quoting old statistics" (p. 7). "The respect for the teaching profession has declined. I used to feel trusted as a professional that we were doing the best we could for the kids. Now it's been twisted and what we're doing is never good enough" (p. 22).

The Alberta Teachers' Association

"Globalization" indeed has strong effects, but care must be taken not to overinflate and therefore reify its rhetorical power. Because globalization is occurring now and because of more widespread awareness of the strategic importance of accounts that challenge the dominant paradigm (e.g. Ball, 1987; Bascia and Hargreaves, 2000; Blackmore, 1999; Harrison and Kachur, 1999; Portelli and Solomon, 2001; Robertson and Smaller, 1996; Whitty et al., 1998), it is possible to chart the process of change and to identify challenges to the dominant discourse. Specifically, we can document how the Alberta Teachers' Association struggled to make sense of what was happening and developed strategies to challenge the forces of globalization.

The ATA emerged initially in 1918, from an earlier organization that first met in Edmonton with a membership of 700. Alberta's Teaching Profession Act of 1935 established the ATA as the legal representative for elementary and secondary, public and Catholic teachers and school administrators. Today, there are approximately 70,000 members. Typical of many teachers' associations worldwide (Fraser, 1998; Young and Levin, 1998), the ATA provides a broad and complex range of services: professional development activities; member welfare supports such as counseling, legal and professional advice; lobbying and consultation activities with governments and other educational stakeholders; and collective bargaining. The ATA's stated objectives are:

> [T]o advance and promote the cause of education in Alberta; to improve the teaching profession; to arouse and increase public interest in the importance of education and public knowledge of the aims of education, financial support for education, and other education matters; and to cooperate with other organizations and bodies in Canada and elsewhere having the same of like aims or objectives. (Flower and Booi, 1999, pp. 134–135)

These intentions are not atypical for North American teachers' organizations, but they suggest particular nuanced understandings, including an expectation that the organization will work alongside and in cooperation with other educational agencies and play a major role in shaping and supporting public education.

Like many other teachers' organizations, the ATA plays a sort of insider–outsider role relative to other educational players, sometimes taking advantage of its status as teachers' legal representative and other times emphasizing its distinction from the formal educational hierarchy. ATA staff boasts that the government "doesn't like us but appreciates the good things we do … it would not think of not consulting with us regarding [certain domains of educational policy]." This statement reflects a tension between government's lack of trust in and reliance on the ATA – again, a not unusual response of government to teachers' organizations. Part of the ATA's legitimacy rests in long-standing relationships with other educational organizations. For example, in the 1940s the ATA led the fight to transfer responsibility for teacher education from normal schools to universities and in 1970 worked for legislation to require teachers to complete a 4-year Bachelor of Education. Today, ATA staff work with University of Alberta administrators and faculty to help develop, oversee and deliver academic programmes in pre-service teacher education, administrative preparation, and graduate studies. The ATA also works increasingly with Alberta's Home & School Association and with several school districts on a range of projects that are described in later sections of this paper. While such collaborative ventures are increasingly common across North America (Bascia, 1994, 1998d), what is unusual is the long history of such involvement in Alberta.

Unlike many other North American teachers' organizations, however, the ATA does not affiliate with provincial labour groups. Its mandate proscribes overtly "political" action – that is, partisan politics that, given Alberta's "hostile political culture" vis-à-vis organized labour and the "essentially conservative" nature of its teachers, would "most certainly produce a pernicious backlash from the public" (Soucek and Pannu, 1996, p. 40).

Further, in this "essentially conservative political culture" (p. 37), and given Alberta teachers' reluctance to strike, the ATA has been unwilling to overtly antagonize the government as some other provincial organizations have done; instead, ATA staff say, the organization has had to focus on "the issues." Some critics view this stance as problematic because it leaves teachers defenseless between "the imperative of professional conduct and a top-down push toward further reduction in their professional autonomy and a lower skill level ... and a simultaneous degradation of their working conditions" (Soucek and Pannu, pp. 41–42). The right to collective bargaining and to strike in Alberta was legislated in 1942, relatively early in its existence; a victory which, on one hand, has placed the organization in a strategically strong position for many years but, according to ATA staff, has also meant that teachers currently in the system have not had to fight for better working conditions and, as a result, are complacent and ignorant about the value of union representation.

The ATA's initial response to the government's "powerful, fast-moving, determined and aggressive" action (Flower and Booi, p. 128) in the early 1990s was cautious and reactive (Soucek and Pannu, p. 54). But as ATA staff claimed in their interviews, "We don't like other people telling us what to do." More than this, the ATA case suggests that particularly acute crises can provide the catalyst for learning, social engagement and action not evident in times of relative social stability. But how did the ATA revitalize itself, find ways to encourage educators to mobilize and take some control of their practice, and redirect the public discourse about education? While luck and strong leadership were clearly factors, something more seemed to have been operating as well: a conscious, explicit recognition of the imperative for ongoing learning at multiple levels and in multiple locations – among individual staff members, within organizational subunits and across the organization as a whole; in its relationships with its members; in the ATA's relationships with other educational organizations; and for individual teachers, school staffs, school councils and other working groups, for school board and regional configurations, across the entire province including urban, suburban and rural contexts in various regions. Rather than working from generic assumptions about educators' occupational needs, the ATA was able to recognize the diversity of its membership – as both novices and veteran practitioners; simultaneously as workers with concerns about working conditions, policy implementers, and subject specialists with varied expertise; and as community members in various contexts across the province.

Processes of struggle and contestation engender social change. Powerful learning can result from such struggles with adversity as well as from the ensuing action. The sections that follow consider strategies employed by the ATA that have been effective in engendering and sustaining ongoing learning. These strategies are described both in terms specific to teachers' organizations in broad terms, and as they might be applied to many types of groups and organizations. A final section considers the multilevel nature of social learning – for individuals and collectivities, for Alberta generally and within the ATA specifically.

Organizational Strategies

Continuous Learning

Many organizations profess a commitment to "organizational learning" in order to suggest that they recognize a need for and can claim an actual adaptation to changing social conditions (see Chapter 10 by Laiken et al. , in this volume). While the ATA does not make this rhetorical claim, it nonetheless demonstrates this commitment in a variety of ways: by seeking information and ideas vociferously and from multiple sources, by deliberate attempts to minimize internal organizational fragmentation and balkanization, and by minimizing boundaries between the organization and the field. In this sense, an ATA staff member's assertion that "professional development drives the organization" should be understood not as the domination of the professional development unit over other units but rather as a commitment to learning that has permeated and made coherent many organizational activities. The ATA works both explicitly and implicitly on an understanding of the relationships between learning, values, structure, power and action.

The ATA works actively to understand what is occurring in the field of education. While it is all too easy for teachers' organization staff, like any administrators or educational bureaucrats, to quickly lose touch with classroom and school practice (and to be viewed by educators as out of touch), the ATA surveys its members frequently; beyond this, ATA staff spend approximately half of their time every week in the field. Each staff member travels around the province to get a feel for what is occurring across diverse educational contexts, and also to ensure that they are visible and that ATA programmes do not look like "Edmonton" initiatives.[2] The ATA also has developed pilot projects such as professional development schools and a mentoring programme for new teachers in several cities in the province. While other teachers' organizations also support such projects, the ATA takes the notion of piloting seriously: rather than merely "first" or "only," it treats such experiments as opportunities to learn about new practices that subsequently can be applied more broadly.

Perhaps even more significantly, careful attention is paid to distributing field knowledge across the association through a range of organizational processes. While many teachers' organizations are constitutionally required to seek direction from their members through member surveys and the decisions made in representative assemblies, most associations do a better job of representing some groups of educators than others. Often organizational priorities are driven by the needs and interests of educators from certain schools or school districts, subject areas (e.g. science or other high status disciplines versus special education and other marginalized programmes), levels (elementary versus secondary), gender, age cohort, role (teachers or administrators) or parts of the province (large urban areas versus smaller rural jurisdictions). This privileging of certain points of view over others, if unquestioned, often becomes more pronounced over time and can lead to the perception that "the union is a 'cabal'" driven by "special interests" and inaccessible and unresponsive to anyone else (Bascia, 1998b, 2000).

Further, teachers' organizations are often characterized by internal structures that in some ways resemble departmentalized, "balkanized" secondary schools (Hargreaves, 1994; Siskin, 1994). Staff members who are associated with professional development, collective bargaining and other organizational priorities tend to interact with distinctly different people (government officials, administrators, "teacher leaders," teachers in trouble) and maintain distinctly different views of the world. Differences in world view can result in a rich programme of organizational "products," but they can also lead to organizational subunits acting in ways that actually undermine the efforts of the others, and specific projects rendered ineffective and invisible by actions and publicized statements that reflect other organizational priorities. Within many contemporary teachers' associations, some organizational priorities, such as professional development, are less valued than others, such as political action.

The ATA actively works against these tendencies to privilege certain groups of educators and organizational subunits over others by carefully attending to intra- and inter-organizational dynamics: by supporting and encouraging a range of special interest caucuses (in this case, subject specialist councils) which act as lobby groups within the organization and interact with the provincial government around curriculum change; by ensuring that staff from different subunits such as teacher welfare and professional development are always on the leadership team simultaneously; by actively recruiting staff from across the province who have divergent views, orientations and skills; by creating complex portfolios so that individual staff members work across organizational subunits; by involving staff members from several units in the development of most initiatives and programmes; and by fostering mutually respectful working relationships between elected officials and professional staff.

Finding and Creating Spaces (Making Lemonade)

Seeking support for its members and political advantage for itself, the ATA has capitalized on the ideas of others and worked in whatever arenas become available. The ATA attended government-initiated regional meetings in 1993 even though it was clear that "the government has already made up its own mind" and consultation was merely a "charade" (Flower and Booi, 1999, p. 126); other teachers' organizations might have refused. Then, when the government released a position paper, "Meeting the Challenge," which presumably reported on the results of the consultations, the ATA sponsored its own roundtables throughout the province, made them accessible to the public and then released its own report, "Challenging the View."

In rebuttal to negative reports on the sorry quality of teaching released by Alberta Education, the ATA initiated an ongoing, multilevel media campaign. More significantly, it established a Public Education Action Centre in 1995 to develop an ongoing, proactive campaign that would mobilize teachers in grassroots activities, promote positive changes in education, build effective coalitions and employ ATA members in schools and locals to promote public education in their own settings (Flower and Booi, 1999, p. 127, 129).

In addition to these public and political activities, the ATA attempted to fill many of the substantive gaps in educational practice resulting from the "decimated" educational infrastructure, particularly in the area of professional development. While other teachers' organizations have argued that it is the school system's responsibility to support teachers' work, the ATA has perceived such gaps as opportunities to challenge the government by asserting its own orientation to teaching and schooling. For example, supporting the government's interest in site-based decision making but finding neither models nor technical assistance forthcoming from Alberta Education, the ATA developed information packets and professional development strategies for school staffs. When the government mandated individual growth plans,[3] it was the ATA that "became the official source of information endorsed by the government" by seeking and winning the contract to develop workbooks and train administrators on their use, essentially defining their purpose and content ("they emphasize professional judgment, they are not just a check list"). Similarly, when the government legislated school councils in 1995, the ATA chose to support the plan and, with the assistance of other stakeholders, including the Alberta Home and School Councils' Association, it developed the official resource manual and provided "meaningful rather than trivial" training for school council participants, essentially managing to determine the shape of this reform (Flower and Booi, 1999, p. 130).

Multiple Strategies

Research that has evaluated teachers' organizations' reform initiatives has consistently demonstrated that no single initiative or strategy will be attractive, meaningful, and effective for a teaching staff or population of any diversity (Bascia, 1994, 1998b, 2000). But because of the costs involved in mounting any project and the intellectual challenge of articulating a complex yet coherent vision of educational practice, teacher organization staff often work with generic notions of teachers' occupational needs and interests, either choosing a strategy they hope will appeal to a majority of educators[4] or selecting a splashy initiative based on its potential to attract media and public attention. The ATA's professional development offerings and other contacts with educators, however, are based on a recognition of members' diversity with respect to developmental needs, learning preferences, personal obligations (and therefore time for extra-classroom activities), social status (and therefore opportunities for organizational participation), programme and subject affiliation (and therefore goals or interests) as well as school, community and school board contexts (and therefore policy pressures and workplace conditions) (Bascia, 1998c; Earl et al., 1998). Rather than attempting to mount the one best programme, the ATA attempts to fill a variety of needs.

This strategy is exemplified in the ATA's wide array of professional development offerings. The association continues to support local and regional annual "conventions" which have occurred since the 1920s and are formally written into Alberta's Education Act. Developed by local committees and based on the results of educator surveys, conventions often include a wide range of workshops, usually of the traditional staff development, technically oriented, skills-based, transmission-adoption variety. But at the same time, the ATA also makes affordable workshops available to school staffs, presented by a cadre of trained workshop leaders on a range of current issues and concerns. Popular workshops include site-based decision making, classroom strategies such as conflict resolution, classroom management, inclusivity, pedagogy and student assessment, professional wellness and professional growth plans. The ATA supports the professional activities of a range of subject specialist councils (over 60% of the province's teachers are members) which sponsor their own subject-based professional development. ATA staff members also pay particular attention to the needs of the growing number of new teachers, mounting an annual new teacher conference in every provincial region and working on a pilot for mentoring new teachers. Beyond these, the ATA is working with several school districts to develop an understanding of how to mount collaborative professional development programmes; working with regional consortia to develop curriculum-based, classroom-focused professional development that occur over several days across a several month period, based on constructivist understandings about teacher and student learning. Teachers try out new practices in their classrooms and report back in ensuing sessions. These sessions, and subject council work, increasingly occur during annual convention sessions since the provincial government has reduced paid professional development days for teachers to one per year.

Where many contemporary educational policies appear to assume simplistic, technical views of teaching and unrealistic assumptions about how to bring about improvement in teaching practice, many of the ATA's professional development offerings involve processes and conceptual structures that build teachers' individual and collective capacities to work effectively in and across classroom, school and community settings. Many are based on sophisticated understandings of learning: Rather than focusing on simple skill development, they are intended to increase teachers' capacity to develop intellectually, socially and politically as well as technically, often all at once. For example, curriculum-based professional development helps educators develop a shared language about practice and get a taste of what it is like to work collaboratively (see Cochran-Smith and Lytle, 1992) – skills and relationships that may serve them well in a range of unanticipated ways beyond the scope and time period of the specific reform. School council training helps participants learn group process and leadership skills. The ATA's public education campaign encourages educators at all levels to develop promotional skills and increase their visibility and contacts with larger groups of people within their communities and organizations.

Reframing the Discourse

Language plays a significant role in framing the basic terms of social engagement: "what can be said and thought, but also … who can speak, when, and with what authority" is defined and maintained through discourse (Ball, 1990, cited in Foley, 1999, p. 15). People participate in their own subordination when they unconsciously adopt and use discourses that contain a logic of unequal power relations. When dominant discourses are used in alternative ways, social relations can be negotiated and redefined. And dominant ideologies can be fundamentally challenged when people who struggle to overcome their subordination come to new conscious understandings and introduce a counter-discourse.

Many teachers' organizations, particularly those accustomed to a one-down position relative to other educational players, have been slow to recognize their power to contribute to the public discourse about teaching and schooling. Certainly, they inform the discourse about teachers and teaching by negotiating many conditions of teaching through collective bargaining, by attempting to influence educational policy, and through statements they make in the press; they may reinforce or assert images of teachers as victims or heroes, technicians, intellectual workers, political activists, and/or professionals (Bascia, 2000; Mitchell and Kerchner, 1983). In recent years, as the dominant discourse has become increasingly anti-education, however, many teachers' organizations have become convinced (or, if you like, have adopted the discourse that prevails in national and international meetings of teacher union staff) that they are uniquely situated to persuade the public to greater respect and support for education. Organization staff members are increasingly self-conscious about their direct communication with teachers and administrators and statements they make in the press. Public relations or "communications" are a common and increasingly active organizational function in teachers' organizations of any size.

The ATA's research and communication teams have collaborated on *Trying to Teach* and *A Report Card on Education*, which reported on conditions of teaching and learning across the province; a *Globe & Mail* reporter called *Trying to Teach* "passionate and disturbing" and said, "if politicians and business people read only one educational document this year, … [this] should be it" (Flower and Booi, 1999, p. 125). Beyond this, ATA staff members read educational literature, attend educational conferences, meet with teachers' organization staff from other parts of Canada and internationally, and may borrow ideas liberally from any of these sources. Because of many teachers' lack of familiarity with educational research (Cochran-Smith and Lytle, 1992; Hargreaves, 1982) and their negative experiences with the wholesale adoption of policies and programmes developed elsewhere (Bailey, 2000), many teachers' organizations are cautious about importing ideas for innovation from out of province, especially internationally. ATA staff members are not afraid to look outside Alberta for new ideas and concepts even though they are careful to couch their examples in Albertan descriptions (e.g. using quotations by teachers about their practice from documents like

"Trying to Teach"). For example, the ATA has adopted the notion of training a cadre of professional development leaders from the British Columbia Teachers' Federation and adapted the National (US) Education Association's strategy of mounting a multilevel public relations campaign.

The ATA has supported a range of public forums and published reports, including *Challenging the View, Trying to Teach*, and *A Framework for Educational Change in Alberta* in direct rebuttal to the Klein government's attempts to justify the reduction of funding for education and the "reinventing" of the educational system. A Committee on Public Education and Professional Practice was established in 1992 to look into factors which are "imposing unsound practices on teachers and creating conflicting and unreasonable expectations of public education" (Flower and Booi, 1999, p. 125). A media campaign based on the theme "Don't cut my future," including news ads, billboards, public transit signs, radio advertising, and support from the Public Education Action Centre (developed in early 1995), has been funded on "emergency" monies for the last 7 years to mobilize teachers in grassroots activities, to make clear the threat to education, to promote positive changes in education, to build effective coalitions and to make use of assistance from public relations professionals. As a result, 40 of the province's 51 local teachers' associations have started promotional programmes. Beyond these public promotion efforts, the ATA works to influence educators' professional discourse through a host of professional development strategies, directly challenging government rhetoric by providing technical assistance to shape how reform initiatives are actually implemented. A provincial rally organized in October 1997, which included a staggering 75% of the province's teachers, is evidence of the ATA's success in this realm, especially given Alberta educators' historic unwillingness to take overt political action. Teachers at the rally were quoted as saying, "We are overworked and underpaid and children are suffering because of it." "I'm here for the kids. They are the ones losing out because of the cutting." "I'm here because I'm proud to be a teacher." "Many of us became teachers because we wanted to help students. Under current classroom conditions this is becoming more of a dream than a possibility." These and other quotes are both evidence of and further ammunition for the ATA's efforts to redirect public discourse about education.

Considering Learning

Some of the specific strategies employed by the ATA may be of interest to other teachers' associations concerned about the deteriorating quality of conditions for teaching and learning and about their own ability to participate in improving them. More generally applicable is what the ATA exemplifies as an organization which has consciously, deliberately and persistently worked over the past decade or so to foster individual, occupational and broader social learning. It seems likely that the ATA's vitality rests in its attempts to work both explicitly and implicitly to understand the relationships between learning, values, structure, power and action.

Earlier sections of this chapter illustrated how the ATA promotes learning for educational change and reassertion of its own role as a political force in three domains. The first is within the organization itself. Beyond mere platitudes about "organizations as learning environments," the ATA has struggled to make sense of the government's dominance over educational policy making, its vision of educational practice, and its own and its members' subordination by attending to internal organizational dynamics to ensure ongoing sharing of information and the application of divergent talents and perspectives to problem solving. Second, recognizing the multidimensional nature of the learning needs of Alberta educators, the ATA continues to develop and provide a wide range of professional learning opportunities that are less frequently restricted to narrow conceptions of classroom teaching and increasingly about accomplishing complex activities in a variety of locations with others. Through such learning experiences, educators can discover and develop their personal strengths and competence and also come to understand their positional power in the larger educational system and in society (Bascia, 2000; Foley, 1999). By engaging educators in practice-based, collaborative learning opportunities that focus on developing new skills and relationships, these activities increase educators' capacity to engage effectively in the educational enterprise. Third, the ATA has recognized the necessity of shaping public understanding about teachers and schooling, contributing actively to public discussions, thus developing an effective counter-discourse that has challenged and re-formed public images of teachers, schools, and students.

ATA staff members are the first to recognize that their organization's capacity for coherent, focused and effective action is context-specific and cannot readily or realistically be expected of other teachers' associations. They sympathize with other provincial organizations – in British Columbia and Ontario, for example – which have experienced "full-out external assaults," which have concentrated their efforts on fighting with their provincial governments and which have even fragmented under the strain. "I'm not sure we wouldn't respond similarly to an external attack," said a senior staff member. "But attacks [on us by the government] have been on certain things we do, not about challenging us fundamentally." At the same time that adversity has compelled the organization to learn and change, "Ralph Klein has pulled the organization together." Complacency, whether collective or individual, rarely provides sufficient impetus for change. The need to struggle can. Individuals and organizations who assume the entitlement to participate, or who discover a need to participate because they have been shut out of decision making that affects their ability to thrive, will do what they can regarding their marginalization (see, e.g. Bascia, 1998b). When they discover opportunities, they will seize them; if and when spaces are unfilled, they will fill them. They will use any idea if it furthers their cause. The ATA is very careful to protect its ability to maneuver. "Unless we're attacked we'll be nonpolitical, we don't support any political party or announce that we're working to defeat the government, we'll be principled — but we'll get nasty if necessary. We want to play."

How these lessons are understood is crucial. For teachers' organizations, it would be a mistake to interpret this literally as whether or not to "get nasty."

Rather, the goal is to gather and consider a range of options and to select those which seem likely to be successful in a particular place, time and dynamic; to understand that the overarching goal is to maintain organizational viability that will serve membership over the long term; and to maintain a stance of continuous and active learning that is intended for, depends on and is distributed across individuals and groups at every level.

Endnotes

[1] Such discursive logic is active at many levels beyond policy making: other researchers have described how the actual names assigned to certain practices and actions within educational organizations shape participants' understandings of their legitimacy – see, for example, Metz (1989); Meyer and Rowan (1977); and Wodak (1995).
[2] Edmonton, where the ATA head office is located, is not generally considered representative of the rest of the province, just as Toronto is not representative of the rest of Canada.
[3] Annual plans developed by teachers that commit them to particular professional development strategies and teaching achievements, and which are part of the formal assessment process employed by administrators.
[4] For example, in some locales in recent years, when the median teacher was in her mid- to late-career, retirement-related issues often took precedence over support for new teachers.

References

Bailey, B., 2000, The impact of mandated change on teachers, in N. Bascia & A. Hargreaves (Eds.), *The Sharp Edge of Educational Change: Teaching, Leading and the Realities of Reform*, Falmer Press, London.
Ball, S., 1987, *The Micropolitics of the School*, Methuen Press, London.
Ball, S., 1990, Politics and Policy Making in Education: Explorations in Policy Sociology. London: Routledge.
Bascia, N., 1990, Teachers' evaluations of unions, *Journal of Educational Policy*, **5**(4): 301–313.
Bascia, N., 1994a, *Unions in Teachers' Professional Lives: Social, Practical, and Intellectual Concerns*, Teachers College Press, New York.
Bascia, N., 1994b, Creating a Culture of Change Initiative, Evaluation Report prepared for Ontario Ministry of Education and Training and the Ontario Teachers' Federation, Toronto, Canada.
Bascia, N., 1996, Caught in the crossfire: restructuring, collaboration, and the "problem" school, *Urban Education*, **31**(2): 177–198.
Bascia, N., 1997, Invisible leadership: teachers' union activity in schools, *Alberta Journal of Educational Research*, **43**(2): 151–165.
Bascia, N., 1998a, Changing roles for teachers' federations, *Orbit (From Reform to Renewal: Beyond Bill 160)*, **29**(1): 37–40.
Bascia, N., 1998b, Women teachers, union affiliation, and the future of North American teacher unionism, *Teaching and Teacher Education*, **14**(5): 551–563.
Bascia, N., 1998c, The next steps in teacher union research and reform, *Contemporary Education*, **69**(4): 210–213.
Bascia, N., 1998d, Teacher unions and educational reform, in A. Hargreaves, A. Lieberman, M. Fullan & D. Hopkins (Eds.), *The International Handbook of Educational Change*, Kluwer Academic, Dordrecht, The Netherlands.

Bascia, N., 2000, The other side of the equation: professional development and the organizational capacity of teachers' organizations, *Education Policy*, **14(3)**: 385–404.

Bascia, N. & Hargreaves, A., 2000, Teaching and leading on the sharp edge of change, in N. Bascia & A. Hargreaves (Eds.), *The Sharp Edge of Educational Change: Teaching, Leading and the Realities of Reform*, Falmer Press, London.

Bascia, N., Stiegelbauer, S., Jacka, N., Watson, N. & Fullan, M., November 1997, *Teacher Associations and School Reform: Building Stronger Connections*, an external review of the NCI Learning Laboratories Initiative, prepared for the National Education Association, Washington, DC.

Blackmore, J., 1999, *Troubling Women: Feminism, Leadership and Educational Change*, Open University Press, Philadelphia.

Carlson, D., 1992, *Teachers and Crisis. Urban School Reform and Teachers' Work Culture*, Routledge Chapman & Hall, New York.

Cochran-Smith, M. & Lytle, S., 1992, Communities for teacher research: fringe or forefront? *American Journal of Education*, May **(11)**: 298–324.

Corson, D., 1995, Discursive power in educational organizations: an introduction, in D. Corson (Ed.), *Discourse and Power in Educational Organizations*, OISE Press, Toronto.

Earl, L., Bascia, N., Hargreaves, A. & Jacka, N., 1998, *Teachers and Teaching in Changing Times: A Glimpse of Canadian Teachers in 1998*, prepared for the Canadian Teachers' Federation, International Centre for Educational Change (OISE/UT), Toronto, Canada.

Flower, D. &. Booi, H., 1999, Challenging restructuring: the Alberta Teachers' Association, in T. Harrison & J. Kachur (Eds.), *Contested Classrooms: Education, Globalization, and Democracy in Alberta*, University of Alberta Press, Edmonton.

Foley, G., 1999, *Learning and Social Action: A Contribution of Understanding Informal Education*, Zed Books, London.

Fraser, C., 1998, Teacher activism in the 1990s (Book Review), *Alberta Journal of Educational Research*, **44(4)**: 265–268.

Hargreaves, A., 1994, *Changing Teachers, Changing Times: Teachers' Work and Culture in the Postmodern Age*, Cassell, London.

Hargreaves, A. & Fullan, M., 1998, *What's Worth Fighting for Out There?* Ontario Public School Teachers' Federation, 2nd edn., Toronto.

Harrison, T., 1999, The "Alberta Advantage": for whom? In T. Harrison & J. Kachur (Eds.) *Contested Classrooms: Education, Globalization, and Democracy in Alberta*, University of Alberta Press, Edmonton.

Harrison, T. & Kachur, J., 1999, *Contested Classrooms: Education, Globalization, and Democracy*. University of Alberta Press, Edmonton.

Jung, R. & Kirst, M., 1986, *Beyond Mutual Adaptation: Into the Bully Pulpit: Recent research on the federal role in education*, Stanford Educational Policy Institute, Stanford, CA.

Kachur, J., 1999, Orchestrating delusions: ideology and consent in Alberta, in T. Harrison & J. Kachur (Eds.), *Contested Classrooms: Education, Globalization, and Democracy in Alberta*, University of Alberta Press, Edmonton.

Lawton, S., Bedard, G., MacLellan, D. & Li, X., 1999, *Teachers' Unions in Canada*, Detselig, Calgary.

Lieberman, A. & Bascia, N., 1990, *Assessment of the California Policy Trust Agreement Project*, prepared for PACE (Policy Analysis for California Education) and the Stuart Foundation, Centre for Research on the Context of Secondary School Teaching, Stanford University School of Education, Stanford, CA.

Lieberman, M., 1997, *The Teacher Unions: How the NEA and AFT Sabotage Reform and Hold Students, Parents, Teachers, and Taxpayers Hostage to Bureaucracy*, Free Press, New York.

Little, J.W., 1993, Teachers' professional development in a climate of educational reform, *Educational Evaluation and Policy Analysis*, **15(2)**: 129–151.

McDonnell, L.M. & Pascal, A.H., April 1988, *Teacher Unions and Educational Reform*, RAND Corporation Publication JRE-02, Washington, DC.

Metz, M., 1989, Real school: a universal drama amid disparate experience, in D. Mitchell & M. Goertz (Eds.), *Education Politics for the New Century: The Twentieth Anniversary Yearbook of the Politics of Education Association*, Falmer Press, London.

Meyer, J. & Rowan, B., 1977, Institutionalized organizations: formal structure as myth and ceremony, *American Journal of Sociology*, **83**: 340–363.

Mitchell, D.E. & Kerchner, C.T., 1983, Labor relations and teacher policy, in L.S. Shulman & G. Sykes (Eds.), *Handbook of Teaching and Policy*, Washington, DC.

Nespor, J. 1997. *Tangled up in School: Politics, Space, Bodies and Signs in the Educational Process*. New Jersey: Lawrence Erlbaum Associates.

Portelli, J. & Solomon, P. (Eds.), 2001, *The Erosion of the Democratic Tradition in Education: From Critique to Possibilities*, Detselig, Calgary.

Robertson, S. & Smaller, H. (Eds.), 1996, *Teacher Activism in the 1990s*. James Lorimer, Toronto.

Siskin, L.S. 1994. Realms of Knowledge: Academic departments in Secondary Schools. London: The Falmer Press.

Soucek, V. & Pannu, R., 1996, Globalizing education in Alberta: teachers' work and the options to fight back, in S. Robertson & H. Smaller (Eds.), *Teacher Activism in the 1990s*, James Lorimer & Company, Toronto.

Thomas, G., Meyer, J., Ramirez, F. & Boli, J. (Eds.) 1987, *Institutional Structure: Constituting State, Society, and the Individual*, Sage, Newbury Park, CA.

Whitty, G., Powers, S., & Halpin, D., 1998, *Devolution and Choice in Education: The State, the School and the Market*, Open University Press, Buckingham.

Wodak, R., 1995, Power, discourse, and styles of female leadership in school committee meetings, in D. Corson (Ed.), *Discourse and Power in Educational Organizations*, OISE Press, Toronto.

Young, J. & Levin, B., 1998, *Understanding Canadian Schools: An Introduction to Educational Administration*, 2nd edn., Harcourt Brace, Toronto.

Chapter 10
Formalizing the Informal: From Informal to Organizational Learning in the Post-Industrial Workplace

Marilyn Laiken, Karen Edge, Stephen Friedman, and Karima West

Introduction

For over a decade, the concept of organizational learning has pervaded the lexicon of workplace learning and change. However, despite legions of books, articles, films, courses, conferences and complete professional and academic programmes on the subject, the concept of organizational learning remains difficult to define and even more difficult to implement in practice. Organizations attempting to integrate organizational learning principles lack specific examples of how these relatively complex notions translate into daily workplace experience.

We conducted a research project to locate and study Canadian organizations that were using organizational learning approaches to embed ongoing learning within actual work processes – whether at an individual, team or strategic level. This research was intended to be a voice for workplaces in which the lives of clients or customers, employees and volunteers have been dramatically affected by new organizational forms. Our hope was that, by providing visibility to such "models" of organizational learning, the research would not only reinforce current best practices, but would also demonstrate the potential of such practices across diverse work sectors, organizational size, and employee populations.

The study initially identified 42 Canadian organizations which either self-reported or appeared in the literature as examples of those attempting to become or demonstrating features of a learning organization. Ten of these organizations agreed to participate in the research and ten randomly selected employees in each completed *The Learning Organization 5 Stage Diagnostic Survey* (Woolner et al., 1995). In response to this survey, five organizations self-identified at mature stages of development as learning organizations in the areas of individual, team and strategic learning.[1] Of the five, four of these organizations – a medium-sized hospital, a large retail chain, a small not-for-profit government funded organization and a large electronics manufacturer volunteered for more in-depth study through individual interviews, focus groups and on-site observation.

Through an online qualitative data analysis programme, twelve primary codes and multiple subcodes which emerged from the resulting data were used to analyse the transcripts from each organization. The results informed a narrative written

K. Church et al. (eds.), *Learning through Community: Exploring Participatory Practices.*
© Springer Science + Business Media B.V. 2008

about each of the cases which was then integrated under common thematic headings to form the body of this chapter.

The data and analyses surfaced key thematic insights, but the research could be further informed by future studies that investigate larger sample sizes in relation to our findings. Additionally, since the data were extracted from work sites in a diverse and relatively wealthy urban setting, the area of inquiry could be expanded by parallel studies in different cultural and socioeconomic contexts. This might provide more heft to the claim that the ideas outlined here are in fact applicable across cultural and economic boundaries. Nonetheless, we are convinced that the results of the study presented in this chapter have critical implications for researchers and practitioners interested in creating cultures of continuous learning within organizational settings.

All four of the organizations represented in this chapter must be viewed in the context of the current turbulent workplace environment caused by globalization, restructuring, reengineering, mergers and acquisitions. Within this milieu of upheaval and transition, which has become endemic in the contemporary workplace, we were particularly interested in discovering what role informal learning might play in contributing to employees' ability to move beyond simply coping with stress to engaging in creative action, individually and organizationally. We were also interested in how these organizations might be embedding informal learning in their very structures and cultures, so that its benefits could be sustained beyond future changes in leadership. Finally, we were concerned about what *kind* of leadership would support and legitimize informal learning approaches and help make them part of organizational "memory," while simultaneously respecting the integrity of employee learning as valuable in its own right. This chapter will explore each of these issues in turn, demonstrating how our case workplaces have been able to create vibrant cultures of organizational learning, despite their late 1990s context characterized by a volatile, technologically oriented, knowledge intensive, globalized economy.

The Case Examples

The four organizations that comprise this research are identified with pseudonyms for purposes of confidentiality. However, all four are currently operating organizations in an urban setting in Southern Ontario, representing the private, health-care and not-for-profit sectors. They range in size from eighty to ten thousand employees, both unionized and non-unionized. The respondents represent a mix of gender, age, experience and roles within the organizations.

Wealthshare is a non-unionized, not-for-profit grant-making organization that was established in 1982 as an arm's length agency of the Ontario Government. Its purpose is to disburse funds to charitable organizations across the province, in order to help build healthy, sustainable and caring communities as a strategic contribution to Ontario civil society. Wealthshare's Mission, Vision and Values states:

> We encourage collaborative and imaginative, holistic approaches to increased community well-being which recognize the important and interdependent role that arts, culture, recreation, sports and social services play, and the underlying value of a sustainable economy and environment. (Organizational documentation, p. 1)

During the year in which our research was conducted with Wealthshare the organization changed dramatically. The budget was increased from US$12 to US$100 million; the staff had grown from 12 to 80; the well-respected CEO had been terminated by the incoming Board of Directors, and had not yet been replaced; the structure of the organization was decentralized and now included regional offices in various areas of the province; and the entire head office physical plant had been completely renovated.

Urban Religious Hospital (URH), as the name implies, is a religiously affiliated hospital operating within a Southern Ontario urban centre. It has a strong community focus and prides itself on its work with its community neighbours, in particular the poor and the homeless. Until 10 years ago, URH was suffering from what seemed to be an irreversible debt crisis. However, over the course of the last decade, URH has succeeded in its quest to become a profitable provider of "excellent quality patient care." The last decade has been one of significant upheaval within the Canadian health care system. Within that system, hospitals have experienced the most dramatic change and have often been faced with unprecedented funding cuts and budget shortfalls. Urban Religious Hospital provides an example of one that has risen to the challenges, maintained its focus on its values, and managed to thrive despite the tumultuous climate.

Homewares is a home furnishings retailer with more than 800 stores in the United States, Canada, Mexico, Puerto Rico, the United Kingdom and Japan. Worldwide, this non-unionized, publicly traded, 39-year-old company employs roughly 10,000 employees and is one of North America's leading specialty home fashions retailers. Its mission includes a strong customer focus which staff members try to support by ensuring that the shopping experience is enjoyable, and that the customer is provided with a varied selection of unique home furnishings and accessories. Homewares also has articulated its commitment to employee learning and to taking a socially conscious approach to business. Its philanthropic endeavors include international, national and local foci through fund-raising and community outreach. Homewares' partnering relationships with organizations like the United Way and UNICEF have resulted in contributions of more than US$17 million to hundreds of worthy causes around the world. With respect to learning, this organization states that having fun at work in combination with training opportunities and a "team learning" environment best describe the intended experience for employees, whether at the store, distribution centre or home office location.

ThermoDial is a leading supplier of building control solutions. Its products include building automation systems for heating, ventilation and air conditioning; comprehensive services for mechanical equipment and building automation; design-build engineering services; integrated security, surveillance, fire and alarm systems; and technical services to assess and improve energy efficiency.

Customers include builders of homes, schools, hospitals, office buildings, museums, airports, shopping centres and other public institutions. Over the past decade, the CEO of a Canadian ThermoDial manufacturing plant has incorporated innovative management practices and learning strategies into the workplace in an effort to streamline and update systems and procedures and improve quality of work life for all staff. As part of a large, diversified, multinational organization, this plant employs 300 people, 200 of whom are unionized, and is a ThermoDial Centre of Excellence for production of valves and actuators that are exported around the world.

Basic Social Processes as an Avenue for Informal Learning

The cases represent organizations that view learning, and in particular, *informal learning* (defined here as that which happens naturally, as part of daily work), as critical to both their effectiveness in achieving their goals and in providing a stimulating, challenging, developmental environment for all of their employees. This concern, supported by the literature in organizational learning and redesign (Emery, 1980; Senge, 1990; Trist, 1981), values the joint optimization of both the social and technical systems – or the achievement of organizational goals through the enhancement of the workplace as a continuous learning environment (Laiken, 1987, 1997, 2002).

Individual professional development (often represented by one-off training events) is valued to varying degrees in all of our case organizations. However, the most sustainable benefits, in terms of both individual and organizational needs, tend to result from "action" or "situated" learning (Revans, 1982; Lave and Wenger, 1991) which is informal, and accrues directly from work-related activities. This is the learning that takes place in the interstices of organizational life – in the coffee shop or during a car pool, in a meeting, or on the shop floor during a production process. It is characterized by relationship and interpersonal interaction through basic social processes such as:

- Formal and informal problem-solving in groups or teams
- Making mistakes, reflecting on the experience, and applying the learning in practice
- Confronting the gaps between organizational vision and the reality
- Dealing directly with conflict or difference in the workplace
- Participating in organizational decision making; filling a leadership "vacuum"
- Learning technical skills from peers through cross-training on the job

Brown and Duguid (1991, 1992) describe this type of workplace learning as a process that occurs through "webs of participation." Wenger and Lave (1998) and Wenger (1996, 1999) have characterized these informal learning webs as "communities of practice," while Boland and Tenkasi (1995) refer to them as "communities of knowing." Rather than representing organizational learning as that which occurs within formal systems, for instance through classroom training, they are concerned with learning which occurs through participation at work outside of formally designed professional development opportunities. Organizations that encourage, or at least do not prevent, these emergent communities, recognize that knowledge transfer and more integrated learning are best facilitated by authentic social interaction.

Individual Informal Learning

Although informal learning through social interaction can be supported and encouraged anywhere, it appears to be more difficult to achieve through strict adherence to traditional formal hierarchies (Lave and Wenger, 1991). ThermoDial's Canadian plant has experimented with a dramatic change in the last decade from a traditional assembly line structure to one of relatively independently operating work teams, each responsible for a complete production cycle. Previously, staff would spend their entire day repeatedly performing one specific operation on a product (e.g. connecting a wire to a screw, or putting two parts together) before passing the parts on to the next worker. Now, teams of five to ten individuals rotate all relevant jobs. For their particular line, each team member must be able to download order and supplies information from the computer system, perform all assembly tasks, inspect the product and make adjustments when errors are found, and prepare finished goods for shipping in a "just-in-time" manufacturing environment.

As might be expected, the roles of staff and management have evolved throughout this transition. Staff are more psychologically engaged and feel responsible both for their own success and for contributing to the overall success of the company. Apart from enhancing job satisfaction, this results in financial gain for all involved, through rewards for skills and knowledge accrued. Commitment is promoted by delegating authority directly to the front-line staff. In the process, learning, through self-direction and through interaction with others, becomes an integral part of accomplishing the task. Concerning their reaction to this approach, research participants say:

> We used to have people working ... overtime and every day doing a repair. Why? Because we didn't care. Somebody else was going to correct our garbage. Now we care because the reject is going to come back to me. I don't want that, so I'm trying to do my job right the very first time. (Line Staff)

> I do new things all the time in my job, so I almost have to learn new things just to keep up with the growing technology. So I usually know what I need before they do, so I'll approach them that I need this, and usually they supply it somehow. (Engineer)

> I feel far more comfortable to ask questions now. If you have a disagreement with something, you know that your opinion is going to be valued. And in my relationship with my manager, I can ask him anything. Absolutely anything, and I would disagree with anything. We trust the people we work with, and we trust their opinions as well. (Production Supervisor)

At ThermoDial, management's role is to support the employees' success by looking for ways to help them incorporate new skills and knowledge into the work. The manager's role is best discussed as what Block (1993) terms "stewardship" and Kofman and Senge (1993) call "servant leadership." Managers view staff as their priority customers, and tailor their support and the environment, whenever possible, to accommodate employees' strengths and needs, in order to enable the most effective achievement of organizational goals. One manager comments about the peer learning involved in this process:

> When it comes to actually doing the job and learning the computer skills … they're side by side with their co-workers, they're not with me. I'm here for them, and they choose who they're comfortable with. … I don't designate someone on the line to be, okay, you're going to train these people, I don't do that. My personal belief is that people need to be able to go to whoever they're comfortable with, because if they're uncomfortable they'll never learn. I think I had seven people who were trained on the new Oracle system. Of those seven people, there are four that are constantly on their feet showing people the new system. (Production Supervisor)

At Wealthshare, the formal structure is more traditionally hierarchical than that of ThermoDial. Nonetheless, like ThermoDial, Wealthshare values individual and team autonomy and maintains an unequivocal respect for learning. Informal learning at Wealthshare usually results from a work-related need. These demand-driven opportunities range from formalized meetings and staff retreats, to more informal hallway conversations, to small self-appointed teams working on a particular issue of importance to all members. Respondents repeatedly offer examples of their learning in this context, noting that even during a formal orientation/training session it is the *informal learning* through social interaction that is particularly significant:

> It was mostly just the discussions among people being trained together – and we were sort of sorting out the issues on our own. (Staff)

> Oh yeah – like in the early stages we did a collective analysis of the application – to provide different views, different ways of looking at an application – it just came out of the group. That's how I learned to do those things. (Staff)

> So no one really knows, so no one is really able to give you any concrete answers. So there's on-going discussion – there are chat lines, and so on – all sorts of stuff about how you interpret things – we teach each other all the time. (Staff)

Team Learning

Team environments, which have become the norm organizationally since the late eighties and early nineties (Boyett and Conn, 1999; Lawler et al., 1992; Katzenbach and Smith, 1993, 2003), provide another site for informal learning through social interaction on the job. Although Wealthshare is committed organizationally to team learning, its success with teams has been mixed. Some of the challenges are directly related to the lack of systemic stability during a time of dramatic change within the organization. However, many of the issues are similar to those experienced in more stable organizations (Katzenbach and Smith, 1993) including two of our other research sites (Homewares and URH). Teams feel that they do not have enough autonomy to make decisions that directly affect them. There is a lack of clarity about decision-making boundaries or a lack of effective team facilitation. There is a lack of willingness to raise conflictual issues openly for fear of hurting feelings, and therefore a failure to set potentially helpful group norms. One Wealthshare research participant comments:

> Oh, they look bored at the meeting, and they don't make notes, and they think, well, didn't we already discuss this? So people try to speed up the tempo, you know, and it's a good thing, because there is work to do … but it's also a forum where you can get a little deeper into some issues. (Staff)

The teams that seem to most effectively provide a context for individual and group informal learning in all of our sites have a number of common characteristics. They meet regularly. Although task-focused, their meetings include time for reflection on their process; the members attend to individual as well as group needs. Meetings are usually facilitated by someone (not necessarily the manager) who has some skill in team leadership and is focused on sharing these skills. These teams support individual professional development to help members learn needed skills, name problems as they arise and deal directly with them, and often act as an on-going community of practice. They do so by providing a forum for dialogue, in addition to problem solving regarding work-related issues. Most importantly, the team members function interdependently, and are collectively accountable for achieving mutually agreed-upon team goals.

Conversely, although Homewares' intention is to function as a team-based organization, it is a negative example of teams as settings for learning. While the organization does not actively discourage teams, efforts to formally support the use of teams is not explicit. One respondent says, "there's nothing formal, nothing developed thus far for Homewares in that regard." Additionally, only one explicit effort to become team oriented consisted of managers attending a retreat where they experienced team-building exercises with strangers. While this is indeed an effort to teach some team skills, it does not meet the conditions outlined by Wenger and Lave (1998) and other theorists (e.g. Revans, 1982; Brown and Duguid, 1991) for truly integrated learning. It did not take place in the context in which it was to be practiced and it was not supported by the organization beyond the initial training experience.

The paradox raised by the Homewares case is that, in order for more informal learning within a team to take place effectively, the organization must provide a context of formal support. (This will be discussed later in this chapter under the heading of "organizational culture.") It must make conscious efforts to clarify what it means by the term "team," rather than simply labeling all working groups as teams (Katzenbach and Smith, 2003). Further, team learning, however informal, must be accompanied by explicit efforts to define the processes and norms for how a team is expected to operate, as well as supported by more formal training in the skills needed for effective team leadership and membership (Laiken, 1993, 1998).

Learning Through Dealing with Conflict: Making and Reflecting on Mistakes

At Wealthshare, there was one area that was both the most challenging for teams, and, paradoxically, the most rewarding in terms of individual and group learning. This is the realm of risk-taking and conflict management, and involves making mistakes, reflecting on the experience, and applying the learning in practice. Sources of conflict at Wealthshare seem typical of most organizations. The most common include differences in status; unclear assumptions; feeling silenced in a discussion; lack of clarity regarding roles, goals and expectations of others; lack of trust; and perceived workload inequities (Laiken, 1994). However, what seems somewhat unique at Wealthshare, and helps designate it as a "learning organization," is the cultural norm that supports confronting conflicts openly and viewing them as opportunities for learning. Nonetheless, here, as in other aspects of functioning, there are individual differences. Some people are more willing to be direct in dealing with conflict than are others.

Confronting conflict seems to be more risky, as might be expected, when the person being confronted is one's manager as opposed to one's peer in the organizational hierarchy. However, at Wealthshare there is a surprising lack of fear in this respect – even new hires seem prepared to call a manager on his/her behaviour – especially when the latter is contravening an organizational norm. This kind of confrontation is not only condoned, but encouraged actively, as part of Wealthshare's cultural values:

> A number of times, people made a courageous step by calling our CEO on some stuff, and in a way that was really helpful for the whole rest of the staff, when they took that step. You know, basically a "time out" – like "I don't think you're respecting my opportunity to speak in this arena." People then acknowledged the courageousness of that step. (Manager)

The underlying belief is that, if people either recognize mistakes on their own, or learn about them through feedback from others, and most importantly, see this as an opportunity to learn and improve in the future, both the individual and the organization will benefit. The most critical principle here seems to be an explicit culture of "no blame" – where employees are supported in viewing mistakes simply as an opportunity for learning (Gephart et al., 1996; Kofman and Senge, 1993). It appears from our research that organizations intent on enhancing learning from experience prohibit, both culturally and procedurally, the use of threat, punishment or blame. As two of our interviewees note:

> We're laid back when it comes to mistakes that happen – we recognize it for what it is, it's a small thing, no problem, no blame ... and we always say ... this is the phrase that always comes back – "next time we'll do it better." (Staff, Wealthshare)

> Everybody's included in all the good things about working in a team environment ... and if you screw it up, we'll fix it tomorrow. So there's no punishment, there's no downside to making a mistake, either. (Production Supervisor, ThermoDial)

Shared Leadership in Support of Informal Learning

Increased individual and team autonomy was an outgrowth of major organizational transition in three of our four cases. URH was suffering from an unprecedented debt crisis due to large funding cuts and budget shortfalls, resulting in overall major restructuring of its systems and processes. ThermoDial's transition to its new approach required additional skills training for all staff, for many of whom English was a second language. It also required a leap of faith to appreciate that a flattened hierarchy and distributed responsibility would be an improvement on the old system, and not simply "more work for the same pay." Finally, the new approach was introduced at a time of downsizing, when most supervisory roles were eliminated. The remaining unionized employees realized that their traditional seniority programme of advancement from assembly to set up to inspection roles would be irrelevant in a setting where all staff would now be required to rotate diverse jobs as part of self-managed units.

At Wealthshare, although the changes were largely positive and the atmosphere generally expectant and charged with the excitement of a growing enterprise, the transition was also difficult. New systems and procedures were evolving but not yet fully in place. Staff roles were shifting, resulting in concerns about loss of the kind of autonomy that had become the norm in the smaller organization. The decentralized structure resulted in central and regional differences that had not yet been reconciled. At a time when strong leadership would have been welcomed, there was no Executive Director, but only an over-worked senior management team struggling valiantly to respond to the varying complex demands of an essentially new organization.

Trust and Distributed Leadership

Whether it was explicitly designed to be a feature of the organization, as at ThermoDial, or was the result of an unanticipated leadership vacuum, as at Wealthshare, the opportunity for more distributed, participative leadership among all employees presented itself as a key enhancer of informal learning.

In our research sites, those on the "front lines" of the organization offered concrete examples of how they were invited to use their skill, knowledge and creativity in their daily work. A critical aspect of such autonomy is the strong sense that employees have of being trusted to act responsibly. At URH a staff member says:

> We follow up with patients. I have my own business cards that I can give to patients so that they can contact me. All the nurses in the clinic have them too. Everyone has a direct link to me as a person. It makes everything more professional.

At ThermoDial, employees say they have gained in both direct and indirect ways from acquiring the new skills associated with increased responsibilities in their jobs, including more confidence in their own judgment and in their potential to learn and contribute.

Respondents comment:

> This has been the biggest learning experience of my life ... people are no longer a great mystery. (Production Supervisor)

> It's good for ThermoDial; it's good for me ... with the computer courses ... [now] I'm not afraid of the computer. When you know how to operate a computer, it's much easier to learn new stuff. So every day we're learning. Right now we're trained for Oracle, the new program that we have here. It was not a big deal because we have so much knowledge of the computer. You know what I mean? It's much easier. Like learning, I mean for me, I'm learning every day. And I have a mind, especially when it comes to computers, I know that now. (Line Staff)

In all cases, the opportunity to participate in organizational decision making through distributed leadership was viewed by research participants as a major contributor to their learning, development and increased self-confidence on the job. Important enablers in this process include accessibility of information, and a sense among employees that they are being trusted to make decisions by using that information responsibly.

At ThermoDial respondents praise the efficiency of information sharing throughout the plant, particularly between management and staff. Line staff obtain an understanding of customer needs through both formal and informal interaction with sales and marketing, internal postings, and information sessions with management. Being kept informed is important to front-line workers, who want to comprehend their contribution to the organization as a whole:

> Because we have the documents, we have the figures and we have the instruction how to do everything, if we see something wrong we can stop the line right away. ... It might be a short time until I see the engineer or something. ... Because the way we work, we're flexible. (Line Staff)

> We have enough experience that, frankly, I could go for a week and never speak to any of them, the world will function just fine. I know the products well enough and have been here long enough, and have such confidence in people doing their job that they don't need me. (Production Supervisor)

At Wealthshare, although some newer employees continue to feel vulnerable and in need of direction, all chose the organization as a workplace in which they could expect personal autonomy and self-direction to be valued. The transitional leadership vacuum provides an invitation to fully exercise this autonomy, and most teams and individual employees have accepted the invitation with enthusiasm. Workers participate in interviewing and selecting new hires. Many appreciate this as a key informal learning opportunity. Recommendations regarding a wide variety of operating issues have been proposed by individuals and teams, and implemented. Employees have found themselves defining their own roles within organizational parameters, particularly in newly designated jobs such as Area Manager. Individuals are offered much room for flexibility through job arrangements such as home working. Interviewees express their enthusiasm for these opportunities in such comments as:

Like mainly, you have a free handle on how to develop your local grant review team. For example, what I did in my region is, I involved them a lot in site visits, as a way of educating them. In our first meeting, we didn't have applications to review, so I invited the Social Planning Council to provide a context. In a way, yeah, I see myself as having the authority or freedom to do things. (Manager)

It's very open, there's a lot of opportunity to participate generally. There is a strong value in respecting everyone's voice. Lots of discussion – changes are not made without striking working groups. It's a very consultative, participative organization. (Staff)

Workers at Homewares also attribute much of their important informal learning directly to the amount of autonomy they experience in their role. A staff person notes that her manager views her desire to take initiative as an opportunity for her to learn some new aspect of the store management. She says, "Many of the operational decisions in the store are up to my own discretion."

Other Homewares staff members gain a sense of autonomy through the freedom they experience to display items in the store using their own creativity, by the receptivity with which their suggestions regarding visual display are met, and through the encouragement to find innovative ways to provide excellent service. One employee comments that associates are given "turf" in the form of sole responsibility for one area of the store, where they are invited to use their initiative.

Informal Learning and Organizational Benefits Through Increased Autonomy

Opportunities for informal learning through increased autonomy clearly benefit individual employees in our research sites. However, of equal importance, such opportunities also appear to also result in improved group cohesiveness as well as greater quality in services and products for the organization as a whole. At ThermoDial, both management and staff indicate that their team approach has improved quality because of a shared responsibility for team output and a commitment to quality by every member of the organization. With ownership for the final product delegated right to the front line, staff are more conscientious about their work:

To me you are a liar if you send out a bad product, just to get the work done. You know something is bad, you don't do it. (Production Supervisor)

You don't have anybody to correct your mistakes, you're doing it, so you're more careful doing it. (Line Staff)

Additionally, shifting ownership to the front-line results in greater work group cohesiveness. Most employees pull together and choose to step in to "get the job done," out of a sense of duty to the organization and its customers and with resulting pride of accomplishment:

As far as the team work, it's good as far as getting the stuff out ... being in a smaller group, so if a problem arises, like I say we're using the wrong something or other, it'll be caught more than it would have the way we used to work with two people here, four people on this job... we've all been trained now to visually look at the things instead of just doing

what you need to do ... so it's all, it's a lot better for the company because they don't have
as many rejects returned. Because we find all the stuff. It's wonderful for that and the
amount we get out now ... it's unbelievable. (Line Staff)

Intergrating the Learning Organizationally

Much research (Ahmed et al, 1999; Bartlett and Ghoshal, 1998; Goh, 1998; Stamps,
1998) supports our most important finding from this study, which is the notion that
organizational climate and culture is critical in creating an environment which enables informal learning and shared leadership in the workplace to thrive. Additionally,
managing the paradox of "formalizing the informal" by embedding it in the structure, systems and processes of the organization ensures that its benefits are largely
sustainable.

We identified three sets of activities as key factors in ensuring an organizational
climate conducive to learning. They are: (1) creating a values-based shared vision
of both the task-related goals and the internal functioning of the organization;
(2) examining and revising systems, procedures and processes so that they clearly
reflect the vision and values in action; and (3) continuously evaluating progress
towards achieving the vision so that the gap between the vision and the current
reality is progressively decreased.

Creating a Values-Based Shared Vision

URH has developed a set of institutional values that embody its commitment to
"excellence in patient care" and service to its unique urban community. All interviewees discussed the central role of the mission and values within the hospital,
making statements such as: "The mission and values guide the hospital in what we
want to do in a larger health care frame." Information about the mission, vision and
values is transmitted formally through orientation and professional development
activities, informally through hallway conversations and team discussions, and
through the day-to-day work in the hospital. Consistent with this, URH has created
a position entitled "Director of Mission and Values" (DMV), whose role is to keep
the conversation about this important aspect of the organizational culture alive. All
research participants mentioned the centrality of the role of the DMV and the
mission and values statements during the orientation programme for new employees.
One person notes: "There was an open discussion of the mission and values, the
history of URH, the importance of caring for the disadvantaged and the commitment
to the poor."

At Thermodial, the entire workplace structure reflects the organization's values-
based commitment to employee participation and distributed leadership, while at
Wealthshare, there exists a strong belief system which originated in the smaller

organization. This vision supports learning and development among all employees, and includes community members as well. There is a deeply held belief about the benefit of helping clients reach their own solutions to issues of concern, as well as a set of values regarding Wealthshare as a nurturing workplace for its employees.

All of our case sites noted that the orientation process for new employees was an initial location for introducing them to the organization's vision and values. At Homewares, although there is no formal orientation programme for non-managers, sales associates are offered a self-directed learning opportunity through videotapes and workbooks, which introduces them to their role in the organization. However, the critical factor in whether or not such exposure is taken seriously by workers appears to be the degree to which the rhetoric is actually enacted in practice within the organization.

Reflecting the Vision in Practice

Most contemporary organizations have recognized the importance of developing a shared vision to help align the work of disparate units or individuals. However, few have as yet managed to integrate this vision within their systems and work processes, so that it is reflected in every aspect of organizational life (Laiken, 1997, 2002; McKenna, 1992; Senge et al., 1999).

Our research sites offer several examples of having achieved this goal: from distributed leadership increasing worker autonomy at ThermoDial to encouraging staff to build links with the community at URH. By creating the position of Director of Mission and Values and securing its place in senior management, URH ensures a "champion" for enacting its vision. The hospital has also reflected its beliefs through its awards and recognition programme for all employees. The rewards have served to create an awareness of the values supported by the organization as well as acknowledging employee achievement and effort in this regard. Staff members explain:

> In 1990 there was nothing in the way of staff recognition or values recognition. Now there are plenty of awards. ... "Most Valuable Player" award is nominated by peers for going above and beyond the call of duty. There are also pictures and names of recognized people.

> Values in Action nominations are more complex and there are awards for individuals, teams and projects. We have a set URH Day. Everyone is honoured, and that is September 29. Everyone is given a memento. ... There is a Values in Action Award that recognizes the 5 values. Each year, one team is recognized around each value.

Finally, values play a significant role in the decision-making process at URH. Staff members repeatedly note how teams and leaders reflect their commitment to excellence and to the community as a framework for planning. For example: "There are strong mission and values. We have worked to keep it alive. We talk about it a lot." Another participant explains, "The values are the heart of the organization. They influence decision making at the leadership level. ... There is recognition of the values in the leadership. It is evident in their behaviour."

ThermoDial's line staff members appreciate the value that supports the inclusion of every worker in creative problem solving and organizational decision making. One staff member says:

> Before ... I felt like a dummy. Nobody was asking me for ideas, talking. They were telling you what to do and that was it. Even though you knew better how to improve things on your job and everything. And it's not because they were bad, because that was the system. But now, if you have an idea, just say it, say your idea and somebody will reward you for that, if it works. ... And you do, believe me, there are a lot of [opportunities] to use your brain. (Line Staff)

At Homewares, the extent to which practice reflects beliefs varies according to the style of leadership in any particular store. What is lacking here is an organizational vision to which all locations have committed themselves. As a result there is a large variation in the extent to which the vision is consistently embedded in day-to-day working life.

In contrast, at Wealthshare the general feeling among interviewees is that while the values are clearly espoused throughout the organization, there is some tension in enacting them. This is partly due to turbulence and structural changes that are not yet firmly rooted. As at Homewares, some supervisory styles are seen as not consistent with espoused values but, for the most part, there is a feeling that Wealthshare is positioning itself to implement its values in action. Much of the learning identified takes place by people becoming aware of the gap between the espoused values and the values in use (Argyris and Schon, 1978; Argyris, 1990), and making attempts to close that gap. There is a recognition that aligned action requires congruence between personal and organizational values, and staff members are learning to be more aware when these are not congruent. A participant comments:

> Everybody in our organization used to report to one person, and so there were times when we did some spectacular things in communities, we had tremendous autonomy in our jobs, and then, at an internal level, there would be some blaming about something that didn't match the kind of autonomy we were feeling in our external roles. (Manager)

Making space for reflection and discussion of the gaps between vision and reality is viewed by most research participants as one of the key activities in sustaining organizational learning, as well as in providing opportunities for informal learning. Once identified, a problem is never ignored – it is seen as an opportunity for learning, and time is set aside to deal with it. One participant provides an example:

> In September we had a Staff retreat. And I would say we had a variety of challenges facing the organization, because we were about to be in this huge transition, but it was like being in a hurry-up-and-wait mode. We'd hired talented staff who couldn't do the job they'd been hired for because some of the approvals weren't in place. So we had disgruntled people, in a way, and we weren't leveraging their potential as well as we might have. And so during the Staff retreat, we wanted to look at the future, but had to address some of those realities. And out of the retreat we did develop a series of working groups that were staff-driven, grassroots. We figured out some parameters, and enabled staff to find their voice through these work groups. (Manager)

Continuously Evaluating Progress

Making discussible the gaps between theory and practice and conscientiously acting on the issues identified emerges strongly as the most significant feature separating our case examples from other, less learning-oriented organizations. This type of reflective activity sets the stage for continuous individual, team and organizational learning.

URH takes a more structured approach to evaluating progress than do the other organizations in our study. Over the years, the hospital has developed a culture that is deeply rooted in reflection and analysis of organizational health in order to improve its performance. As one employee notes, "There is an underlying thirst for knowledge," and another says, "We are measuring things constantly. There are lots of indicators."

For example, URH has turned its diagnostic sensibilities upon itself and has committed to learning more about the experiences of its employees. In addition to generating a better understanding of how individual employees view their work and the hospital, the organization also conducted a study of its own organizational culture.

Additionally, URH is working to better understand its clients' experiences through a continual assessment of patient satisfaction, patient outcomes and waiting time. Finally, the hospital has established a community advisory committee to address specific inner city programme needs. A critically important aspect of this activity is the fact that these data are fed back to the employees directly involved with the clients in question. This places responsibility for problem-solving and continuous learning squarely on the shoulders of those who are in a position to take immediate action for improvement. As one respondent explains:

> There is a patients' complaints process. There is a designated person who deals with this as the Patient Satisfaction Coordinator. She is the "survey queen" and reports back to staff. (Staff)

Conclusion

The cases reviewed here shed light on the role of and potential for informal learning within the process of organizational change. This chapter illustrates concrete approaches for ensuring that learning is integrated into the broader change processes at individual, team and systemic levels. We believe the research illustrates that these strategies can be applied to organizations in private and non-profit sectors alike.

For individuals, action learning on the job is enhanced by legitimized opportunities to view mistakes or problems as an opportunity for learning through reflection and subsequent application of new insights. For both individuals and teams, framing conflict and difference as a source of creativity, and being encouraged to directly confront issues within an atmosphere of "no blame," provides the safety workers require to engage in such potentially risky ventures. Leadership modeling appears to be particularly significant in this area.

Teams thrive as a learning context when they meet regularly (either face-to-face or virtually); are skillfully facilitated to balance task and process; incorporate individual needs into shared team goals which require members' interdependence; clarify roles and expectations; and are aided by organizational support such as opportunities for skill development. Team learning occurs in teams that are differentiated from natural working groups (such as a unit or department) by the fact that they are meeting to work on specific goals for which they are mutually accountable.

Systemically, shared or distributed leadership enables continuous informal learning through autonomy on the job and opportunities to participate in organizational decision making. The outcomes for individuals include increased technical and interpersonal skill, as well as enhanced self-confidence and creativity. The critical enablers are: management trust in worker responsibility; continuous and unrestricted access to job-related information; and, working within a "whole job" concept which allows employees to pursue a complete project from beginning to end.

Additionally, what we have termed "formalizing the informal" seems to be essential in order to embed the learning organizationally. Organizational culture and climate are crucial in creating an environment for informal learning to thrive. Three sets of activities were identified as core in this enterprise: creating a value-based shared vision; examining and revising systems, procedures and processes to clearly reflect the vision/values in action; and continuously evaluating progress towards achieving the vision within the context of day-to day working life.

None of the organizations represented in this study would identify themselves as a fully developed "learning organization." What became abundantly clear as we listened to workers' stories is that there is no end point to the processes that were being examined, for either the individuals or the organizations involved. This is lifelong learning writ large. It seems not to be a question of who has *done* it, but a question of who is *doing* it – with the journey characterized by a continuous cycle of understanding, implementing, reflecting and sustaining. Kofman and Senge say: "The best constructs for explaining and organizing the world will imitate life itself. They will be in a continual state of becoming" (1993, p. 15). However, our own research participants express the concepts best with such statements as:

> For me, organizational learning incorporates some of the other levels of learning – it is how the organization is accessing information, knowledge resources – and interpreting them in a way that moves them forward continually – enabling the organization to achieve best practices, to reflect on what it's doing. ... So it's macro – but it also requires individual and team and other types of learning for it to actually work ... and, for an organization to do that, it needs to have in place a vision and values that link back to reality. It's one thing for one or two people to hold those kinds of values – if the organization itself doesn't serve these issues through its mission, vision and values, and then practices underneath that – policies and practices that are supported – then it won't happen. (Wealthshare Staff)

Endnote

[1] Woolner et al. (1995) define a "stage 5" organization as one in which business strategies are based on a shared collective vision; structures and functions are flexible and responsive to organizational needs; there is direct information sharing and a constant questioning of assumptions and testing of reality; and work and learning are fully integrated.

References

Ahmed, P., Loh, A. & Zairi, M., 1999, Cultures for continuous improvement and learning, *Total Quality Management*, **10(4/5)**: S426–S434.

Argyris, C., 1990, *Overcoming Organizational Defenses: Facilitating Organizational Learning*, Allyn & Bacon, Boston, MA.

Argyris, C. & Schon, D., 1978, *Organizational Learning: A Theory of Action Perspective*, Addison-Wesley, Reading, MA.

Bartlett, C.A. & Ghoshal, S., 1998, Beyond strategic planning to organization learning: lifeblood of the individualized corporation, *Strategy and Leadership*, **26(1)**: 34–39.

Boland, R. & Tenkasi, R., 1995, Perspective making and perspective taking in communities of knowing, *Organization Science*, **6(4)**: 350–371.

Block, P., 1993, *Stewardship: Choosing Service Over Self-Interest*, Berrett-Koehler, San Francisco, CA.

Boyett, J.H. & Conn, H.P., 1999, *Workplace 2000: The Revolution Reshaping American Business*, Penguin Books, New York.

Brown, J.S. & Duguid, P., 1991, Organizational learning and communities-of-practice: toward a unified view of working, learning and innovation, *Organization Science*, **2(1)**: 40–57.

Brown, J.S. & Duguid, P., 1992, When change is constant, maybe we need to change our own eyeglasses, Paper presented at *the Learning in Organizations Workshop*, University of Western Ontario Business School, June 21–23, London, Ontario.

Emery, F.E., 1980, Designing socio-technical systems for "greenfield sites," *Journal of Occupational Behaviour*, **1(1)**: 19–28.

Gephart, M., Marsick, V., Van Buren, M. & Spiro, M., 1996, Learning organizations come alive, *Training and Development*, **50**: 35–45.

Goh, S.C., 1998, Toward a learning organization: the strategic building blocks, *S.A.M. Advanced Management Journal*, **63(2)**: 15–22.

Katzenbach, J.R. & Smith, D.K., 1993, 2003, *The Wisdom of Teams: Creating the High-Performance Organization*, Harvard University Press, Cambridge, MA.

Kofman, F. & Senge, P.M., 1993, Communities of commitment: the heart of learning organizations, *Organizational Dynamics*, **22(2)**: 5–23.

Laiken, M., 1987, *Taking charge: the impact of organizational restructuring on learning and change within self-managing teams*, Unpublished doctoral thesis, University of Toronto, Toronto, Canada.

Laiken, M., 1993, The myth of the self-managing team, Organization Development Journal, **12(2)**: 29–34.

Laiken, M., 1994, Conflict in teams: problem or opportunity? In Lectures in Health Promotion Series No. 4, Centre for Health Promotion, University of Toronto, Toronto, Canada.

Laiken, M., 1997, Collaborative processes for collaborative organizational design: the role of reflection, dialogue and polarity management in creating an environment for organizational learning, *Organization Development Journal*, **15(4)**: 35–42.

Laiken, M., 1998, The Anatomy of High Performing Teams: A Leader's Handbook, 3rd edn., University of Toronto Press, Toronto.

Laiken, M., 2002, Models of organizational learning: paradoxes and best practices in the post-industrial workplace, *Organizational Development Journal*, Fall, **21(1)**: 8–19.

Lave, J. & Wenger, E., 1991, *Situated Learning: Legitimate Peripheral Participation*, Cambridge University Press, Cambridge.

Lawler, E.E. III, Mohrman, S.A. & Ledford, G.E., 1992, *Employee Involvement and Total Quality Management: Practices and Results in Fortune 1000 Companies*, Jossey-Bass, San Francisco, CA.

McKenna, S.D., 1992, A culture instrument: driving organizational learning, *Leadership and Organization Development*, **13(6)**: 24–29.

Revans, R.W., 1982, *The Origins and Development of Action Learning*, Brookfield Publishing, England.

Senge, P.M., 1990, *The Fifth Discipline: The Art and Practice of the Learning Organization*, Doubleday/Currency, New York.

Senge, P., Kleiner, A., Roberts, C., Ross, R., Roth, G. & Smith, B., 1999, *The Dance of Change: The Challenges to Sustaining Momentum in Learning Organizations*, Doubleday/Currency, New York.

Stamps, D., 1998, Learning ecologies, *Training*, **35(1)**: 32–38.

Trist, E.L., 1981, The evolution of socio-technical systems: a conceptual framework and an action research program, *Issues in Q.W.L. No. 2*, Ontario Ministry of Labour, Ontario Quality of Working Life Centre, Toronto.

Wenger, E., 1996, Communities of practice: the social fabric of a learning organization, *Healthcare Forum Journal*, **39(4)**: 20–26.

Wenger, E., 1999, *Communities of practice: learning as a social system*, Unpublished paper, presented in Toronto, April 1999.

Wenger, E. & Lave, J., 1998, *Communities of Practice: Learning, Meaning, and Identity*, Cambridge University Press, Cambridge.

Woolner, P., Lowy, A. & Redding, J., 1995, Learning Organization 5 Stage Diagnostic Survey and Workshop Version, Woolner Associates, Toronto.

Author Index

Subject Index

.

Printed in the United States
132075LV00009B/3/P